In search of management

In Search of Management looks at the nature of managerial work and how people are managing to be managers in the difficult circumstances of the 1990s. By observing the lives and experiences of managers struggling to succeed in a business organisation facing major strategic challenges, Tony Watson considers basic questions about the nature of management. He argues that management is best understood as the component of work organisations concerned with longer-term organisational survival; individual managers carrying out their specific tasks within this broader strategic responsibility. This is not necessarily what happens in practice however, to the possible detriment of both the individual's experience and the performance of the organisation.

Working alongside managers as a participant observer, Tony Watson reveals the rewards and pains managers experience as they cope with both traditional business pressures and the newer ideas of pursuing 'excellence' through changing cultures and 'empowering' employees. Written to appeal equally to those with a practical, academic or general interest in the subject the book argues that management is a social and moral activity. In spite of their stress on practicality, managers are shown to work out their own theories as they shape their identities, values and careers. By looking at these issues, Tony Watson assesses the personal and organisational problems which can arise as managers struggle to control their lives and jobs.

Tony J. Watson is Professor of Organisational and Managerial Behaviour at Nottingham Business School.

In search of management

Culture, chaos and control in managerial work

Tony J. Watson

INTERNATIONAL THOMSON BUSINESS PRESS
I ⓣ P An International Thomson Publishing Company

London • Bonn • Boston • Johannesburg • Madrid • Melbourne • Mexico City • New York • Paris
Singapore • Tokyo • Toronto • Albany, NY • Belmont, CA • Cincinnati, OH • Detroit, MI

In Search of Management

Copyright ©1994 John J. Watson

 A division of International Thomson Publishing Inc.
The ITP logo is a trademark under licence

British Library Cataloguing-in-Publication Data
A catalogue record for this book is available from the British Library

First published by Routledge 1994
Reprinted by International Thomson Business Press 1996, 1997 and 1999

Typeset by J & L Composition Ltd., Filey, North Yorkshire
Printed in Croatia

ISBN 0-415-09231-0

International Thomson Business Press
Berkshire House
168–173 High Holborn
London WC1V 7AA
UK

http://www.itbp.com

Contents

Preface

In the course of this 'search for management' I worked alongside managers in 'ZTC Ryland' and I spent a great deal of time talking to them both informally and in formal interviews. I dedicate the book to all of these men and women, with immense gratitude for their help, support and, indeed, inspiration. I cannot thank anybody by name, because of my promises of confidentiality. Much of what was said to me and much of what I observed was of a confidential nature. This means that a lot of effort has gone into writing in such a way that individuals will not be embarrassed. False trails have been laid so that personal confidences will not be broken. All names of companies and individuals have been changed throughout to preserve anonymity. There are one or two cases where it has been impossible to disguise completely the identities of the people concerned. In each of these cases the individual concerned was not interviewed by me under conditions of confidentiality. As a result of similar pressures to protect people, there are occasions in the study where I have been more vague about details of events than I might have preferred. This has again been to protect the feelings and interests of individuals.

Introduction

'So who do you think is going to read your book then?'
   'Oh, lots and lots of people.'
   'Go on – who for example?'
   'My father will, I am sure. He reads a lot. And my mother . . .'
   'Seriously though. You've told us that you are writing a book about managers, about us lot. So who is it for? Is it for people like us? I mean, you know, will thick people like us understand it?'
   'What do you mean 'thick', that's not . . .'
   'What I am saying is – I mean what I am asking is: are you writing it for your academics or for managers and other ordinary people?'
   'Well, my Dad's an ordinary person . . .'
   'Can't I ever get a straight answer from you, Tony?'

ACADEMICS, MANAGERS AND ORDINARY PEOPLE

This piece of banter was one of the thousands of dialogues which I had with the managers I worked with and studied for this book. It is the first of many pieces of dialogue I shall be using as part of my exploration of what managerial work is and how people in managerial jobs are *managing being managers* in the changing circumstances of the 1990s work organisation. And, like much of the dialogue used in the book, these words are taken to be more significant than they might at first appear. The above conversation is at first sight just a piece of light-hearted chatter between the researcher and one of the people being 'researched'. I am being asked a serious question. But I don't answer it. I joke. As I will argue later, there is no such thing as 'just a joke'. Human beings typically joke about that which, deeper down, bothers them. We treat things lightly precisely because they might otherwise be too heavy. And the question for me about whom my book could be written for and who would read it, was one which weighed heavily on me. I could not answer the question when it was asked by my management friend because I could not easily answer it when I asked it for myself.

   Why should there be an issue here? Why is there a problem for any academic wanting to write about management in a way which will be valued by both fellow academics and practising managers? Did I have to write exclusively for one group or the other? Couldn't I have it both ways? It would be a challenge to try. It often seems to me, as someone who regularly moves back and forth between industrial organisations and academic institutions, that managers and academics sometimes seem to live in two different worlds, and speak two different languages. There is prejudice on both sides (Watson 1994a) and I can sympathise with the concerns of people on both sides of this unfortunate fence. But it is a fence which needs to be broken down; it is a foolish and dangerous error to maintain barriers between 'thinkers' and 'doers' in any kind of human activity.

I hope to appeal at the same time to a managerial and an academic readership, as well as to the general reader interested in a social science analysis of an important modern activity. I have therefore carefully crafted this book to avoid what Charles Wright Mills (1970), in his discussion of intellectual craft work, criticised as the 'dense and turgid' style of much academic writing. This does not mean that I have suspended normal standards of academic rigour. It seems to me that good sociology which is meaningful and enlightening to the non-academic reader is a realistic possibility. Theoretical complexities do not have to be skated over and necessary technical terms do not have to be avoided – as long as all terms and all conceptual developments are carefully explained. I have tried to follow this principle throughout. And I have also carefully structured the book so that theoretical themes, considerations of methods and the main 'meat' of the work are not served up in separate lumps, but offered at the appropriate time in the sequence of what I hope to be an enjoyable as well as a digestible feast.

After an initial chapter which sets the scene, the theoretical themes unfold throughout the book and reflections on the research methods used are introduced at various points where they become relevant. Conceptual and methods issues are too integral to the story to be set apart in separate theory or methods chapters.

SHAPING, SEARCHING AND STORYTELLING

In Search of Management tells a story. I believe it is an important story for anyone interested in what is going on in the contemporary world of work and production. And it is unashamedly concerned with theories, too. One of the key arguments of the book, in fact, is that managers themselves, however much they tend to scorn the very idea of theory, are inevitably theorists of a sort. I am concerned to bring out the theoretical thinking which lies beneath the surface of the practical activity of managerial work. And in the process of doing this I have found that there is a lot to be learned. In many ways this book is the product of the managers with whom I worked as much as it is my own creation. That is not to deny the extent to which I shape the record of their thoughts and insights. But the managers helped shape the study more than they could ever have been aware. A conversation with a manager on the way into work one morning, for example, helped me in the early stages of shaping the research project. He also took me towards its eventual title. As I walked down the corridor on my way to my office on the ZTC Ryland site I was greeted by John Stapleford:

'Dr Watson, I presume?'
'Come off it, John.'
'Yeah, it's a bit predictable isn't it? Do you get it all the time?'
'Not really, but it's better than "elementary, my dear Watson". Anyway isn't it meant to be "Dr Livingstone, I presume?"'
'Of course it is. But what can you expect; I'm only an ignorant engineer, aren't I? What did Livingstone have to do with Sherlock Holmes, anyway?'
'Nothing, you ignorant sod.'
'I know: he was an explorer, wasn't he – Africa and all that.'
'Yeah.'
'Oh well, off to work we go. And good luck with your search for the Nile.'
'See you later.'

I almost uttered, as my parting shot in this typical early morning banter, 'Out of the mouths of fools, babes and engineers'. I resisted this but was rather taken with the idea that there was insight, wisdom even, in John Stapleford's simple quip about the search for the Nile. Rushing to my desk to record the interchange in my field notes, I imagined myself not so much crossing the yard of a twentieth-century telecommunications factory as hacking my way through the African jungle. I was an explorer. I was in search of the source of the Nile. Well, I was an explorer anyway. I was not looking for the source of a mighty river. I was – what? – yes – in search of management. That had a ring to it. It might not be a very romantic mission, but the boldness of the idea helped to make me feel important and to make sense of what I was doing in this industrial jungle, away from the safety of my academic desk.

The phrase in 'search of management' was also attractive because it echoed the title of one of the most influential books ever written about management. The publication and immense popularity of *In Search of Excellence* (1982) by Tom Peters and Bob Waterman marked a significant shift in the way many managers thought about running businesses and other organisations. The book helped popularise the notion of managing an organisation as much through *culture* as through traditional structures and procedures. The book has been much criticised, on the one hand, and much cited as an influence on managerial practice, on the other. But what interested me and formed a key research question for me was the extent to which the implications of that book, and its sequels, have been fully appreciated by the many managers who have spoken so freely of their intent, for example, to 'change culture' and 'empower employees'.

During my year of participant observation research at the ZTC Ryland plant I used to joke to colleagues that I chose the company for my study because the factory was just a twenty-minute walk from my house. Again, as with all jokes, there was a serious element to this. But the most significant factor in choosing ZTC Ryland as a research site was that its management had engaged in a whole series of change initiatives of the type associated with the 1980s and 1990s 'search for excellence'. There was an explicitly formulated corporate culture which the company was trying to engender and there was a whole series of 'progressive' management initiatives, ranging from 'total quality management' to team briefing, team working, personal development programmes, performance-related pay, and so on. Not only this, but the company had based its distinctive approach to strategy development and culture-building on the work of consultants who were also academics. This was a gift to me as a researcher, because it meant that I could turn to the published work of these consultants to discover the principles upon which some of the company's key policies were based. It also meant that the study could contribute to our general understanding of corporate strategy issues.

ZTC Ryland is a plant of three thousand or so employees engaged in developing, making and selling telecommunications products. It is one of several plants owned by ZTC, a company made up of what were formerly rival telecommunications businesses. It presented a superb opportunity to look closely at a fairly mainstream British company with many of the problems generally besetting manufacturing companies in Britain (instead of the over-cited and typically American or Japanese-owned companies which regularly star in accounts of 'excellent' companies). It provided an oppportunity to look at how some of the fashionable management ideas are impinging on the lives of managers who are attempting to put them into practice. At the same time I could apply my interest in trying to relate academic ideas to the practicalities of managerial work. I was in search of management in both an intellectual and a practical sense; continuing to tackle a question that had preoccupied me throughout my career, that of how could one best understand management, as a peculiarly and characteristically twentieth-century form of occupational activity, and how such an understanding might be of help to those who want to learn how to be effective, or more effective, managers.

In the process of handling broad questions like this, however, one could also possibly throw light on what looked like contradictory accounts of how managers in contemporary organisations are experiencing the pressures of life in such organisations. Whilst Scase and Goffee (1989) have painted a black picture of the working lives of 'reluctant managers', Dopson and Stewart (1990) have been more optimistic about how changing ways of structuring organisations have affected the experience and satisfactions of managerial work. I hope to throw light on this apparent conflict by looking more closely at the lives of managers in just one organisation, a focus which allows greater account to be taken of the particular circumstances in which they work and live.

In looking at both these broad and these more specific matters, I was not searching for some fundamental *truth* about the world, or about managerial activity in that world. It was more a search for a way of giving an account of, or 'putting across', what management is, in a way which might be closer to the 'realities' of the managerial experience than much of what is on offer in management textbooks and courses. The traditional conceptions of management as an activity involving planning, controlling, commanding and the like had long seemed to me to amount to little more than idealised aspirations of management writers who saw the world as a much more malleable and controllable place than it turns out to be when we actually try to manage aspects of it. Whether or not it has been fully appreciated by those managers who talk so much of cultures and cultural changes in their organisations, it was this kind of dissatisfaction with conventional ideas about management which set off the whole trend looking at cultural variables in the management of work.

The project was also shaped by a notion which had long been in my mind. This was the feeling that many managers conceive of their jobs as primarily concerned with managing their own departments or staff, as opposed to helping run the organisation as a whole and ensure its long-term survival. Yet I suspected that, at the same time, many of them hankered after a more 'strategic' role than this former conception would suggest. My own understanding of the role and purpose of managerial work is that it is most usefully regarded as an activity which contributes to the directing of the organisation as a whole towards long-term viability. I believe, and shall be arguing the case in this book, that the more a set (or 'team') of managers operates in these terms, the more effective it will be. As a researcher, though, I also wanted to ask the straightforward question: to what extent do managers think and act in these terms?

This concern about the way many managers see their jobs was shared by the people in ZTC with whom I negotiated taking a management role as part of my one-year secondment from my business school. The personnel director and organisation development executive at the ZTC Ryland plant were keen to have help in looking at this issue and in identifying ways of encouraging all their managers to see themselves as 'business managers', rather than as specialist or departmental managers. One of my key tasks was to develop a scheme identifying and expressing the management competencies which ZTC Ryland would use in selecting and developing its managers for the future.

This shared perspective between myself and my 'sponsors' in ZTC, and the tasks I was asked to perform, provided me with an opportunity to explore certain questions which had always fascinated me – questions about how managers generally think about their work and how they relate their personal lives, values and priorities to the work they do. How do they 'manage themselves' at the same time as managing their jobs as 'managers' of others? What part is played by the theoretical understandings which lurk beneath the surface of their everyday pragmatic behaviour? Why is it that people in the managerial world often seem to be so bad at putting to use what they already know? ZTC seemed to me to be an exemplar of what I have seen in many organisations: a lot of impressive thought and action going into efforts which were less than impressive in their effects. To understand matters like this one needs to look closely at the thoughts and ideas of managers and at how these relate to the specificities of an actual organisation. This requires getting close to managers as individuals and involving oneself in their organisational context. All of this suggests an ethnographic or participant observation research method, something which has rarely been applied to managers, since the classic American study, *Men Who Manage*, by Melville Dalton published in 1959.

INTO THE FIELD: REVEALING THE ETHNOGRAPHER'S HAND

Ethnography has traditionally been associated with anthropologists going to live over the seas for a year or two with 'primitive' or 'exotic' tribes. Nowadays it is sometimes seen simply as a way of collecting 'data' through a process of *participant observation* in which the researcher becomes an active member of the group which is being studied. It is, however, increasingly seen as more than this. John Van Maanen argues that an ethnography is a 'written representation of a culture (or selected aspects of a culture)' (1988: 14) and Michael Rosen has stressed that in doing this in an organisation the ethnographer lives among the 'subjects' and tries to 'learn the subjects' rules for organisational life, to interact with them for a frequency and duration of time "sufficient" to understand how and why they construct their social world as it is and to explain it to others' (1989: 5). In ethnography, then, there is a coming together of the 'everyday' thinking of the 'subjects' of the research and the body of academic knowledge to which the researcher has access. And there is attention to meanings and the processes through which the members of particular worlds make those worlds meaningful to themselves and others.

A good ethnography will add to the general body of knowledge about the human social world and, at the same time, inform the practical understanding of all of those involved in the activities it examines. Phil Strong and Robert Dingwall note the tendency of sociologists to be critical of 'a worldly concern for efficiency and effectiveness, the stock in trade of the manager or policy maker' and call for ethnographies to be developed which address such issues and show more concern with 'the general properties of social institutions than the constant celebration of their uniqueness' (1989: 65–7). This does not have to mean that we adopt an uncritical ethnographic style, however. An ethnography should represent the existing views of those who are studied. But it should also engage with those views. Ethnography can raise questions about institutions and practices which we take for granted and thus contribute to a critical and emancipatory use of social science (cf. Alvesson and Willmott 1992).

The present study can be read as, in part, a critique of certain aspects of contemporary organisational practice. But it is a critique which *emerges* from my dialogues with organisational managers, rather than one imposed on the world by a holier-than-thou radical or critical sociologist. This is not to deny, however, that the account of all of this is written by me. It is my construction – anxious as I am to represent the views and feelings of others. This is why it is vital for me, or any other ethnographic researcher, to 'reveal the hand' behind the text when writing my research report. I was no neutral fly-on-the-wall in ZTC Ryland and I was not 'collecting' attitudes and other data like a naturalist netting butterflies. Like any other social researcher I was influencing those I was researching and I have endeavoured to be honest about this *reflexivity*. In my stress on dialogue, symbolically flagged by my starting every chapter with a reported conversation, I am making this evident. I make no claim to be a neutral reporter but I attempt a degree of objectivity by allowing readers to judge for themselves something of the way I influenced the events and accounts I am writing about.

How representative of managerial work is this research among managers in just one work organisation? It could be said that all my arguments about managers and managing can only apply to the sample of the hundred or so individuals I was involved with, and my generalisations about organisations could be said only to apply to a sample of one – ZTC Ryland. This is to miss the point of detailed ethnographic or case-study research. Getting very close to managers in one organisation is a means of generalising about *processes* managers get involved in and about basic organisational activities, rather than about 'all managers' or 'all organisations' as such. It is a matter of generalising 'theoretically' rather than 'empirically', as Robert Yin puts it (1984).

One of the leading researchers on managerial work, Rosemary Stewart, argues (Stewart 1989) that to find a 'way forward' in management research we need 'a good theoretical base so that progress can be made'. She also suggests that, to clarify 'what is distinctive about managerial work' and to 'seek to develop concepts for describing managerial activities', we have to turn to 'intensive qualitative research' and 'try and understand the constructs that particular individuals use to think about their jobs'. These research agenda are ones I have tried to fulfil. I hope, too, to tackle the complaint made by David Weir, the head of an important business school. He says 'There is not enough 'simple ethnography' in management research, so we do not know in enough useful detail what management is, what it is like to manage' (1993: 22). But he goes on to say that simple ethnography 'of course, is not simple at all but relies on an ability to use language, to observe, and to empathise, above all to listen quietly, and to reflect over a long period'. Whatever abilities I have in these areas, I have striven to use them to the utmost.

Ethnographic research involves feeling one's way in confusing circumstances, struggling to make sense of ambiguous messages, reading signals, looking around, listening all the time, coping with conflicts and struggling to achieve tasks through establishing and maintaining a network of relationships. But this is what we all do all the time as human beings. This is how we cope with our lives. And it is what managers do in their more formalised 'managing' roles. This is a key theme of my *search for management*. In conducting this search I have plied the researcher's craft, something I have come to see as very similar to the craft of the manager (Watson 1994b). Both crafts involve close attention to language. Research is done through listening, reading, speaking and writing as well as observing. And it is through language, formal and informal, official and unofficial, that the bulk of the business of management is conducted. It is through speaking to each other that all of us make sense of the worlds we move in, whether we are trying to make sense of things as managers, as researchers or as part of our ordinary daily lives.

Chapter 1

Managing and making sense
Culture, control and dialogue

'I love this job. But sometimes it nearly drives me mad. I think I am a good manager. There is satisfaction in that, real satisfaction. But at times I think I'm totally wasting my time. I reckon I work with some of the best people around. We've got all the brains, all the skills you could want. But where is it getting us? In this business nobody can do it better than us. When we pull our fingers out we can do the impossible. Yet in many ways we are just floundering.'

'What's missing then?'

'That's the sixty-four thousand dollar question isn't it? We're undoubtedly up against it in the market-place – the recession and all that. But I just don't think we are getting it together. But why aren't we? We do all the right things. I mean just look at it. We've had the lot: total quality management, a winning culture, customer focus, continuous improvement, business improvement plans, decentralisation, business action teams, harmonisation, blah blah blah. Every bloody consultant in the world has given us advice. And what does it add up to? We ought to be one of these so-called "excellent" companies. But I don't think we are.'

'What does it add up to, then?'

'That's the trouble – it doesn't. Everybody is working flat out and working very competently – at their own thing. All the pieces of the puzzle are there, but we're not getting our picture together. Everybody's singing very nicely. But we are not singing off the same hymn sheet.'

'Why?'

'That's what we have got to understand. Every time we try to make sense of what is going on we just seem to make it more complicated. We shoot off in one direction, then another direction and then another. I'm not saying we can ever make it easy but I do think sometimes that we ought to just sit down and discuss what we are here for. We could then come to some sort of agreement about what we need to do. Then we might just all start moving in the same direction.'

THE SIMPLICITY OF MANAGEMENT

In my *search for management* among the managers of ZTC Ryland I had many conversations with managers who were, in their own ways, trying to make sense of what they were doing as managers in a company struggling to make its way in the business of developing and manufacturing telecommunications equipment. When I went to work and research with these managers, I had a lot of my own ideas about management and I had a lot of questions about it. My ideas about managerial work and the questions which troubled and excited me derived in part from my earlier experience of working within the management of a British aerospace company and in part from years of academic research and teaching in the management field. Conversations like this one with Bob Sherwood, some informal and some in interviews, helped me sharpen up a lot of my questions and make better sense of managerial work. The conversation with Bob Sherwood, a senior technical manager, had a particularly strong impact on me. I too was struggling to understand why an organisation in which so many modern and fashionable management innovations had been applied was not achieving anything like what had been hoped for. And I was intrigued by the notion that the problem had something to do with a tendency to make everything more complicated than it needed to be.

Implicit in Bob Sherwood's words is the idea that management is essentially a rather simple matter, and that we forget this at our peril. This indeed is a conclusion that I have come to. Managing an organisation is a simple process. But this is not to say it is an easy process. Because it is difficult to do we tend to see it as complicated. And the more complicated we believe it to be the more we make it complicated by piling initiative on top of initiative, reorganisation on top of reorganisation and new policy on top of new policy. Why does this happen? It is because management involves dealing with a lot of human beings: customers, clients, employees, investors, suppliers, regulators, and so on. The complexity lies in the web of relationships which the managers of organisations have to cope with, not in the basic processes which managerial work entails. To put this another way, we could say that managerial work is very simple in principle but that the practice leads us to experience it as a complex matter because we become intimidated by the large number of human interests and the great variety of personal foibles we have to contend with when we try to do it.

Management can be seen, I suggest, as *simply a matter of running an organisation so that the variety of people who want something out of it will go on supporting it in such a way that it is able to continue its existence into the future*. This initial definition begs the question of what an organisation is and what is meant, for example, by 'supporting' the organisation. This will all be considered later on as the search unfolds. At this stage I simply want to suggest that a valuable starting point for trying to make sense of managerial work is to try to get down to basics. This simple conception of the managerial task supports my claim that management is at the same time both simple in principle and difficult in practice.

KNOWING EVERYTHING AND KNOWING NOTHING

I do not think that managers themselves are unaware of the idea that managerial work, when we get down to basics, is a simple matter. And

they are certainly fully aware that it is no easy matter to carry out. I have
long had the suspicion that managers have a much better idea about what
they are doing, or might do, than tends to be suggested by what we see of
their actions in the actual setting of the everyday pressures and ambiguities
of work organisations. What we need to do is to bring out these basic
understandings, or 'theories in practice', and put them into a form which
is meaningful to managers and which is also sufficiently academically
rigorous to encourage academics to incorporate them into the material
they present to managers and would-be managers who seek their guidance
by attending their business schools and reading their books.

We also need to give managers confidence in the understanding of the
basic principles of managerial work which I believe many of them have,
albeit in an often ill-formed and only partially articulated form. The role
of the academic researcher is not to discover new truths or make basic
theoretical breakthroughs. As Alistair Mant once so powerfully put it:

> We do not, it seems to me, require one penny more spent on
> fundamental research into the 'unknown', but to understand why we are
> so bad at putting to use what we know already.
>
> (1979: 207)

To put this into a neat, if paradoxical, formula, we might say we know all
we need to know about management, yet, at the same time, we know
nothing.

Something similar to this is implied by two of the most influential
managerial evangelists of the 1980s, Tom Peters and Bob Waterman. It is
reported that a member of a three-day seminar looking at their research
and prescriptions said that it all amounted to 'a blinding flash of the
obvious' (Peters and Austin 1985: 3–4). The researchers agreed that what
they were offering was indeed common sense. Another seminar member
commented, however, 'I guess the obvious must not be so obvious or more
would practise it'.

The work being considered in this seminar was that appearing in the
immensely significant book, *In Search of Excellence* (Peters and Waterman
1982). We will return shortly to look closely at this book but, for the
present, we can note the summary of what Peters and Austin claim was its
common sense 'message'. This amounted to:

> giving everyone in the organisation the space to innovate, at least a little
> bit. Answering the phones and otherwise behaving with common
> courtesy towards customers. Making things that work. Listening to
> customers and asking them for their ideas. Then acting upon them.
> Listening to your people and asking them for their ideas. Then acting upon
> them. Wandering around: with customers, with your people, suppliers.
> Paying attention to pride, trust, enthusiasm – and passion and love.
>
> (1985: 4)

This is a clear statement of the simplicities of managerial work. Yet we know that such a reality can all too rarely be seen in practice. To some tastes the last words in this statement might be somewhat sentimental. Yet look back to the opening words of Bob Sherwood, who spoke of *loving* his job. This was far from unusual among the managers in ZTC Ryland. But equally far from unusual was his feeling that all the love and enthusiasm that many people were putting into the company was not leading to either the achievements or the satisfactions that they would have liked. We need to work out why this was. To achieve this understanding we have to bring together the thoughts and experiences of these managers themselves and some of the key ideas that social scientists have developed as resources for analysing the social and organisational world.

GETTING DOWN TO BASICS: EVERYBODY HAS TO MANAGE

The picture which is developing here is one in which the distinction between the academic researcher and those who are researched is blurred. Both, in effect, are theorists of a kind, for example. This insight can be taken further to argue that all human beings are practical social scientists striving to understand the world around them and work out guiding principles on which to base their behaviour. And, in a sense, all human beings are managers too; people struggling to cope, to manage, to shape their destinies.

The view of the world which suggests this argument is not a comfortable one. I believe that it is one that also frames some of the most significant changes in management thought which have unfolded in recent years – changes making prominent use of the concept of *culture*. But it is a view which, I feel, has been appreciated by too few of those who have started to talk about 'managing through culture', 'changing organisational cultures' or 'thriving on chaos' (Peters 1989) in the way encouraged by these developments. What is this view? It is one that takes the world to be a confusing, ambiguous and always potentially chaotic place.

Given the complexity of the world around us and its unpredictability, and given the limited mental ability of the human animal to gather and process information about the world, we can never really know what is going on around us. Neither can we ever be sure what the outcome of any action we take will be. Yet to survive in the world we have to manage our situation; to meet our material needs and to stay sane we struggle to exert some control.

Notice the language used here: 'we have to manage'. This suggests that all humans are managers in some way. But some of them also take on the formal occupational work of being managers. They take on a role of shaping aspects of human social structure and culture in parts of our societies – those parts we call work organisations. But these managers are not supermen and women. They have all the human anxieties, inadequacies and needs for meaning to be found in those whom they are meant to 'manage'. Managers' work thus involves a double essential task: managing others at the same time as managing themselves. But the very notion of 'managers' being separate people from the 'managed', a notion at the heart of traditional management thinking, undermines a capacity to handle this. Managers are pressured to be technical experts, devising rational and emotionally neutral systems and corporate structures to 'solve problems', 'make decisions', 'run the business'. These 'scientific' and rational-analytic practices give reassurance but can leave managers so distanced from the 'managed' that their capacity to control events is undermined. And they also tend to leave managers isolated from the essentially human community which the organisation might be. This can mean that their own emotional and security needs are not handled, with the effect that they retreat into all kinds of defensive, backbiting and ritualistic behaviour which further undermines their effectiveness as people moulding and maintaining a 'healthily' and productively cooperative organisation.

This perspective gives us a start in tackling the question, posed earlier, of why it is that managers do not effectively apply the principles of managerial work which are generally understood. But it is only a start, and the insights set out out here will be applied in the course of our search for management and our investigation of life in one real-life managerial setting. However, as I have already suggested, the insights making up this perspective have already been introduced into management thinking by those writers and consultants who have brought the social scientific concept of 'culture' to the centre of fashionable management discourse. I shall be arguing that just how deep and dangerous the waters this thinking takes us into is often underestimated. But first we need to examine the key work which set this bandwagon rolling.

THE SEARCH FOR EXCELLENCE AND THE REDISCOVERY OF CULTURE

In Search of Excellence by Tom Peters and Bob Waterman has probably been the most widely read management book of all time. By the time its sequel appeared, *A Passion for Excellence*, three years after the original, five million copies had been sold around the world (Peters and Austin 1985: xi). Numerous imitations and sequels have followed over the years and I know of more than one organisation which, not unusually I understand, bulk-purchased the book and circulated it among its managers. Certain of its key concepts have entered the argot of modern managers, who talk of giving their organisation a 'bias for action', or insist that it should 'stick to its knitting'. But the most significant effect has been to encourage the use of a language of 'corporate culture', 'changing the culture', 'managing through values'.

The book's authors, Peters and Waterman, were associated with the McKinsey consulting company, as were other authors whose work helped popularise 'culture talk' among managers (Deal and Kennedy 1982, Pascale and Athos 1982). This company had very much been identified with advising organisations to improve their performance through structural changes such as the divisionalisation of the enterprise. The shift in thinking towards cultures and cultural change could be seen as a form of 'new product development' among these consultants. There was indeed, as the 1980s approached, a market for new solutions to managerial problems. As Clutterbuck and Crainer (1988: 210) put it, 'unemployment was rocketing, manufacturing declining rapidly and people, especially in once self-assured America, were anxiously looking for solutions. The Japanese seemed to have it right, but how could their best practices be brought to the Western world?'.

This new culture-excellence style of thinking can also be seen as a partial return to some of the more humanistic concepts of management practice which had been associated with earlier popular writers such as Douglas McGregor (1960) in the 1960s and those associated with the 'quality of working life' movement in the early 1970s (Work in America 1973, Wilson 1973). Michael Dixon (1986: 14) argued that as the 'western economic climate turned cold' in the later 1970s there was the adoption by many organisations of what might be called 'macho-management'. Dixon was suggesting that in the 1980s there was a growing disenchantment with an all-out macho approach 'which is one of the reasons why millions of them are turning to the more humanistic theses of the new gurus'. Perhaps more significant than this, though, is the possibility that managers were also becoming disillusioned with popular business school ideas of management as a highly rationalistic and analytical type of work involving the use of complex and, typically quantitative, management techniques. Peters and Waterman signalled a move away from this approach in having, as Dixon put it, 'acknowledged the essentially intuitive aspects of good management in practice' (1986: 14). Peters and Waterman criticised American businesses for losing focus on 'product or people' because they focus on something else: on an 'overreliance on analysis from corporate ivory towers' (1982:40). This leads to over-caution, 'paralysis-induced-by-analysis', inflexibility and an inability to innovate through experimentation.

How widely understood this questioning of the idea of managers as number-crunching analysts and meticulous planners-of-everything has been is unclear. Nevertheless, it was probably part of the appeal of new culture-excellence writing, as was its demystifying of managerial work. There was the appeal of the common-sense nature of much of what was written, and there was an attractive injunction to 'keep things simple'. The book's suggestion that managers should involve themselves with people's feelings, desires and values may also have resonated with something which managers often suspect but rarely fully articulate (as I shall argue in later chapters): that management has a moral dimension to it as well as a technical one. It is doubtful, however, whether many of the managers who took up the ideas of books like *In Search of Excellence* with such enthusiasm fully grasped intellectually the significance of what was beginning to come out into the open about the value-soaked nature of managerial work.

Peters and Waterman and their associates were writing about excellent organisations as ones which have 'strong cultures' in which people were directed more by shared values – articulated by 'leaders' and absorbed by employees – than by rule books, commands or formal procedures. In this, they were taking us into questions about profound matters like the human need for meaning and into questions concerning what is right and wrong in human behaviour. To talk about 'managing through values' sounds straightforward in its glibness. But we have to remember that 'values' are notions of what is good and bad, right and wrong. These are deep waters indeed.

The theoretical grounds for taking management thinking in this direction are set out in *In Search of Excellence* and need to be carefully considered because they draw on some strands of social science thinking which have enormous relevance for any understanding of the nature of managerial work. In spite of the authors' urging of readers to consider the theoretical chapters of their book, one fears that too many took up the apparently reluctantly offered invitation to skip these chapters if they so wish (Peters and Waterman 1982: xv). One can read the culture-excellence literature as taking up some very significant ideas which were available in the organisation theory literature and then illustrating these with 'evidence' from real companies. But the more normal reading, and the one encouraged by the writers, is that the research fieldwork in the so-called excellent companies produced these ideas as 'research findings'. The rhetoric of searching for excellence is one which implies the undertaking of relatively naive investigations which 'discover' the roots of such excellence, after which the researchers 'buttress [their] observations on the excellent companies with sound social and economic theory' (Peters and Waterman 1982: xxvi).

I am suggesting, then, that the authors of *In Search of Excellence* can be seen as having made a shrewd reading of developing ideas in organisation theory in order to produce a new and usable 'product' to be offered to the market for new management ideas. But to make this material credible, it was presented as if it had been 'discovered' by scientific research. As a consequence of this and of the almost indiscriminate throwing-in of theoretical points, regardless of their origin or degree of relevance (cf. Carroll 1983), attention has been drawn away from valuable theoretical ideas. Critical fire has been drawn towards the highly questionable research credibility of the claimed fieldwork investigation (ibid., Saunders and Wong 1985) and the attention of practitioners towards the simpler-to-understand 'eight characteristics of excellence' such as 'bias for action', 'sticking to the knitting', 'hands-on, value driven', 'close to the customer'.

The most important concept put forward by Peters and Waterman is the final of their eight characteristics, and it is one which can be seen as providing a conceptual underpinning for all the rest. It is the idea of *simultaneous loose–tight controls*. The excellent organisation has loose controls, in the sense that people are not tightly constrained by supervisory surveillance, by corporate rules, by detailed performance measures or by closely prescribed roles. Yet, in these organisations, people do not wander away from serving the key purposes of the organisation's founders or leaders. The tightness of control comes from people *choosing* to do what is required of them because they wish to serve the *values* which they share with those in charge. These values, typically focusing on quality of service to customers, are transmitted and manifested in the organisation's *culture*. This culture uses stories, myths and legends to keep these values alive and people tend to be happy to share these values and subscribe to the corporate legends because to do so is to find meaning in their lives.

Peters and Waterman (1982:75) quote Bruno Bettelheim's (1976) *On the Uses of Enchantment: the meaning and importance of fairy tales*, in which he argues that the greatest human need and challenge is that of 'finding meaning in our lives'. They note his emphasis on the 'historically powerful role of fairy tales and myths in shaping meaning in our lives'. They later (1982:77) say: 'So strong is the need for meaning, in fact, that most people will yield a fair degree of latitude or freedom to institutions that give it to them.' This, they suggest, does not mean that people must surrender a sense of control or autonomy to the organisation. Meaning comes from adherence to key values, with people left free to make choices over particular actions.

The idea of managers shaping and communicating values to be shared throughout the organisation in which they are managing is not a new one. Peters and Waterman draw it from the classic management writing of Chester Barnard (1938) and from the social scientific work of Philip Selznick (1957) who wrote of managements moulding the 'character' of their organisations. More recent social scientists such as Henry Mintzberg and Andrew Pettigrew are also cited, but perhaps the important theoretical move forward by Peters and Waterman is their connecting of this to the idea of a basic human need for meaning and, also, to the view associated with James March and Johan Olsen (1976) and with Karl Weick (1979) that the world is an essentially ambiguous place in which we cannot realistically make detailed plans. The implication of this latter work (to which I will return shortly) is that we need to manage through broad values and culture, rather than through detailed plans and tight rules, because the world is too unpredictable and ambiguous a place for these latter methods of control to be viable.

The thesis I am extracting from *In Search of Excellence* is that, in managing organisations, loose–tight controls – using culture and shared values – work better than traditional 'tight' ones. This is, first, because it fits with what human beings are essentially like (meaning-seeking creatures) and, second, because it fits with what the world is like (an unpredictable and ambiguous place).

DEEP AND DANGEROUS WATERS?

The political and ethical implications of all this have to be confronted directly: there is a clear manipulative potential in the notion of managing organisations through values. As Carol Ray (1986) argues, in relating this literature to the ideas of the classical sociologist, Emile Durkheim, there is a suggestion that work organisations take on the role of managing the sacred dimension of social life. And to take on such a role necessarily has political implications, too. One view of these implications can be seen in Jim Silver's (1987) powerful attack on the ideological principles underlying *In Search of Excellence*. He sees the book as part of a 1980s Reaganite 'neo-conservative revival of faith in traditional American values', with an 'ideological thrust' which is 'a throwback to an earlier, much less sophisticated period' when the focus was on changing workers' attitudes 'without changing the nature of the job, without making tangible concessions to labour, and especially without increasing worker participation' (ibid. 126).

Because we are sailing in deep and potentially dangerous waters, we must be alert to the political and ideological implications of the concept of managing through cultures and meanings. Peters and Waterman's work may have overtones of 'new right' politics, as Silver (ibid.) suggests. They may, as he also argues, be 'the new sellers of snake oil', peddling fake medicines to the dupes of a system dedicated to the interests of 'capital'. But the underlying concepts of the thinking cannot be dismissed. Paul Thompson and David McHugh (1990) recognise this, going as far as suggesting that there is something 'tragic' about the suspect qualities of *In Search of Excellence* because 'we have a lot to learn from studying organisational cultures'. We cannot be diverted from such important matters just because we reject either the ideological or the academic credentials of much of the work that has brought the concept of culture to the fore. These authors want to jettison 'impoverished notions of culture which mistake style as substance':

> Creating a culture resonant with overall goals is relevant to *any* organisation, whether it be trade unions, voluntary groups or producer co-operatives. Indeed, it is more important in such consensual groupings.

Cooperatives, for example, can degenerate organisationally because they fail to develop adequate mechanisms for transmitting the original ideals from founders to new members and sustaining them through new shared experiences.

(1990: 235)

This statement is important because it suggests that although we may disagree with or dislike the values or purposes of particular organisations which are managed through key attention to culture (say, a viciously exploitative commercial company, a suspect religious cult or a totalitarian political party), it does not follow that we reject the basic proposition that the organising of complex human tasks over an extended period of time *necessarily* involves the organisers in attending to matters of meaning, culture and value. Those who entirely reject the idea of managing work through culture because of particular humanistic values are rejecting the potential for the successful functioning of organisations which they may favour as much as they are attacking those they dislike.

If we are going to take seriously the possibility of the managers of work organisations manipulating and shaping the cultures of those organisations, we must fully recognise the significance of the 'variables' we are dealing with. We must have full charts of the deep and dangerous waters in which we are sailing. To create such charts we have got to look at four interlinked issues, each of which, if not appreciated, can act as a rock on which our understanding, and hence our practice, might founder. First, we have to consider our understanding of human nature. Without this we can have little appreciation of the role that culture plays in human life, and I shall bring onto deck to help us here a modest little hedgehog. Second, we have to recognise how limited or bounded is our human rationality. Much of the time, in organisations and in life generally, we are navigating our way in the dark. Culture again provides resources to find our way through the dark and the fog. Third, we need to look at the concept of culture itself and the key role played in it by story-telling. Fourth, we must consider the importance of language, not just in human communication, but in the very process of human thinking and decision-making. These are all themes which will be developed as the search for management unfolds in subsequent chapters. But, if I may deploy the nautical metaphor just one more time, I shall end this chapter by laying the keel of the theoretical vessel whose superstructure will be built up as the journey proceeds. To put this in more traditional scientific terms, I shall reveal my basic conceptual framework: a set of framing ideas I call my *strategic exchange perspective*.

OF HUMANS AND HEDGEHOGS

The way we think about and deal with other human beings is inevitably informed by assumptions about human nature. This was famously pointed out with regard to managerial work by Douglas McGregor (1960) when he encouraged managers to move from 'theory X' assumptions, which regard people as essentially lazy and inclined to avoid responsibility, towards 'theory Y' assumptions about people as naturally responsibility-seeking and as having considerable creative and imaginative talents waiting to be tapped. To understand the role of cultures in human life, however, we need to consider much more basic matters than these: 'human nature' is something that can follow either of these two directions, depending on the circumstances we are considering (Watson 1986: 111, 154–7). To go to a more basic level we can start by comparing humans to other animals.

All animals, other than the human one, act on the basis of instincts combined with some limited and rather mechanical reasoning and learning. As Edmund Leach (1982: 38) says, anthropologists from the start needed a concept to differentiate 'man from no-man'. Culture, as opposed to nature, is the concept to do this. And central to culture is language.

The human capacity for language creates the 'possibility of making value judgements and exercising moral choices' (ibid. 104). With Leach, we can put aside the experimentally trained chimpanzees who have been made by humans into something 'betwixt and between humans and apes' (ibid. 103). Let us consider the much more typical hedgehog I can see from my window as I write. The small hedgehog I can see on my lawn is not likely to be worrying about whether or not it should eat another worm or whether it is a good or bad thing to walk across someone's lawn. It has neither the words nor the concepts of good and bad, let alone those of worm and lawn. Its 'hedgehogness' is built in; it hedgehogs its way through its life. It neither needs nor has the capacity to worry about rights and wrongs. To be a hedgehog is to be a hedgehog.

A male hedgehog does not worry about what is the appropriate behaviour, way of walking or way of dressing for a male, any more than the female hedgehog experiments with different clothes or styles of expression to be seen as appropriately feminine. The hedgehog does not worry about whether or not its mother loved it or in what kind of esteem it is held by other hedgehogs. Neither does it agonise about the inevitability of its eventual demise: it has no word for death, no concept of mortality. Hedgehogs neither debate with nor evangelise to others about the possibility of life after death. Heaven, as humans conceive it, may have a place for hedgehogs but hedgehogs have no place for heaven.

The point of all this reflection on hedgehogs is a simple one; it is to bring out something essential about the human condition. Hedgehogs do not agonise over all these matters, but humans do. Humans do not have guidelines for behaviour and interaction with others 'wired into' their brains. Humans have continually to 'work on' their humanness. They have to achieve humanness. They have to think about what it is to be female or male, a parent, a teenager, an ageing individual, a husband, wife, lover, friend, enemy, brother, sister, manager. We have an awful lot we need to make sense of to survive mentally. And we could not handle alone all these sources of anxiety. Our capacity for culture, language and concepts partly creates these problems. It makes possible, through the provision of the very words, for example, the question 'who am I?' or the question, 'Why should I follow this managerial instruction?'. But it also assists us with handling them.

FEELING OUR WAY IN THE DARK: THE LIMITS OF HUMAN RATIONALITY

Human beings, to a vastly greater extent than any other animal, are *choosing* creatures. Related to this is the advanced human capacity for reasoning: working out in any given circumstance what the most appropriate means might be to achieve a particular end. But, here, we hit a further problem for the human animal: its capacity for reasoning, considerably greater than that of other animals though it is, is nevertheless massively limited. This is recognised in the classic work of Herbert Simon (1957) and his concept of *bounded rationality*.

The human mind, Simon points out, is severely limited in the amount of information it can take in, and once it has acquired information it can only do so much with it. We simply cannot know 'all the facts', or more than a tiny fraction of them, in any decision-making situation, and the processing of that information has its own limits. In deciding whom to marry, or in making a business decision to go into a new market, we cannot know very much. The uncertainties and ambiguities are vast and so we fall back to a considerable extent on recipes, formulae, legends, folk tales and intuition to make sense of these situations. Culture again becomes a resource, with all its stories of what has happened before and its notions of good and bad (a 'good wife', a 'badly run business'). We can do no other. We cannot 'know' our environment. Its ambiguity is so great we can only, as Karl Weick (1979) puts it, 'enact' it – make and act upon our own interpretation of it. And it is a recognition of the force of this kind of theorising that strongly encouraged Peters and Waterman (1982), as we saw earlier, to turn against the image of managers as analysts and system builders.

 Culture can be understood as a human creation which helps human beings avoid the dark abyss of disorder and chaos into which they might otherwise fall. The cultures we develop also assist us in making decisions. In managing our personal lives as well as our business ones, we are always, in a sense, in the dark. Where our cultures help us here is in assisting us to feel our way in the dark. We are not left to whistle to keep our spirits up; we can talk to all of those who have gone before us by invoking the principles, guidelines, norms, values and precedents recorded on the cultural tape recorder. Cultures provide powerful guidelines for human action as well as resources to help us shape and justify actions which promote or defend our interests.

THE NEED FOR CULTURE AND THE SIGNIFICANCE OF STORY-TELLING

I define culture as

> the system of meanings which are shared by members of a human grouping and which define what is good and bad, right and wrong and what are the appropriate ways for members of that group to think and behave.
>
> (Watson 1987: 83)

A culture is, in part, a moral system. It not only defines values (ideas about what is good and bad, right and wrong) for those who subscribe to it, but contains assumptions about the nature of the world and of human beings (cf. Schein 1985). It also helps people construct their identities. The culture of our society provides resources for the individual to create an answer to the question of who they are; it offers various types of haircut one might adopt to 'be' a man or a woman; various modes of dress one might wear to be a manager, a musician, a holiday-maker; various ways of behaving to be a parent, a son or daughter, a senior citizen. We all work on our identities all the time: making meaning through a dialogue with the culture (or cultures, in so far as we are parts of several groups), its norms, values and symbols. Through our actions we are contributing to culture as well as taking from it. Cultures are human-made and we are constantly remaking them as we interactively devise new ways of going about our lives. But cultures help us with more than the provision of resources of clothes, hairstyles, behavioural cues. They provide resources to help with more profound existential problems about the nature of obligation to others, the meaning of death, the character of love. Daniel Bell (1977) sees these questions as ones arising for every human culture and points to the role of religions in providing ways for people to handle these problems.

Without the resources of culture, whether given a religious expression or not, we could not survive. We do not all go through our daily lives agonising directly about the significance of mortality, the nature of love, the meaning of fidelity or the 'good life'. But these are issues for us; we need help with all of them. In a sense, we handle these things by continually 'talking to our culture' about them, thus allowing our culture in part to 'do our worrying for us'. How? It is done through looking at, reading about, engaging in stories in novels, newspapers, films, jokes and gossip – stories about love, death, hate, infidelity, illness, bliss. The average twentieth-century person may not consciously worry about their inevitable death (or the possibility of immediate death by sudden accident or murder) every day of their lives. But they *engage* with these matters daily in the stories of murder, accident and war offered by plays, papers, books, film or television screens – fact and fiction alike.

This engaging with stories in popular culture, high culture, fiction, reportage and gossip to help us handle our deeper existential anxieties parallels the idea associated with Sigmund Freud (1900) of our dreams functioning as vehicles for the working out of problems which we do not recognise in our conscious lives. The 'mythic' element of all these cultural products functions like fairy tales do for children (Propp 1968, Silverstone 1981, Bettelheim 1976). Our anxieties are raised as the ogre storms from his castle, the murderer creeps up behind the victim, the adulterous seducer slips in, and out, of the bedroom of the erstwhile faithful spouse. But order and calm is restored to our lives as the fairy tale ends with 'and they all lived happily ever after', the murder film comes to a close or we shut our newspaper and go to empty the dishwasher. These same cultural sources provide us with human figures and groups with whom to identify: detective heroes, football teams, rock groups, ethnic or national groupings, religious or political leaders. All of these, and many others, provide possible sources of meaning in our lives, some anchor for identity. The culture-excellence writers are keen to add hero managers, legendary business leaders and our own employing organisations to this list.

This is partly why we are going into these complex matters in a book about management. To talk of culture and values and, even more seriously, about changing cultures in organisations, has become central to management thinking and we need to realise the deep and difficult waters we are getting into. Corporate cultures only play a partial role in our lives but, in so far as the leaders of work organisations follow the exhortations of the culture-excellence writers discussed earlier to influence employees through making meanings for them, they are dabbling in matters traditionally left to the other guardians of the sacred, the churches and leaders of religions. And in writing on these matters here I am developing some of the theory left implicit in *In Search of Excellence*, explaining just why 'strong cultures' seen in some business organisations' 'stories, myths, and legends appear to be very important' (Peters and Waterman 1982: 75). They do indeed 'convey the organisation's shared values, or culture' (ibid.: 75). They are attempting to influence their employees' ideas about commitment, good and bad, right and wrong, just as do the parables of big religions or the moral fables of pop culture.

Culture in its broadest sense, and in Peter Berger's terms (1973), is a human and social construction which creates *nomos*, order, out of *chaos*. It saves us from madness through the provision of a shield against terror:

The socially established nomos may . . . be understood, perhaps in its most important aspect, as a shield against terror . . . The anthropological presupposition for this is a human craving for meaning that appears to have the force of instinct. Men are congenitally compelled to impose a meaningful order upon reality. This order, however, presupposes the social enterprise of ordering world construction . . . Separation from society . . . inflicts unbearable psychological tensions upon the individual . . . The ultimate danger of such separation, however, is the danger of meaninglessness. This danger is the nightmare par excellence, in which the individual is submerged in a world of disorder, senselessness and madness . . .

Seen in the perspective of society, every nomos is an area of meaning carved out of a vast mass of meaninglessness, a small clearing of lucidity in a formless, dark, always ominous jungle.

(1973: 31–2)

This, I suggest, is the context into which we need to put the words of those best-selling management writers quoted earlier, stressing that 'so strong is the need for meaning . . . that most people will yield a fair degree of latitude or freedom to institutions that give it to them' (Peters and Waterman 1982: 77). A culturally transmitted sense of order, or *nomos*, is humanly constructed and our very sanity is based on our relationship to it. At the heart of this process of constructing a sense of order is language and processes of dialogue; not just dialogues between people and their cultures, but dialogues between individuals themselves – even dialogues between ideas within our own minds.

TALKING TO OTHERS; TALKING TO OURSELVES: DIALOGUE AND RHETORIC

Human beings are not passively moulded by their culture. I have referred to people *engaging* with their culture and to culture providing resources which people use in the process of achieving their humanness and making sense of their lives. People, to shape their lives, give to and take from the cultures around them. But this cannot happen literally, because cultures are not persons. We can only exchange with other people; our dialogue with our culture is a dialogue with others. It is not just a matter of face-to-face dialogue, though: our very process of thinking and decision-making involves us in a dialogue in our minds with the arguments of human others, whether these be remembered arguments of particular people ('My mother always said brown shoes don't go with a dark suit') or cultural norms ('In this company you always wear black shoes'). Thinking and deciding ('What shoes shall I wear?') has a dialogic form.

I have already revealed the key role that my own dialogues with managers have played in the development of my thinking about managerial work. This relates to a view of human beings as *rhetorical* animals (Harré 1980, Billig 1987, Leith and Myerson 1989) and of human life as essentially *dialogic* (Bahktin 1981). In the essential spirit of this idea, we can illustrate this idea of thinking as rhetorical in the sense of engaging with the ideas of others with a small event from my fieldwork: the case of the manager's second lunch-time pint of beer.

A small number of managers taking a lunch break in a public house a mile or two away from the factory had all finished their pints of bitter. All but Sid Breaston were ready for a second drink; he sat staring at his glass.

> 'Can't you make your mind up, Sid?'
> 'Sandra says I drink too much. But I am damned thirsty. Then again, it's me who's driving, so perhaps I . . .'
> 'Come on, are you having one?'
> 'I never work very well if I have more than one drink before the afternoon. But Sandra did say the other day when I went to the pub that I deserved a break now and again.'
> 'Sid, for goodness sake.'
> 'OK. I'll have a half pint then.'
> 'And will you tell Sandra?'
> 'I'll say I really like the way she cares for me . . . that she's the perfect secretary . . . and because she's so caring she'll appreciate that I deserved a drink after that bloody control meeting went on all morning.'

As this reporting to the company of Sid's mental debate reached its conclusion, another full pint of beer was put into his hand.

In this thinking process ('should I or shouldn't I?'), Sid was engaging with the arguments of his secretary and with those who say 'it is illegal to drive a car if you drink more than a certain amount'. But he was even more directly 'debating with himself' when he engaged with his own argument, derived from his past experience, about the problem of working effectively after drinking beer. He was arguing with himself, as if he were another person. And Sid's rhetorical thinking turns to rhetorical speaking (or the planning of it) when he constructs the argument to be put to Sandra on return to the factory. I do not know whether he ever spoke these words to his secretary but, if he had, we would have seen an action commonplace enough but one getting close to a central element of managerial work: persuading others, justifying decisions, seeking support.

If one looks at this piece of pub dialogue or at the various other pieces of dialogue I have reported so far in the book, the use of a particular style of analysis should be visible. It accords with Michael Billig's injunction that, to understand the meaning of words and sentences,

> [one] should not examine merely the words within that discourse or the images in the speaker's mind at the moment of utterance. One should

also consider the positions which are being criticised, or against which a justification is being mounted.

(1987: 91)

To think and to speak is to engage with counter-thoughts and counter-arguments. It is part of the process whereby we negotiate reality with others through the cultural medium of discourse and through which we justify and make sense, to ourselves and others, of what we do.

This book itself, as an expression of the thinking of its author, is an outcome of various dialogues. My thinking involved hundreds of dialogues with managers as well as mental dialogues with the arguments offered in previous academic and other writing (including my own). The 'processing' of these arguments in my mind has led to the formulation of further arguments; the ones which constitute the present 'text'. This is to suggest that the book cannot wholly stand outside the social processes it is analysing. It is not some remote analysis of the world from the outside by a scientist who is no part of the world he is studying. This book is, in Paul Atkinson's words (1990: 2), an 'artful product'. As he says of another study, 'the narratives and descriptions, the examples, the characters and the interpretative commentary are woven together into a highly contrived product' (ibid.: 2). The book is a rhetorical product; it is a set of artfully crafted arguments in which I am trying to persuade my readers to accept the plausibility of my view of the world and my view of management. It could not be otherwise.

Social science writers, in crafting their work, must have some kind of scaffolding with which to work, even if it is a scaffolding which they build up piecemeal as the edifice rises from the ground. The conceptual framework helping shape the present work was developed in this way. But I need to reveal its bare bones at this stage. It is the skeleton which holds together what is to follow in subsequent chapters and give shape to the whole enterprise. I hope, too, that it might be used as an apparatus for subsequent studies by myself and, indeed, others.

THE STRATEGIC EXCHANGE PERSPECTIVE

The strategic exchange perspective is a way of looking at individual and social human life in a way which draws on a range of ideas from social theory. It tries to deal with the essential two-sidedness of social life: the side in which individuals can be seen to initiate, choose and shape their world, and the side in which they can be seen as being constrained and shaped by influences external to themselves. Human actions, in the managerial context or any other, have patterns to them which arise from an interplay between deliberate choice or purpose and the social, political economic circumstances in which they find themselves – circumstances which involve a constant struggle to cope and survive.

Central to all human interactions are processes of exchange, by which is meant, in the words of the *Oxford English Dictionary*, 'the action, or an act of, reciprocal giving and receiving . . . of things in general'. Thus two people, or two organisations (as coalitions of human actors), may exchange goods for money. But, equally, an exchange can be other than material and can be other than immediate in its fulfilment. We can see an example of this in the notion expressed by a manager in ZTC Ryland:

> 'I give all the people in my department a lot of respect and I always treat them with courtesy and consideration, however hectic things might get. It therefore seems reasonable for me to expect them to help me out when the pressure is on.'

Exchange, in this usage, covers the symbolic and the abstract as well as the material and the concrete. To see human society and relationships in terms of exchange is not to imply a cynical view of crudely self-interested individuals calculatingly and constantly trading for short-term or specified returns. Love, affection, respect and caring are exchanged by people where the 'give and take' is not necessarily of a measured or even of a balanced kind. Exchanges which might be labelled as calculating, short-term or selfish frequently occur, of course. To so label action is to take a particular moral position on those exchanges. But however we may label any given exchange, we have to recognise that exchanges between human individuals and human groupings do not occur randomly. They are related to the interests, purposes and projects of those who engage in them. Exchanges tend to be *strategically shaped*.

As in my use of the term 'exchange', I am using the concept of strategy in a broad sense. Whilst being sensitive to the danger of the ideological baggage carried by the word 'strategy', with its origins in the notion of generalship, helping to legitimate hierarchical relationships in society (Knights and Morgan 1990), I see it as an appropriate term to capture that much broader quality of human action whereby our specific actions have some relationship to a broader purposive scheme of things – however vague or emergent that scheme may be. The human individual, on the one hand, and the work organisation, on the other, have to survive in a challenging and risk-filled world, and there tends to be some pattern to the approach taken by any person or particular organisation to achieving that survival.

I see human action as being strategic in so far as it is *shaped* in some way by the need of individuals or of groups to cope with the challenges of their environment. And organisational activities are strategic in so far as they shape the organisation to help it cope with the challenges of its environment and hence to survive into the future. Such a usage reflects, as Martin Shaw puts it, 'an increasing self-perception of individuals, and basic social groups such as families, as embattled agents, in constant tension with other individuals, groups and institutions, in a competitive social environment' (1990: 467). But the shaping to which I refer here is that which comes about as a result of the interplay between the intentions of the person acting and the constraints (and opportunities) of their circumstances. Hence, we can talk of a person's career strategy in the present sense of strategy as a pattern which can be discerned in a person's life as a result of intentional choices mixed with the jobs which did (or did not) become available at particular times. And this directly parallels Henry Mintzberg's notion of corporate strategies as realised strategies: 'Strategy is a pattern, specifically a pattern in a stream of actions' (1988: 14).

These *shaping* processes are equivalent to what Anthony Giddens (1984) calls 'structuration'. Human initiative ('agency') is not simply constrained by the circumstances in which it occurs ('structure'); it may equally be enabled. The structures and circumstances in which humans find themselves partly shape what they think and do, yet humans also shape those thoughts and circumstances (the extent to which they are able to do this varying with the power associated with the position in which they find themselves). The managers of a business organisation may, for example, be constrained in what they can produce and sell by what people out in the market-place will buy. But demand does not exist independently of the behaviour of producers; those managers may try to influence the market through such activities as market research, product development and advertising. The 'market' is both a constraining and an enabling phenomenon. To manage an organisation is to shape it to take account of this dual aspect of its structural context. At a more individual level we might see an individual manager potentially constrained in their desire to advance their career by, say, a culture which encourages discrimination against their gender. They might try to shape those circumstances to their 'strategic' advantage by exploiting certain expectations of their femininity or masculinity.

One of the most significant things I am trying to do in developing this strategic exchange perspective is to relate strategic exchanges engaged in by *individuals* to ones involving *work organisations*. Central to the processes whereby individuals engage with each other are ones of exchange whereby people trade material and symbolic resources with each other. Thus, I may exchange money with another person for a pint of cask-conditioned beer, which simultaneously deals with my thirst and transmits the message to others in the bar that I am an individual with good taste. Equally, I may exchange a joke with a manager to establish that I am a friendly person and a person worth talking to, as opposed to an interfering consultant or nosey researcher. And moving to the organisational level: central to the processes whereby organisations engage with their environment are ones of exchange whereby the organisation trades goods, services, revenues, corporate image and so on with various parties inside and outside the organisation in order to obtain the resources necessary for it to survive within its environment into the long-term. Thus an organisation rewards its employees with an appropriate level of cash, security, job interest and the like to gain the quantity and level of effort and commitment required to keep it going. At the same time it trades goods and meanings (through, say, product image) with its customers.

Because organisations are effectively the outcomes of the actions of human beings, as opposed to entities existing entirely separately, the way they shape themselves is dependent on the way the people with whom they 'trade' go about shaping themselves; moulding their projects in life and their identities. Managers are among these individuals. But not only are managers themselves parties 'trading' with their organisation, they are also charged with the task of shaping the organisation. This makes them especially interesting and the strategic exchange perspective would suggest that if we wanted to understand, say, how the strategy of a particular business had been reshaped we would need to look not just at all the interested parties that the management had needed to take into account in making that change, we would also want to look at these individuals to see how these moves related to their specific interests, personal priorities and views of themselves. A group of managers uninterested in technology, for example, might pull things in a different direction from managers who were deeply fascinated by technological innovation.

AND SO, FORWARD

Our search for management is concerned with the various ways in which managers both shape themselves and shape their organisations. Although there is ambiguity among managers about what it is that they do, we shall search through that fog of ambiguity for ideas, theories even, which if brought out into the light of day might help managers to be more confident in what they do and hence to do it to better effect. The next chapter will look at the nature of management itself, taking into account both developments in management thought and the ideas emerging from dialogues with managers in ZTC Ryland. The chapter following that will focus on managers' personal attempts to shape their lives, before I return to the organisational level to look at processes whereby ZTC as an organisation has itself been shaped and reshaped through managerial processes. After this we can concentrate on the various ways in which managers can be understood as people who simultaneously manage their own lives and, in their jobs, manage to manage.

Chapter 2

Management

An activity in search of itself

'You know when you're a kid, people ask what you want to do when you grow up?'

'Yes.'

'Can you imagine a kid saying "I want to be a manager when I grow up"?'

'That's a good question. Don't you think they would?'

'Of course they wouldn't, would they, seriously though?'

'I suppose not. But why wouldn't they?'

'Well it's not a job is it? No . . . I mean . . . of course it's a job. But it's not a job a kid would know about, is it? At school you might say "I want to train to be a scientist" or "I want to learn to be a pilot". I can remember saying those things. There was a kid in our class who said he wanted to train to be an accountant. I remember that quite well. I think I had a vague idea of what an accountant was. But being a manager is not something you set out to do is it?'

'Are you sure?'

'I think it's much more that you sort of just become a manager, don't you? You know, you start off doing a real – I mean a – you know, an actual job and then you end up getting promoted. And then you're the manager. You see what I am getting at, don't you?'

Laughing, I replied, 'Yes, you're saying that you don't have a real job any more. Writing software was a real job and now you've given up real work.'

At this, Steve Loscoe leaned forward and slowly banged his head on his desk,

'I certainly don't feel like I've given up working but I have to admit, all joking aside, I really do wonder what my bloody job is sometimes. I say to myself "I'm in charge of this office and the office in Birmingham" but then I ask whether I'm really in charge of even myself when it comes down to it. I get told to jump here, jump there, sort this, sort that, more than I ever did before I was even a section leader.'

MANAGEMENT AS AN OCCUPATION?

This conversation between myself and Steve Loscoe, a ZTC technical manager, sets managerial work alongside other occupations and raises questions about the extent to which management has a clear occupational identity. To look at a type of work in occupational terms is to locate it within the overall division of labour of a society and examine the consequences of the ways in which members of society see involvement in that work as constituting membership of an identifiable group within society.

Management can be said to be an occupation, in the formal sense that people are frequently categorised as managers, not just within the organisations which employ them but also in official employment surveys and statistics. It would also be categorised as an occupation if we applied to it a sociological concept of occupation as entailing 'engagement on a regular basis on a part or the whole of a range of work tasks which are identified under a particular heading or title by both those carrying out these tasks and by a wider public' (Watson 1987: 122). However, management is less unambiguously an occupation than the classic vocations of butcher, baker or candlestick-maker. Steve Loscoe's comments in his conversation with me suggest that it is less meaningful a category than those of scientist, pilot or accountant. But he goes even further, to suggest to us that even when one is a manager, one can be very unclear about just what one's role is. He goes so far with this that he uses language implying that management is not a 'real' or an 'actual' job compared with, in this case, the job of software engineer.

Why should this matter? Could one not argue that this ambiguity is of little importance – a matter of mere academic quibbling, another example of what one managerial colleague referred to as 'this ridiculous need of all you academics to label everything and pin everything down'? It could be argued, as indeed it was by the person who made this comment, that as long as managers 'get on with the job and do it well', then it matters little whether we can define the nature of the beast. But there is a powerful response which can be made to this: how can one get on with the job if there is not some clarity of what the job really entails? This was a matter of practical importance to me in my own job within ZTC. I had to develop a scheme of managerial competencies – indicators of the characteristics to be sought in and developed in ZTC Ryland managers. This meant that I needed to have an idea about what 'doing the job well' would mean. But perhaps more important here is the need for managers themselves to have a clear concept of what managerial work is, so that they can judge for themselves whether they are doing the right things and are doing them well.

There are broader reasons why management as an occupational activity needs to 'search for itself', if I may continue with this metaphorical notion of management as a lost soul searching for an identity. We can identify several reasons why it needs to present itself to the world clearly and meaningfully. A clear image of an occupation is necessary if it is going to attract and recruit appropriate people and a clear conception of the occupation is vital if people are to be educated and trained to carry it out. Also, since management is very much involved with issues of control and social power, it needs to establish its legitimacy as an activity within the community (cf. Anthony 1986), an argument we will return to in the final chapter. This means that it needs to know what its 'role' in the world or, rather, in the broader division of labour is. You have to be clear about what you are doing in life before you can justify it to others. Furthermore, such clarity plays a role in helping members of the occupation to 'place' themselves socially: people like to be able to tell other people fairly simply what sort of work they do.

To help throw light on these issues, and how management stands with regard to them, I will be looking at how the managers in the study talk about what their involvement in managerial work means to them. But, in the spirit of maintaining a 'dialogue' between 'theoretical' and 'practical' thinking, this needs to be set in the context of the existing formal and academic thinking about the nature of management. This thinking plays its part in helping, or hindering, the understandings of management held by people living in the societies in which it is taught and otherwise disseminated. 'Management thought', as this kind of material is sometimes known (Child 1969), has, I believe, made its contributions to the confusions surrounding our concept of what management is. Nevertheless, there has been a useful trend in academic thinking in recent years towards overcoming this. It entails a recognition of managerial work as *organisational work*; managers manage work organisations to enable them to survive.

THE LOGIC OF MANAGERIAL WORK: SHAPING ORGANISATIONS TO SURVIVE

Human beings do not simply need to solve the problems of meaning which were discussed in the last chapter, in order to survive. They must also find food, shelter, physical comfort and material gratification. None of these things are separate from the cultural side of humanness: they are all drawn into the interpretative web which human beings weave. What we aspire to, which foods we eat, what sort of dwelling we prefer, how we subsist relative to others, all these things are culturally significant. But to produce and distribute the goods and services which handle these interwoven material and symbolic needs and wants, humans make structural arrangements in their societies. And among the social structural devices of classes, states, and the like are work organisations; characteristic institutions of the division of labour in modern societies.

Societies have been developed through human history to cope with problems of human existence; providing cultures and social, economic and political structures through which people meet material needs and make sense of the world. But the evidence of history, with all the miseries, sufferings, wars and human tragedies which punctuate the successes and degrees of contentment which have been achieved, suggests that chaos is *[margin note: POWER VIOLENCE & INTIMIDATION]* only being held at bay. The building of societies and the creating of cultures is a process which involves power, violence and intimidation, and which regularly sees some human groups winning out over others in the competition for scarce and valued resources, for power and for the freedom to define meanings for others. Against this background of struggle, power and inequality as well as of natural disasters, humans strive to keep a degree of order in human relationships and struggle to maintain a sense of order in the way they come to terms with the world. Work *[margin note: MGT AS BRINGING ORDER TO CHAOS]* organisations play their part in this and are as vulnerable to chaos as any other part of human society. To avoid it they have to be managed.

Managerial work happens in work organisations such as schools, businesses, hospitals, prisons and administrative bureaucracies. These institutions represent a segment of this broader human world. But they are especially interesting, not just because they are microcosms of the wider human world, but because they are segments of broader social and cultural organisation which are deliberately designed and formally managed. In a sense, the managers of modern work organisations are creators and manipulators of miniature human societies. They actively devise social structures and cultures within which people relate to each other and find at least some of their life-meanings.

Organisations are *sets of ongoing human relationships utilising various technologies in which people cooperate to achieve tasks which would otherwise not be possible, either at all or from an equivalent resource base.* These technologies range from typewriters to robotic tools, lecture-giving to document-filing. Organisations have focal tasks such as producing cars, treating patients, educating students. But the people who contribute to the organisation through investing in it, say, or by becoming employed by it do not necessarily do so with a primary interest in meeting these purposes. Contributors have a multiplicity of purposes, to make a profit, to earn a wage, to make life interesting, to gain status, and so on.

Productive cooperation, therefore, has to be striven for. It has to be brought forth from the working-out of the vast diversity of projects being pursued by the various people in and around the organisation. Within the organisation every employee, managers included, has their own *orientation to work*, an ever-shifting set of meanings and priorities which they attach to their participation in the organisation and which influences their behaviour. Managers' work orientations will be a key concern of Chapter 3 but, for the present, we need to recognise that the variety of orientations *[margin note: PROBLEMATIC]* among managers and all other employees, and the range of expectations held by other stakeholders, means that the productive cooperation which gives work organisations their rationale is essentially problematic. This is why there has to be 'organisational work' or management.

[margin note: MANAGERIAL WORK] Managerial work is concerned with shaping the productive cooperation of individuals and groups within the organisation and matching these

efforts with the demands of those outside the organisation with whom there has to be 'trading' for the organisation to continue in existence. At the heart of the managerial role is the task of orchestrating a series of exchanges with internal and external parties in order to achieve long-term organisational survival (an argument to be developed in Chapter 5). Managerial work is thus about strategic exchange: those directing the organisation are trading and balancing meanings and resources across all those constituencies whose support is needed for the continued existence of the organisation – whether these be junior employees, key customers, senior managers, shareholders, state agencies or pressure groups.

The implication of this analysis is that managerial work is, in effect, organising work. To pull the argument together, we can say that the conception of managerial work which is emerging from all this is one of an activity carried out in organisations to develop and maintain structural arrangements and cultural understandings about appropriate behaviour which are necessary for exchanges to occur whereby resource demands by groups inside and outside the organisation (employees, managers, share-holders, the state, customers, for example) are met to sufficient a degree to enable resource requirements to be supplied (work efforts, investment, legal approval, revenue), allowing the organisation to continue in existence into the future.

This analysis develops a shorthand statement of the nature of management I have used previously:

> Managing is organising: pulling things together and along in a general direction to bring about long-term organisational survival.
>
> (Watson 1986: 41)

Organisational activities have to be shaped so that the organisation sufficiently satisfies the requirements of all those parties who must supply the organisation with resources to enable it to continue in existence. To shape human activity in this way involves setting up systems and procedures, rules, rewards and structures. But human beings, who join work organisations with all sorts of interests, wants and needs of their own, will not be drawn together into the sort of positive cooperative effort typically required in modern organisations by systems and rules alone. To contribute initiative and give commitment to a broader purpose shared with others, the work needs to be made *meaningful* to people.

MANAGEMENT AS FUNCTION, ACTIVITY AND TEAM

The kind of ambiguity about the occupational activity of management seen earlier in the words of Steve Loscoe can be related to a basic confusion arising both in everyday lay talk about management and in more formal discussions. This is a confusion between, first, management as a general function necessary for the successful production of goods and services in an organisation and, second, management as a complex and varied set of activities which are carried out by managers. This confusion is only added to by the tendency to use the expression 'management' or 'the management' in a third way as a collective term for the people in charge of an organisation. There tends to a lack of clarity much of the time about whether we are talking about what the occupation of management is 'for' (what it does within the broad division of labour in society), what members of the occupation actually do, and who the members of the occupation tend to be.

Such confusion comes about in part as a result of a linguistic problem: we use the term 'management' to mean rather different things at different times. And this is not only an issue for the broad question of the identity of the occupation. The broad issue relates to very specific and immediate ones: there are very good practical reasons for clarifying which sense we are intending when we use the term. This was illustrated by a distinction I found myself making in an early conversation with a group of managers, when I found myself suggesting that the 'management here is not too successful at the moment', yet spoke of my impression that 'there are some very good managers around here'. That dialogue was part of my own process of clarifying what the issues were for me in working out my own contribution to 'improving' managerial performance in ZTC Ryland. This distinction was developed and my own thoughts were further clarified in a dialogue which took place as part of a conversation with an especially influential ZTC director. He asked,

'What do you think of our management so far, then?'

I responded: 'Well, to be honest, things aren't going too well, are they?'

'You think the management here is crap then, do you? Do you reckon I ought to get rid of a lot of them – or all of them?'

'Oh no, from what I can see at the moment you seem to have a lot of very able and very committed managers.'

'I'm not sure that you're making sense. Are you saying that the problems are not managerial, that they're to do with the recession and – ?'

'No, I am sure there is a managerial problem. The management of the company, in the sense of the way the company is being moved forward, looks problematic to me – and to plenty of others, you must admit. But this is not to say that the management, in the sense of the people who make up the management team, are not capable of running the company well.'

'Go on.'

'Well, look at it logically, we need to distinguish between problems caused by us having – well, what shall I say – the wrong managers, and problems caused by having the "right" managers who are, nevertheless, doing the wrong things.'

The implication of the kind of distinction I was making here is that there are three senses in which we use the word 'management':

1 *Management as function*: as the overall steering or directing of an organisation.
2 *Management as activities*: as a set of activities carried out in order to bring about the overall steering or directing of the organisation.
3 *Management as a team of people*: as the group of people responsible for steering or directing the organisation through carrying out the various activities which make this possible.

What I was suggesting in this conversation was that to change management in the first sense you needed to decide the extent to which it would be a matter of changing management in the third sense (what this individual went on to describe as 'sacking half the bastards and replacing them with some half-decent blokes') and changing management in the second sense; keeping the managers you have got and getting them to do things differently ('putting fireworks up their arses rather than sacking them' was the 'macho manager' suggestion made to me here).

I went on to argue that I saw the issue in ZTC Ryland as one of reviewing the way it was managed, rather than considering whether or not the individuals they were employing were the 'right' ones. In spite of my impression that there were some managers, especially at the very senior level, who were unlikely to change their behaviour in a direction appropriate for the company's healthy survival, I decided early on that I would have no part, if I could possibly avoid it, in damaging any manager's career. I made an ethical decision that I should devote my efforts to helping improve the performance of the managers who were currently employed. This ethical decision also had pragmatic advantages: by making it clear to managers that my interest was in assisting people to manage better, rather than judging and 'reporting' on them, I could maintain their trust and, hence, their cooperation.

Fundamental to this discussion about how we use the term – or the terms – 'management', is the argument that the 'theoretical' work of clarifying the nature of management has considerable practical implications, in that the conceptions held by managers of the work they do will affect how they do it. But to help overcome the confusions about management to which I have been referring, we need to understand how they arose.

BEYOND POSDCORB?

This peculiar expression – POSDCORB – is likely to be meaningful to generations of managers who have attended traditional management education courses. Such courses play their part in the 'occupational socialisation' of managers and have some influence on how the work comes to be understood. POSDCORB is a mnemonic for remembering the words 'planning, organising, staffing, directing, coordinating, reporting and budgeting' (Gulick 1937). It was intended to help management students remember the functions of management and was a development of the approach introduced by Henri Fayol, an even more famous name in management education circles. Fayol provided management teachers, students and textbook writers with what has probably been the most frequently used definitions of management ever. This said that to manage is 'to forecast and plan, to organise, to command, to coordinate and control' (Fayol 1916/1949).

By the early years of the twentieth century, large work organisations had become well enough established as characteristic institutions of industrialised societies for formal attention to be paid to identifying the tasks, roles and requirements of those who would design and run such bodies. Figures such as Fayol and Gulick, often nowadays identified by textbooks as belonging to a 'classical school' of management thinking, helped provide guidance to managers and would-be managers about what they should do. However, the emphasis in this material on these rather grandiose functions meant that it was left unclear what the actual tasks would be of the managers who were to fulfil these functions for their organisations. The inference was widely made that managers would actually spend their time carrying out activities of planning, commanding and the rest. This was not an unreasonable inference to make and led to the popular adoption of a stereotype of managers as cool, reflective, objective individuals, systematically planning tasks which they pass down to subordinates in order to fulfil clearly stated and unambiguous organisational objectives.

This image of managers as rational and analytical planners, decision-makers and issuers of commands does not stand up to scrutiny when researchers examine what managers actually do. A whole series of studies (Burns 1955, Carlson 1951, Dalton 1959, Mintzberg 1973, Pettigrew 1973, Kotter and Lawrence 1974, Stewart 1976, Watson 1977 and 1982, Kotter 1982) has shown something quite different. The picture painted by this now quite extensive research is summarised by Rosemary Stewart:

> The picture that emerges . . . is of someone who lives in a whirl of activity, in which attention must be switched every few minutes from one subject, problem, and person to another; of an uncertain world where relevant information includes gossip and speculation . . . It is a picture, too, not of a manager who sits quietly controlling but who is dependent upon many people, other than subordinates, with whom reciprocating relationships should be created; who need to learn how to trade, bargain, and compromise.
>
> (Stewart 1983: 96).

Research, and especially that of Stewart herself, has also shown that the work that managers do varies enormously from one manager to another.

Stewart (1991) points out that managers' work varies not only according to such things as hierarchical level, function (production, marketing, personnel, finance, etc.) but also in the characteristics of the people the manager works with, the amount of discretion or power they have, the time pressures exerted upon them and the cultural context in which they operate. On top of this we see that each manager has their own particular way of carrying out the roles assigned to them.

One effect of all this research has been to question the validity of the traditional or 'classical' notions of what management is. Henry Mintzberg (1975) wrote of empirical research destroying what had been prevailing 'myths' about managerial work. But we can see something of an over-reaction in all of this. As Michael Reed put it, we saw the '"Platonic" view of the manager as the global planner and controller' being 'superseded by the "Machiavellian" conception of the manager as a situational operator and fixer' (1984: 278).

The challenge facing us is one of finding an alternative to either of these unrealistically one-sided conceptions. This means finding a way of accounting for the fact that managers indeed rarely exhibit the rational, analytical, planning, coordinating and commanding type of behaviour implied by 'classical' (and still popular) definitions of management whilst recognising at the same time that, for an organisation to survive and flourish in its environment, there has to be steering, coordinating, shaping and directing.

My suggested solution to this difficulty is that we recognise that management as a *function* does indeed have the various sub-functions of planning, coordinating, commanding and the rest. Yet we should equally recognise that the *activities* which bring about these functions do not fulfil them in as obvious or as direct a way as people once thought. Because of all the factors looked at in the last chapter – pervasive ambiguity, bounded human rationality, the existence within organisations of a multiplicity of often conflicting interests and purposes – planning, coordinating, 'commanding' and the rest can only be done by what amounts to 'feeling the way in the dark'. And this involves the incremental processes of incessant negotiating, guessing, manipulating, and speculating which researchers observe as central to managerial behaviour. Managing is essentially a process of strategic exchange because it shapes the overall activities of the organisation and how it functions in its environment through the continual and continuous exchanging of information, favours, material and symbolic resources.

The research on what managers do need not, then, lead to our dismissing the 'classical' functional approach to understanding what management is. Carroll and Gillen suggest that the newer conceptions of what management is are 'less useful than the classical functions in achieving understandings of how organisations function and what managers do since they do not clearly differentiate activities by *purpose* or *function* in relationship to the survival of the whole organisation' (1987: 49). The so-called classical approach helps us grasp 'the essential essence [*sic*] of large numbers of discrete activities in terms of larger ends' (ibid.: 49). Colin Hales similarly criticises more recent studies of managerial behaviour for their 'reluctance . . . to locate managerial work *practices* carefully within the broader context of the *function* of management in work organisations' (1986: 104), whilst Hugh Willmott accuses them of abstracting the activities of individual managers from 'the institutional arrangements in which and through which they act' (1987: 249).

Looking forward, Michael Reed calls for an approach which is sensitive to the diversity and ambiguity characterising managerial practices whilst recognising that their rationale is one of ensuring that 'collective social action becomes sufficiently structured to take on a coherent and a reasonably stable institutional shape in the form of "complex work organisations"' (1984: 279). He proposes a conception of management as a 'secondary social practice' (1984, 1989) which makes possible the functioning of work organisations, an approach which corresponds with that of Richard Whitley who argues that the distinctive characteristics of managerial activities 'derive from their constitutive role in establishing, maintaining and changing . . . organisations as relatively distinct and semi-autonomous units of resource combination and use' (1989: 209).

The message of all this recent theorising about the nature of management is a simple and important one: to understand what management is we have, first, to recognise that its basic rationale is one of establishing and maintaining work organisations as complete entities. My strategic exchange approach is an attempt, along with those of the other sociological writers I have mentioned, to recognise the place of the management occupation in the division of labour of modern societies as the occupation concerned with holding together and sustaining work organisations. And at this point I come to what I regard as a very significant argument indeed: the fact that there is a further division of labour within the management occupation (into junior and senior managers, production managers and marketing managers, warehouse managers and contracts managers, and so on) leads to a serious misunderstanding on the part of many managerial practitioners about the logic of their role. It leads managers to see their job as managerial because they are 'in charge' of a number people, of certain resources or of a department. What needs to be recognised, instead, is that a job is a managerial job in so far as it is concerned with 'shaping' the activities of the work organisation as a whole to bring about its long-term survival.

There are two profound implications of this view of management as 'pulling things together and along in a general direction to bring about long-term organisational survival' (see p. 33) which have immense practical significance. First, it suggests that the managers in any given organisation should see their primary role as contributing towards the overall performance of the organisation as a whole. One is a manager in an organisation by virtue of one's being a member of the management 'team' who direct the organisation through its environment. The tasks managers do in their specific roles are secondary: their functional or departmental roles are simply means towards fulfilling that primary role.

Second, this approach suggests that the management of an organisation, in the sense of the people who carry out the managerial function, can logically be just one person, a team of people, or everybody in the organisation. No organisation can survive without management. But whether that function is carried out by a single person, by a team, or by the democratic involvement of every member of the organisation is a matter of choice (choice, that is, within the constraints of such contingent factors of technological complexity, organisational size and so on). And, similarly, there is choice about the way the work of managing is divided up among those who are to do it – whether this be a large or a small team, or everybody.

In my negotiations with the personnel director and the organisation development executive of ZTC Ryland about my joining the company, the latter identified a management development priority for the company:

> 'It is an absolute priority for us to get all managers thinking of themselves as business managers. They must think first and foremost about how they and their people are contributing to the business. At the moment they see themselves as engineering managers or operations managers or marketing managers. This is what we have to overcome.'

This is a lay expression of the sort of prescription about the essence of managerial work which I have been developing here from basic principles. In interviewing and talking to a wide range of managers, I was keen to learn the extent to which those labelled by the company as managers, at whatever level and in whatever function, would define their work in this broad way. I would then be able to set whatever I learned about this against the managers' perceptions of the circumstances in which they operate. For managers to operate in the way identified by my senior personnel colleagues and myself as 'desirable', two conditions would need to be met: a defining of their work in holistic corporate or 'business' terms, and a felt freedom and desire to act in a way fitting such a conception. The circumstances and opportunities for such action will be the concern of subsequent chapters. In the present chapter, we can examine the accounts managers give of their understanding of what management is all about.

MANAGERS' ACCOUNTS AND MANAGERIAL BEHAVIOUR

The people I worked with, interviewed, argued with and discussed things with in ZTC Ryland were people identified in the company as managers.

They were an enormously varied set of individuals and they did a considerable range of different tasks. From my analysis of what human beings, the social world and work organisations are like, I have constructed an account of what managerial work is – in principle. The analysis implies that for an organisation to be successful as a long-term survivor in its environment, its management team needs to work together to shape the productive cooperation of individuals and groups within the organisation and match these efforts with the demands of those outside the organisation with whom there has to be material and symbolic 'trading' for the organisation to continue in existence (p. 33). For this to occur we would expect to hear those managers speaking a common language, or a language common enough for them to operate sufficiently in concert. How people construct their world and account for what they do in it necessarily influences how they behave; the categories used in their speech and thought are channels through which decisions are made about how to act. But this is not to say that how people think and speak in any way determines how they act. Specific actions are always the outcomes of an interplay between the thoughts, wants, values and priorities of an individual and the circumstances in which they find themselves.

Thus, in turning to what ZTC managers said to me about how they see management, I am not going to say: 'This is what they say, so this is what they will do.' If we find that most managers speak of management as contributing to the overall performance of the business, for example, it does not mean that they will necessarily behave in terms of such a priority. They might not be allowed enough information or enough discretion, say, to act in this way. However, if we were to find managers conceptualising their role in such a way, we would be identifying a greater potential or likelihood of their acting within corporate rather than sectional priorities than if they did not 'theorise' things that way.

The core interview programme with sixty of ZTC's Ryland managers was intended to give me reasonably systematic material which I could use to identify patterns in the way managers talk about themselves, their work and the company. This material complements the much more informal information gathered by my participant observation work and by the numerous personal conversations held with managers who were outside my interview 'sample' as well as part of it. It is important to note, however, that I am not treating the interview material in the same way as a social scientist working within the more traditional 'survey' or quantitative tradition might. Although I look for patterns in the accounts managers give me, I do not assume, like the traditional user of questionnaires, that every respondent's answer to a particular question is equivalent to every other. Even though a question may be identically put to each person interviewed, every person will frame their answer in the light of circum-stances unique to themselves: their attitude to the interviewer, the particular overtones for them of any given word, the time of day, their personal background, priorities and current state of mind, and so on.

A second qualification I must state about my interview material is that I do not take the words uttered by people to be a direct reflection of what are commonly described as 'attitudes'. All statements or 'accounts' are reactions to other statements made in that context, or taken to be implicit by the speaker, as I argued in Chapter 1 in discussing the rhetorical nature of speech and thought. This is not to say that everything any person says is solely a product of that moment. It may well indicate certain predispositions towards action. It is also consistent with what I suggested above about the way that language provides categories within which decisions to act are framed. However, we must recognise that a person speaking always considers to whom they are speaking and what the personally strategic implications might be of what they say. A manager said to me, for example:

> 'When I had my appraisal with Bill the other day I told him that I had been getting really up-to-date with my management reading. I know he likes that but I know that he doesn't actually read much at all himself, in spite of what he makes out. And I have actually read a couple of things. But, for God's sake, don't you ask me to tell *you* about what I read. I'm not going to try that crap on with you.'

This speaker is making explicit here the fact that he tells his manager one thing about his management reading, and me another. This is an unusually explicit recognition by a speaker of the way the listener needs to 'situate' their statements in a context of interests and strategic self-presentation. We must always be sensitive to such matters in interpreting what people say. This is made far more possible here than in much research by my technique of carrying out interviews within an organisation with which I was becoming intimately familiar as a participant observer and where I could cross-check accounts, follow up statements and generally locate individuals and their accounts in the social and political processes of the organisation. My revealing to the reader my own role in events and conversations as far as I reasonably can is done in the same spirit. It should enable the reader to make their own judgements about the ways in which my personal presence, style and words influence the accounts which people give me.

GETTING THINGS DONE THROUGH PEOPLE

In all my core interviews I asked the deliberately imprecise question, 'What does it mean to you to be a manager?' as a way into exploring issues about individuals' personal orientations towards managerial work and, especially, their conceptions of its nature. This question was already contextualised by earlier questions about their job title and their 'role in the organisation'. The question was followed up by a further one about what they saw as 'the essential difference between managerial and non-managerial work'. These were simply my basic questions and they were typically added to by various 'prompt' or follow-up questions appropriate to the particular individual.

Bearing in mind the qualifications I have stated, I will venture to suggest a broad pattern which I have discerned in the accounts given to me by ZTC managers when asked these types of question. The most common conception of managerial work is very similar to that of one of the earliest management writers, Mary Parker Follet (1941). This is the notion of management as 'the art of getting things done through people'. Interestingly, this appears to be a very popular definition of management in recent student texts on management, both British and American. The authors of a recent British management textbook, for example, refer to this as 'probably the best known definition of management' (Torrington and Weightman 1985: 5). This conception relates tasks to be done to the activities of the manager's subordinates, but implies little about what larger ends those tasks are managed towards.

An emphasis on 'getting things done through people' was most common among managers in 'line' roles where managers themselves had a group of largely non-managerial staff directly 'reporting' to them. Accounts which related managers' jobs to the broad direction of the business were more likely among senior managers, those whose role was one explicitly associated with 'business development' and those in more junior posts who were ambitious and were looking towards more senior jobs in the future. There was not, however, strong emphasis on more 'business strategic' matters in more than a small minority of accounts, and these were from people at very senior levels.

Among the large number of people who saw their work as getting tasks done through their subordinates there were a few who gave initial emphasis to 'task' aspects. Henry Dunkirk, who described his role as one of 'being in charge' of a circuit-board testing area, when asked what it meant to him to be a manager, unusually stressed targets:

'As a person, I see my job at the end of the day getting the target out at the end of the month and making sure that the people who work for me are doing their utmost to reach that target.'

He identified the only real difference between himself and those he managed in terms of his 'telling the others what to do'. He was a 'hands-on' manager, something of a first among equals:

'I am what you could call a hands-on manager; I like to be involved, you know, in a do-it-yourself sort of thing. Others like to stand back and delegate everything – I like to get involved which is probably why I tend to be more pally with the people I work with . . . that is the way I work.'

In this statement we can see a useful illustration of the rhetorical dimension of ordinary speech (pp. 23–5). Here, Dunkirk is engaging with the argument that managers should delegate. I am aware that he had frequently been told this by managers senior to him. He is keen to persuade me that his approach is legitimate, using several rhetorical devices to do this. He not only implies that his approach succeeds (with the phrase 'the way I work' carrying overtones of 'it works') but by suggesting positive and cooperative activity with the expression 'get involved', and social legitimacy with the notion of being 'pally'.

In spite of the fact that Henry Dunkirk put initial stress on tasks rather than people, his account soon moved to one consonant with the idea of getting things done through people. Typically, however, the stress tended to be from the start on the 'people' aspect of line managers' jobs. My conversation with John Stapleford, an engineering manager who described his role in the organisation as 'guiding all the people who work for me in mechanical design, equipment engineering design and guide them down the path that leads to a good product' included the following:

'What, then, in the light of your experience of it, is management?'
'It is akin to moulding people, to driving or guiding – no, not driving – people down a path within certain boundaries.'
'What are these boundaries?'
'They are ones that are perceived. They are not things you are taught but are things that you grasp as you go along. It is a learning curve I think. I don't believe you can be taught. Management courses just set certain things in your brain ticking but at the end of the day the manager is yourself.'
'So what is the difference between you as the manager and the people here who are not managers?'
'Well, we are all managers at the end of the day. The one thing you might learn about me today is that I believe in the team thing. I am a team man. On that basis I don't believe in the structure such as sets me up as the manager.'
'How do you mean?'
'I am happy with the four walls of this office only for confidentiality. I need the office because of a lot of the things I deal with. But I don't believe in it for setting yourself on a pedestal. So when you talk about managers and "the others" I'm not happy. They manage.'
'But if all those people out there are managing, what are you here for?'
'I am prepared to make decisions. I don't think everyone else is. At the end of the day it is the parent–child syndrome to a certain extent with certain people. They want the confidence of knowing there is someone there to lean on, if you like. That is where managers come in.'
'But surely your staff are making decisions all the time?'
'Yes they are but there are certain ones that won't. A lot of the time the people out there need me to give them the confidence to make decisions.'

John Stapleford is clearly uncomfortable with the social implications of the idea that a 'member of management' is someone set apart from others, and he can be seen as struggling somewhat to identify what his being a manager actually amounts to. Such an interpretation accords with something said to me about John Stapleford by a more senior manager:

> 'John's an excellent manager who really cares about his blokes. He really looks after them and gets excellent work out of them. I've got to get him, though, to see beyond this; to give more thought to the things his team are doing. I've a gut feeling that some rethinking is needed in his area. But I've not got time to take this on myself. I want to be able to look to him to take it on. How do I get this over?'

PERSONS AND PERCEPTIONS: THE SORT OF PERSON I AM

The starting point for answering this question about John Stapleford may lie in inferences we can make from what he said in his interview with me. John Stapleford was anxious to establish that his notion of managing was a facet of the sort of person he was. On various other occasions he said things to me which accorded with some terms he used in the interview:

> 'I have come up though the ranks. I am a grass roots guy. I have made the coffee. I've done all the filthy things in life. I believe I relate to these guys outside.'

This colourfully rhetorical statement is reminiscent of the earlier words of Henry Dunkirk, who distinguished himself from managers who like to delegate. Throughout the accounts we can see a relating of an individual's expression of what management is to what they wish to say about themselves as a person. For example, Charles Bunny, who was widely seen as especially ambitious and as very self-confident, said:

> 'It's about achieving specific objectives through my own and my people's efforts. It's also about stretching the capability of myself and my people.'

Charles Bunny saw as important to him the way his career enabled him to 'stretch' himself. Management was about doing this simultaneously for oneself and for others and hence getting things done. Bunny believed he could get people to do what he required of them if they could be shown that they, like him, would find reward in continually extending their capabilities. He observed:

> 'I can't really operate any other way. It comes down to what I'm like – the sort of individual I am.'

Managers are often 'searching for themselves' in the way they think about and do their managerial work. They are maintaining and developing their concept of who they are or 'what sort of person they are' in reflecting on their occupational activity. This theme will be taken up in subsequent chapters, but needs to be considered here because it implies that the stance managers adopt on the nature of managerial work has personal 'strategic' elements, in the sense that it helps individuals shape their own lives. It therefore has to be recognised that managers' interest in attending to corporate strategic elements, seeing their work as helping shape the organisation as a whole, must be related to their personal priorities and conception of self. A clearly value-based version of this is suggested by the account of Ed Strelley, a senior executive who borrowed a 'servanthood' concept from his Christian background:

> 'Uhm, what is management? It is not an easy question. The first thing that comes to mind is that being a manager is being a servant because, to a degree, I believe that managers serve the people that they work for as well as serving the company that they work for. By virtue of that he has to understand people's individual needs and how they operate as a group of people. Essentially a manager is there to get the best out of people so that their contribution to the company's objectives can be best placed. He is somebody who is managing a resource and that resource is people and it is machinery and it is time. This can apply to a project manager as well as a line manager: he has to pull together the resources of the company to meet the objectives of his project.'

This broad account is similar to others given by senior managers, apart from the 'servanthood' imagery which can be connected to a significant pragmatic aspect of managerial experience identified by Ed Strelley: that of the manager's dependence on others:

> 'A lot of what makes the manager's job different from that of those who are not managers is to do with how much his job is dependent on other people fulfilling their part in order to enable him to accomplish his objectives. If he is in some way dependent on those people he will have in some way to manage those people – whether it is directing, influencing or encouraging them or motivating them.'

'BIG M' AND 'SMALL m' MANAGERS

Ed Strelley's account refers to both company objectives and individual objectives but treats the objectives of his job as *givens* – rather than as matters which he can significantly influence. This suggests that he conceives of his managerial role as one primarily involving him with his particular area of the company, and not with ZTC as a whole. However, we should not assume that his speaking in this way in a particular context means that this is a position he prefers to take. One may decide to concentrate on one's own territory because one is not encouraged or allowed to contribute in a broader way. This seems to be the case with Ed Strelley; that it is his circumstances which push him towards an emphasis on his functional responsibilities, rather than on his role as a member of the broader ZTC 'management team'.

I took up this matter in a conversation with Ed Strelley on another occasion when he happened to raise with me his difficulties in influencing basic business decisions about his part of ZTC. He argued that he was 'very much a strategic thinker', illustrating this claim with details of suggestions he was putting forward to the company, but that there was not a 'lot of receptiveness at the top' to such suggestions. This is important because it 'situates' the account given to me in the interview; the absence in the account of the nature of managerial work of a creative strategic element reflects the current reality of the individual's situation, rather than a lack of interest in making such a contribution.

We can contrast Strelley's situation to that of a man at an equivalently senior level but in another part of the business. Geoff Clifton's job was as a 'marketing and business manager' for a particular technologically innovative area I will call XYZ:

> 'I am looking at the opportunities presented by XYZ; looking at the overall strategy; directing the product requirements in the light of that strategy; looking at the business development aspects of XYZ – what it will mean – market volumes, trends in the external environment, competitive pressures. It's all this kind of thing for the product area; for a number of products which will profoundly change the nature of the telecommunications products we produce within our side of the ZTC business. It involves a major change in the way we transfer traffic. This means taking advantages of technology to drive costs down (and hopefully not prices down at the same rate).'

When asked what being a manager meant to him, Geoff Clifton stressed the importance to him of 'being in a position to influence and direct the nature of the business we are in'. He also identified as important his role in supporting current activities in his field of interest and observed that an 'important part of management' to him was 'the management of people and all the human interface aspects'. And even closer to the general view of himself as an individual which he stressed on various occasions was the statement,

> 'There is a degree of being close to the centre of things so that one knows what is happening. So you get a broader view of the business, rather than sitting in a compartment. Personally I can't stand sitting in a compartment. I tend to spread across boundaries – sometimes ones I am not meant to spread across!'

I later learned that Geoff Clifton had indeed become involved in arguments about straying into the 'territory' of other managers. However, in the part of ZTC where he had most of his contacts there was, partly as a result of the style of the director in charge of it, considerable scope given to managers to contribute on broad business matters beyond the scope of their immediate responsibilities. This was quite different from the area in which Ed Strelley worked where, Strelley said, there was limited 'receptiveness at the top' to such contributions. Hence, Clifton's more 'business strategic' account needs to be situated in the context of his having greater opportunities to look beyond his specific responsibilities. His stated conception of managerial work is partly a reflection of the circumstances he was in.

Geoff Clifton was suggesting a conception of management as involving, potentially at least, something much more than getting things done through people. He neatly expressed this in an answer to my question about the essential difference between a manager and a non-manager:

'It is all a question of what you see as a management job. As soon as you have responsibility for some people you are a manager with a small m. So I have been a manager in that sense for a lot longer than the time I have been a manager with a capital M.'

This distinction is interesting because it suggests that the more corporate-strategically oriented manager is more of a manager than the 'ordinary people manager'. At various times it was suggested to me that there is more than one type of manager; for example:

'A manager can range from a consultant type of person, with specialist technical skills, to people who actually coordinate a group of people to achieve a particular output by a particular date to a particular budget.'

Similar to this, from Leonard Hilton, was,

'I used to be a manager. I've had quite large numbers of people working for me at times. I'm more senior in some ways now but I am really a sort of consultant. I am trying to change some of the management systems.'

This prompted me to ask:

'So are you saying you are not actually part of the management?'
'No, I am part of the management but I am a consultant to the other managers, rather than a manager myself.'
'So does that mean that you are the same as all the other consultants that are brought in?'
'God no! Well, perhaps it does. I have to say I do not feel that I am really a manager, you know, not having people to manage. How do you see it?'
'My view is that people like you are managers because you are part of the team which manages the business. And even though you are not directly managing people you are part of a team which is.'
'What bloody team? You must be joking.'

Leonard Hilton, it turned out, was resentful of having been, as he later put it, 'promoted out of management', a fact which tended to reinforce his notion of being in 'the management' without being 'a manager'. But his questioning of the existence of a management 'team' as such in the company draws attention to a question to which we will return later; that of whether senior management in ZTC did in practice encourage a view of all its managers belonging to a team sharing a concern with steering the business.

One director did take this kind of view, however. The position taken by Martin Hillside implies that, in Geoff Clifton's terms, all managers should to an extent be 'capital M' managers and none of them 'small m' managers. I asked,

'What does being a manager involve, as you see it?'

'It always needs to be seen in a business context, yes, that's the way I would put it. It means having an understanding of the business and then translating the circumstances with which one is faced into an acceptable – no ... yes – into an acceptable way of running the business from the point of view of shareholders, other managers and people who are employed. Yeah. And managers need to spell out what they expect from people who they are managing and to ensure, having spelled it out, that it's delivered. How's that?'

'Very clear.'

'I'm sure I'm not saying anything very original here. Isn't this the sort of thing most people tell you?'

'Not really. It's a broader view than I find many managers take. They tend to see management mainly in terms of being responsible for the people reporting to them.'

'You manage much more than people; you're managing resources. It has to be seen as part of running a business. Some managers' jobs involve more of an entrepreneurial element than others, but they are all involved . They all have resources to shepherd. And they have relationships, which might be inside or out-side the business, to create and develop in order that their business can flourish.'

I was keen at this point to investigate why Martin Hillside should express a view of management which differed from that of most others:

'It's interesting that I find this an unusual way for managers here to talk. It could be just you or it could be your business education. But it might be because you are a director of the business. In what way does your being a director influence your perception of what management is, do you think?'

'It doesn't. Being a director just means it's more difficult. This is partly because there are fewer people "up there" managing you. It's only more difficult. I haven't changed my views since becoming a director.'

'Is it to do with your business education, then?'

'It could be, but I think I always had those views, particularly having had a lot of experience talking with employees who were not managers – union reps and so forth – and putting across the views of the wealth-creating sector in which I have always worked. It is all about, industry that is, wealth creation. It has to be done to provide all the good things that people want from society.'

Here we are back to seeing an individual's account of how they regard the nature of managerial work being related, by implication, to personal values. I will follow up these elements of Martin Hillside's orientation to work in the next chapter but, for now, wish to look at one more manager's words on the issue of what management is. In Mark Cossall's account, we see an element of reflection on how an individual's view may change as they move from job to job. We see especially clearly how the way a manager's conception of what management is connects to their individual circumstances when we come across a manager who is able to think back to how they saw it at different stages of their managerial career. Mark Cossall's background was in engineering and, later, in quality management. I asked him what it meant to him to be a manager:

'I need to think. I don't want to give you the old textbook stuff. My base perception has always been of a manager as someone who manages people.

That's what I've grown up with – from when I was on the bottom of the heap on £1500 a year. You looked up and said they're managers and what do they do? They manage people. To some degree going up through the organisation I've always seen it that way. Yet I've had doubts.'

'Such as?'

'Well, when I took on my own first job with the title "manager" a lot of what I was doing was not actually managing people. It was initiating ideas, much as at the moment. It was about facilitating, about educating, about motivating, doing lots of things to get the thing moving. I had people working for me – only three people. So the people management part of it took little time, in spite of how I'd seen management before as about the traditional manager–subordinate role.'

'But haven't you just described what you did in such terms – motivating, facilitating and so on?'

'Uhm but what occurred to me was that I just saw them as part of my team; they were people a day ago I'd worked with as equals. I was a manager on Monday, not having been one on Friday. The way I approached it, they were still the same people who had been there on Friday. The relationship was slightly different in that I had to guide them and think about strategic vision. I didn't go round saying, "Me Tarzan, you Jane".'

Here we see a recognition of a 'corporate strategic' dimension to the manager's job developing, in place of a stereotype of a figure controlling and directing subordinates. A tension between two rival images was suggested further on in the interview:

'What is the essential difference between a managerial and a non-managerial job, would you say?'

'Gut feel says to me: in a managerial job you have some aspect of controlling other people – directing things. I don't like the words I am using here but if I'm actually honest, it's about directing other people. Even if I try to soften it by saying "being responsible for guiding other people", my inner voice says "directing". How I see it and other people see it is that you have an element of directing other people. My gut feel says management is directing people, signing important documents, checking through reports and other sorts of things. That is my stereotype. But from what I actually know of the organisation, that isn't how it is at all. Managers and non-managers fundamentally do similar sorts of things, but it's just the level of detail that differs and the breadth of vision and the view you have of life that differs. When I started I used to write detailed reports. But as I've worked up the organisation I've learned that you have to take a different view and pull out the more important elements – the key elements. You move out of the detail and bring out the salient points.'

'What are these?'

'As you go up the organisation the salient points (a) become bigger points and (b) may have a change in emphasis. Take Peter – he's in a managerial position but he focuses on too much detail. He gets pressed by Dave for less detail and more breadth of understanding. At the bottom you are looking at nuts and bolts; the mechanics and methods of what you're doing. At the top, your view would be much broader: maybe directed towards the financial implications or the strategic implications of what you're doing.'

Of particular interest in this account is a suggestion of the power of what Mark Cossall calls 'stereotypes'. I suggest that what he is referring to here is a basic public image of the occupation of management as involving being in charge of people. This is the 'occupational stereotype' of management. His talk of 'gut feel' implies that this is something deeply ingrained. He has clearly found the image resistant to easy alteration in the light of experience. Going back to the conversation with Steve Loscoe at the beginning of this chapter, we can see a suggestion of something similar. When he was casting around for something to help make sense of his role as a manager, the best he could manage, it would seem, was, 'I'm in charge of this office and the office in Birmingham.'

MANAGING RESPONSIBILITY

'Being in charge' has echoes of the notion of responsibility. This, in fact, was the concept most often used by managers in answering my question about what it was that made managers different from non-managers. For example:

> 'It's the level of responsibility, the ownership of the job you are doing; you are rewarded for the success or failure of the operation.'

> 'The responsibility, for all aspects.'

> 'It has to be responsibility – you have to take everything that bit more seriously. This is not just to the company but to the people you manage. When you are not a manager, someone else carries all this for you.'

> 'Responsibility is probably the biggest thing but, equally, authority.'

> 'The essential thing is having responsibility.'

> 'Taking responsibility – being able to direct people and stand or fall by the decisions you make.'

The frequency with which managers speak in these terms reflects, I suggest, the very direct way they experience being managers:

> 'When you know you are a manager is when you have to account to people for things. You get bloody Ted asking why the department's not got its output or you get your blokes or women moaning why aren't they getting decent boards to work with. "It's down to you mate", that's what you have to say to yourself. It's probably somebody else to blame. But it goes down to you.'

This type of response was found across the range of managers in the company – it was not associated with any particular function or level. These accounts seem to suggest something widespread and basic to the experience of doing managerial work, whatever the manager's specific role in the organisational division of labour. It is an everyday reality and can be seen as one of the pressures on the individual manager to give attention and priority (where their level means that they are not formally charged with directing the business as a whole) away from the overall organisational issues of long-term corporate survival, which I have argued are central to the rationale of the work of all managers. It is an experienced reality pushing the manager towards matters of short-term departmental or functional performance. As we have seen, there was a concern within ZTC Ryland to get managers to adopt the longer-term and broader perspective, and a key thrust of this whole book is an argument that effective management of any organisation requires all its managers to share this broader conception of their role. It is therefore important to consider what factors encourage managers to take a more 'local' as opposed to a corporate conception of their role. A range of factors, involving matters of organisational structure and culture will be looked at later but, here, I wish to point to the role of the processes whereby individuals enter managerial work.

ENTERING MANAGEMENT

Looking at the processes whereby people enter particular kinds of work has always been important to social scientists applying an occupational perspective to work. But although the processes through which people are recruited to occupations is never simple, we can say that entry into managerial work is much less straightforward a matter than with most other occupational areas. This is because, as we saw earlier in this chapter, people tend not to have as clear a conception of managerial work as something that they might go into, as they have of butcher, baker, scientist or accountant. And this is closely connected to the fact that one typically moves into managerial work from something else. As Steve Loscoe put it, 'being a manager is not something you set out to do . . . it's much more that you sort of just become a manager'.

A managerial appointment is a stage in a person's hierarchical career in an organisation, rather than an entry into an immediately distinctive and clearly identifiable occupational activity. And the evidence I gathered in ZTC suggests that, even as a stage in a process of movement up a hierarchical structure, the taking on of the 'manager' label may well not mark a change in circumstances that is clear-cut enough to prompt a clear appraisal of the tasks and purposes of the new role – let alone a request for appropriate briefing and training. The most significant experience associated with 'becoming a manager' is thus finding oneself answerable to people further up the hierarchy – experiencing, as we saw above, a sense of now having 'responsibility'. But let us now look at how, more specifically, managers report their entry into this kind of work and ask to what extent they speak of this 'entry' as a distinct shift in their circumstances – a shift which might prompt a fundamental consideration of their role in relation to the overall 'steering' of the company.

Apart from the relatively few managers who had been recruited into the company from managerial posts elsewhere there were no direct entrants into managerial jobs in ZTC Ryland. The nearest thing to this, it occurred to me, might be in the area of graduate recruitment to the company. A manager very much involved in this process explained to me, however, that:

'. . . obviously most of the graduates we recruit are going into technical or professional areas of work initially. They have to prove themselves as engineers, radio specialists, business planners or whatever first. Of course there is an understanding that they can be the "managers of the future", but we are keen to avoid them getting too above themselves with such ideas. I'm careful about this in personnel as much as anywhere else. I emphasise to graduates joining me that they are coming into personnel *work*. They might, or they might not, become personnel *managers* later. I'm not creating any hostages to fortune.'

This view appeared to accord with that held by managers who had entered the company through the graduate recruitment route. For example, I asked Nicola Mapperley:

'Your degree was in . . .?'

'Management sciences.'

'So you expected to become a manager in ZTC at some point.'

'I don't think I thought like that. The idea of being a manager seemed rather remote to me.'

'But surely the fact that you had a qualification – '

' – a qualification with management in its title. I didn't see myself as qualified in management. Andrew's degree is very similar to mine and it is called Business Studies. That seems more accurate to me. And it fits the way I think most of the arts graduates I knew saw things: we were coming into business careers. Whether we would become managers as such – well?'

There was one manager who had been a 'trainee manager' in an earlier career in catering, but he had left his career in catering management to join ZTC in a non-managerial job, only later moving up to a managerial post. This accords with a common theme among managers, that of 'moving up through the grades', for example:

'I progressed up through my job as a technical quality manager.'

'I've just gone through the system, you could say. I started on the bench and because I was quite good at the job and because I liked what I was doing, I was made into section leader. I did several other things like this but when they set up the priority build unit they put me in as manager.'

'I came here as a purchasing expediter. I was then a buyer and, from this, I became purchasing manager.'

A common route 'through the grades' for managers with a technical background appears to one of becoming a 'project manager' – taking charge of a set of tasks with a finite time horizon – prior to moving into something with a more fixed position in the hierarchy. Alan Bridgford explained how he moved into a project management post:

'It is very vivid in my mind. It goes back to 1974 in the TXE2 days. There was the miners' strike of 1974 and because of the state of the business at the time they were looking to get as much money in within the financial year as possible and of course you only got paid when things were installed. So they were looking for volunteers from the engineering organisation to go out into the blue yonder with their knowledge of the problems of the then fairly new TXE2 and get these sites commissioned as soon as possible. I drew the short straw! It was an opportunity; people said it was the right place at the right time. We did not have children at the time and the prospect of unlimited overtime seemed like a good idea. So I trundled off to the coast for a four-month period and I commissioned the exchange, getting it into acceptance by the end of the financial year. That gave me an extra attribute which a lot of other people did not have. In other words, they were just pure designers: I now had actually seen the design in the field, how the product came together. Then we saw at that time a niche market in terms of transportable exchanges – this having good potential for getting into an export market – the concept was disaster scenarios. We bought a Portakabin and we installed all these TXE2s in Portakabins. This had started and then when I came back, they said the logical thing was "Let's put Alan on to commissioning this product". This was my first project management task: to put that exercise together.'

This account, like all such accounts, attempts to make sense of the individual's biography for both the speaker and the listener. Its production is part of the ongoing shaping of the individual's life, a revealing of an emergent life strategy. In the course of this making sense of the past (and connecting it to the present) there is a degree of equivocation visible which is strongly indicative of the 'emergent' quality of such accounts. This is seen in the following of the words, 'I drew the short straw', which imply chance and bad luck, with 'it was an opportunity; people said it was the right place at the right time', which suggests the opposite: good luck, albeit in the context of chance again. Out of this work in commissioning a telephone exchange, the account suggests, comes a changing self-concept in Alan Bridgford, one which pushes him towards a broader concept of his work as something more than purely technical. This involves 'seeing design in the field' and 'how the product came together', a set of words which are immediately followed by reference to some decisions of a business strategy nature, in which opportunities were recognised for the company to supply portable exchanges to countries hit by disasters. However, it is unlikely that Alan Bridgford would have been party to that thinking. Yet he uses the words '*we* saw . . . a niche market', a statement we can interpret as a retrospective identification with business-level thinking. I suggest that Alan Bridgford is making sense of his past in the light of his current concern with being seen as a manager within ZTC who is especially concerned to 'think strategically' (as I heard him express it on several occasions) and to 'look for market opportunities'. Temporal consistency in the account is further sacrificed to help achieve this: he uses 'we' when he says 'we bought a Portakabin', implying his personal involvement in this action. Yet he then reveals that he could not actually have taken part in this when he says 'this had started and then when I came back . . .'. He was not in Ryland when these moves were made.

The past of this individual is further made sense of with the suggestion that it was 'the logical thing' for him to be put in charge of this project. In these words we see an expression of what is a common quality in people's accounts of their work careers: a recognition that their career is neither a direct outcome of specific ambitions or choices on their part, nor the result of a career plan made for them by their employer. Instead there is a process in which inclinations on the part of the individual become actualities in the light of circumstances which happen to arise; the phenomenon of being in a certain place at a certain time. We can see this continuing in the case of Alan Bridgford's account as he goes on to explain how he became more and more a manager as the circumstances of the production of portable exchanges pushed him increasingly towards a people management rather than a 'commissioning' role:

> 'I had inherited a cabin with the bare frame racks in there, with the basic tables. We rolled out about forty of these. Then the following financial year we were in trouble again and we were given the weekend shift to help the factory get these out of the door. Although ostensibly doing commissioning, I ended up the weekend shift leader, saying "Right this is what we will do over the weekend – you do this cabin, you do that". From there it just went on and on and it became more and more management and less and less technology. It was something I was happy to go with.'

This illustrates the notion developed earlier of the individual strategically 'shaping' their life; their personal career strategy being understood as 'a pattern which can be discerned in a person's life as a result of intentions or choices mixed with opportunities which arose (or did not arise) at particular times' (p. 27). Managers' accounts frequently suggest the adventitious nature of their entry into a managerial post, for example:

> 'I could say I was lucky but – no – I was certainly in the right place at the right time. I started a function with someone who was a manager: the pair of us set up the function together – an incoming goods function. He found a lot of comfort in having someone to debate things through with. But he left after three months to go into the police force – he was not happy doing this. I spent two years running the function as a chief technical officer, answering in to someone who was two steps removed. But there was this obvious gap. I worked hard and did all the right things and made recommendations, and along came the offer.'

But there is, too, in this, the choosing on the part of the individual: a shaping of performance and attitude which brings the individual and the role together.

There are frequent references in managers' accounts to replacing bosses who have moved on, such as 'I worked directly to a manager who moved on and I was appointed to manager of the group', and there are frequent references to restructurings and reorganisations. But there is often, within the accounts which mention these circumstantial factors, a sense of anticipation or preparation for such an eventuality. Ron Hucknall, for example, explained how he did a range of jobs in his department, having been told 'Keep your nose clean and you'll do all right'. Then, he explains:

'There was a reorganisation of Jim's first line and it was announced that I was to be the manager for the whole part of this operation. I had designs, you might say, prior to this but I was surprised how quickly it happened.'

The preparation, however, is normally rather tentative, in no case I came across involving the individual in seeking managerial training *prior* to appointment. Dick Mansfield was not untypical in reporting:

'I had this expertise buying machine tools and the bloke who was managing the department was what I would call a flying career man; he was always looking for bigger jobs and while he was there all he did was look for something bigger. So they lost him quickly. They had no one else to do it so they asked me and it was as easy and simple as that really. So I replace my boss, no training, nothing: "This is your job now, get on with it".'

This analysis so far might be read as implying that, although there was a large amount of chance and little formal preparation about individuals' entry to managerial jobs, there was nevertheless a degree of clarity about the point at which they had in fact become managers. This is, however, anything but the case. To explain this we can return yet again to Alan Bridgford, whose biographical account I had to interrupt at one point to get clarification of when it was precisely that he 'officially' became a manager. He explained:

'It was about 1976, because by that time I had gone through the export experience leading to a contract for Moscow, and I virtually ended up, well, um. This is where grading structures come in. Because at that time my level of overtime earning would have made amortising that into a management grading difficult. It would have made a very expensive package. They were in effect saying we will make you a manager, but not yet. There would have been such a loss of earnings, because managers were not paid overtime at that time. I was doing 140 hours a month overtime. So you end up doing pseudo-management tasks without the handle of manager. Once the overtime came down, that was the trigger for me to be made officially a manager.'

In some cases people were regraded as managers simply to enable them to be financially rewarded at what was felt to be a fair level. Jane Trowell illustrates this:

'It was to get the salary due. A job description of my work was put in and it came back that this was a marginal management job but that the person doing it, in spite of the fact that that is not meant to matter, is only such an age. The only way round it was to swap jobs with someone who already had a management grade. This is how things used to be done. It's not so bad now. I was a little bitter.'

The extent to which an individual sees themselves as a manager at certain stages of their career often does not fit the official definition. This may be where the title is absent but the self-perception present:

> 'I was managing years before I was called a manager. And I think my ego wanted me to be called a manager. Everybody knew I was managing, but it got to a point where if I was not called a manager it was a sort of slight on my ability. I was a section leader.'

Or it can be the other way round:

> 'After four or five years I became a manager. That was a title, but as far as I was concerned the reality was as when I had joined; there were ninety people in industrial engineering and one manager. That was a manager. These days seventy out of the ninety would be called managers. They don't have section leaders any more. I was a section leader really.'

Don Smalley felt he had been called a manager before he was one in his own terms. Eddie Elton, on the other hand, was put into a management role, he suggests, as a means of advancing his earning power:

> 'It started when I eventually came on what was known then as top pay or top money – maximum merit money etc. I was only about twenty-five. I went to my boss then and said "I hope you don't mind me sitting here and . . .". Well I asked, "Where do I go from here, now that I have reached maybe the top?". He said "Well we will see what opportunities come up", but these were very limited in the toolroom at that time. So he said that there was not a lot he could do, but "I have listened to your story and we will see what we can do to take any opportunity that arises". Not long after that, unfortunately, one of the managers, supervisors if you like, died so I actually filled a dead man's shoes. That really was the only way then – about 1970.'

There is an ambiguity about this account which is typical of many informal autobiographical narratives. Was Elton simply seeking more money in following this strategy with his then boss? Or was he simply adopting the appropriate language to be used within a shop-floor subculture when seeking advancement? If it was more than money that was being sought, was Eddie looking for a managerial post as such, or just something that amounted to a better-paid job? I investigated this point in a later conversation which arose when discussing issues about gradings of his own staff. He said:

> 'I don't think you work to a sort of life plan, do you. You sort of want something better perhaps. So you push a bit and you see what happens. Now take Kevin. He's a really good craftsman. I'd like to bring him on and he's pushing me. But I tell you what: if I said to him I am moving on and you are going to take over my job, he'd mess himself.'

In addition to bringing out what I hope are worthwhile insights into the personal strategic exchange and self-defining processes which characterise career patterns in general, these accounts of entry into management suggest that these transitions are not seen as putting the individual into a new relationship with the overall 'steering' of the organisation. The typical entry into a management post takes a form whereby the individual is unlikely to see themselves as entering a team charged with directing the business as a whole (something which I and other senior managers in ZTC Ryland, as explained earlier, felt to be an important requirement in the company). New managers either felt, as one put it, 'There was nothing very new to me about my new job' or, more typically, that the key issue was learning to relate differently to former colleagues, trying not, as Mark Cossall put it earlier, to 'go round saying, "me Tarzan, you Jane"'. Eddie Elton may have had this partly in mind in worrying about how Kevin would adjust to a managerial promotion. His experience was that:

> 'I found it very difficult to be suddenly working with friends and being the boss of friends, being suddenly on the other side of the fence or straddling the fence. I never really went over the other side straight away – or ever, I suppose, fully. For many years I found it very very difficult to man-manage people who had been colleagues and friends with me for many years.'

Either way, new managers find themselves focusing on local and short-term matters, rather than on the contribution that they, through their new specific responsibilities, might make to the performance of the business as a whole. This point should not be over-emphasised, however. It is in what we might call the natural order of things for all individuals to pay primary attention to immediate matters in their everyday context. But it is central to the argument growing throughout this 'search for management' that, if management is to have real meaning as an occupational category, it has to be carried out by people who recognise that the logic of their job is to direct the component of the organisation for which they take responsibility not in a direction to suit themselves and their staff alone, but to help pull the whole organisation 'together and along' in a direction to ensure its survival into the future.

What is becoming clearer as we see just how much management is an activity 'in search of itself', is the extent to which managers' views of what I conceptualise as their contribution to the basic strategic exchange processes of the organisation has to be seen in the light of their personal strategic exchange processes. How managers act in their jobs is as much a matter of working out, shaping and expressing their identities and interests as it is of helping shape and steer the organisation. Managers, we can say, are 'in search of themselves'. This will be the concern of the next chapter which will be followed by a return to a consideration of their organisational context as we look at how ZTC, like all other organisations to varying degrees, is an 'organisation in search of itself'.

Chapter 3

Managers in search of themselves

'You didn't plan a managerial career, then?'
  'No, I don't think I did.'
  'You're not sure?'
  'Well, I always wanted to get on. That was understood – in my upbringing, if you know what I mean. I suppose having ended up in the industrial end of technology, I suppose the way to get on was to become a manager. If things had worked out differently I might have been a, you know, a boffin type. I don't know, though.'
  'How do you mean, you don't know?'
  'I don't think it would have suited me. I like to . . . well . . . I like technology and all that. But I like – I think, yes, I like to have influence on things in a more immediate way. Or perhaps it's that I like dealing with people more than I like dealing with things. I don't like sitting on my own for a long time, I reckon. Mmm, I like to be on the move, dealing with all sorts of things, having an influence on what's around me. I suppose it's the sort of person I am.'

IDENTITY AND THE EMERGENT SELF

Jeremy Sneinton's account introduces several of the themes of this chapter. And one of the discursive resources he uses is central to our concerns: that of 'the sort of person I am'. What we should notice about the way he introduces this idea is the words 'I suppose'. In the process of speaking he is speculating about himself; he is working things out. In talking to me about his career, he is also making sense for himself of who he is, what he is doing, what he finds 'rewarding', in the broadest sense, in his job. And very noticeable in this piece of discourse is the repeated use of terms like 'I suppose', 'I don't know', 'I think', 'I don't think'. Jeremy Sneinton, in the process of speaking, is doing 'identity work'. In the process of answering my questions and trying to make sense for me of the relationship between what he does in his work and what 'sort of person' he is, he is also making sense for himself of who and what he is. This, I suggest, is part of the normal way in which the human animal maintains a concept of 'self'. It is a concept always in process. Our idea of self, or identity, is neither pre-given when we are born, nor does it become fixed in the process of our 'growing up'. It is always *emergent*; it is part of the continuous process through which we come to terms with our changing world through a process of shaping our 'selves'. Processes of talking (always intimately bound up with processes of thinking, as I argued in Chapter 1) are vital to the ways in which we do this.

A basic theme of this book is the way in which, in order to understand managerial work, we need to relate the strategic exchange processes whereby organisations are enabled to survive (through processes of material and symbolic exchange with various parties) to the processes whereby managers engage in personal strategic exchange processes. Managers are portrayed as essentially being concerned with *shaping* the organisation in which they are employed, and I am suggesting that we can only understand how they do this if we relate the way they carry out this managerial work to the ways in which they shape themselves as individual human beings.

The conception of human beings as creatures continually having to realise themselves and make sense of their place in a potentially chaotic world was established in Chapter 1. In Chapter 2, I showed that the conception which managers hold of managerial work itself (an important factor influencing how they actually manage) is related to their own ideas of who they are; to what we might call their conception of self.

Managers' ideas about the nature of management were, however, also seen to be related to their personal situation. Notions of self which managers have are themselves always related to their personal situation inside and outside the organisation, and I shall be looking in later chapters at the interplay between managers' notion of self and what they do in their daily work. In this chapter, I shall concentrate on the managers as individuals and on what their work means to them. A key assumption, encapsulated in the concept of work orientation, is that what a person's work means to them is a key influence on how they perform it.

BEYOND PERSONALITY

This emphasis on meanings and the centrality of discourse to the ways in which people are continually shaping their conceptions of self through processes of exchange with others is in contrast to traditional psychological thinking which uses concepts like 'personality' or personality type. It might be argued that what I am concerned with in this chapter is managers' personalities. I am anxious, however, to distance myself from the style of thinking with which this concept tends to be associated in the social sciences.

A classic expression of the mainstream notion of personality is that of Hans Eysenck (1953), who defines it as 'the more or less stable and enduring organisation of a person's character, temperament, intellect, and physique that determines his unique adjustment to his environment'. Each individual is seen as possessing a series of traits which make up their personality, something which, in another classic formulation, 'permits a prediction of what a person will do in a given situation' (Cattell 1966). There are alternative models of the human self in the social science mainstream, such as that to be found in sociological 'role theory', which sees people's selves as the outcome of the 'parts' they play on the social stage, and the humanistic psychology of such people as Abraham Maslow (1968) and Carl Rogers (1961), which views human life as a search for the 'authentic' self; for 'self-actualization'.

All of these approaches treat the 'self' of the individual subject as something that can be pinned down, one way or another. It is a thing; as Jonathan Potter and Margaret Wetherall point out in their critique of such thinking, it is an 'object to be discovered' – it 'is the *centre* of experience, an initiator of action, a coherent whole, separate from other distinct selves' (1987: 101).

Potter and Wetherall describe and contribute to what they call a 'critical movement' away from these conventions, attempting to 'displace attention from the self-as-entity and focus it on the methods of constructing the self':

> It is suggested that methods of making sense are the key to any kind of explanation of the self, as people's sense of themselves is in fact a conglomerate of these methods, produced through talk and theorising.
> (ibid.: 102)

Jeremy Sneinton, in the piece of discourse examined earlier, was engaged in talk and theorising in this sense. Through my conversation with him we get a glimpse into his personal process of biography creation and shaping of identity. This can be understood in terms of meeting the basic human 'need for meaning' discussed in Chapter 1, a need which, as Baumeister (1986) argues, implies needs for justification and self-worth, needs which, he says, are met in part through autobiographical narratives which are part of a negotiation between the idea of self and the external world. This connects with my stress on the rhetorical or persuasive elements of speech; justifying what we 'are about' to ourselves and others is part of our maintaining our personal self-esteem which, in turn, is part of our making sense of our position in the world and thus achieving the sense of control which is essential to our sanity. Harvey, Weber and Orbuch look at the ways in which self-esteem is managed through 'the accounts we tell ourselves and others', observing that:

> Self-esteem is a fragile commodity in our lives as social beings. It is so easily damaged, sometimes almost beyond repair. We, therefore, exhibit a lot of effort and spend a lot of time simply trying to hold constant or bolster our sense of worth.
> (1990: 13)

Sociologists of work have often used the notion of 'subjective career' to conceptualise the way individuals make sense of the sequence of structural situations through which they pass in their lives, accepting, as Audrey Collin puts it, 'the proposition that people seek to achieve overall stability in the outward life and coherence in their inner world' (1986: 22). The notion was established by E.C. Hughes, who referred to 'the moving perspective in which the person sees his life as a whole and interprets the meaning of his various attributes, actions, and the things which happen to him' (1937).

WORK ORIENTATIONS AND IMPLICIT CONTRACTS

To sharpen this focus on the link between the meanings which people attach to their life and their work context, by considering the way people regard how their work connects to how they are predisposed to act, we can introduce at this stage the concept of *orientation to work*. This was introduced into the sociology of work by John Goldthorpe and David Lockwood *et al.* (1968), in part as an alternative to popular ideas about 'motivation' which sought to identify the sort of motives which people generally are trying to satisfy at work. Instead, the focus was to be on the particular set of rewards which particular people in specific personal and work circumstances were seeking to meet. The concept has been further developed by various writers, and in my own work I define it as 'the meaning attached by individuals to their work which predisposes them both to think and act in particular ways with regard to that work' (Watson 1987: 290).

Central to this work orientation is the way the individual perceives the *implicit contract* which is made between the employee and the employer. This is 'the largely tacit agreement made between the two parties with regard to what will be given by each and what each will take from the relationship' (ibid.: 100). What I call the 'implicit contract' corresponds with the concept of 'effort bargain' (Baldamus 1961) as well as that of the 'psychological contract', a concept used by a number of writers, but especially by Edgar Schein:

> Through various kinds of symbolic and actual events, a 'psychological contract' is formed which defines what the employee will give in the way of effort and contribution in exchange for challenging or rewarding work, acceptable working conditions, organisational rewards in the form of pay and benefits, and an organisational future in the form of a promise of promotion or other forms of career advancement. This contract is 'psychological' in that the actual terms remain implicit; they are not written down anywhere. But the mutual expectations formed between the employee and the employer function like a contract in that

if either party fails to meet the expectations, serious consequences will follow – demotivation, turnover, lack of advancement, or termination.

(1978: 112)

With this notion of *implicit contract* we have crystallised the broader concept of individual strategic exchange by focusing on the individual's notion of the current balance between what the individual is 'putting into' the organisation by way of effort, time, commitment and the like, and what they are 'getting out' by way of material rewards, status, career potential, opportunity to realise personal values, and so on.

Each manager, I am suggesting, has particular wants – material and symbolic – which they take to their work, in return for which they are prepared to make certain types and degrees of effort. Their perception of this tacit contract will affect how they behave in their work – it influences their 'motivation'. However, an individual's orientation to work is never static; their life circumstances and the specific circumstances prevailing in the work situation influence what they are looking for and what they expect to get. For example, we might see a manager strongly oriented towards career advancement who finds that opportunities for such progress are no longer available. He or she may therefore decide to concentrate on the intrinsic satisfactions of their current job. Equally, they may seek employment with another organisation, or they may decide to concentrate on having an easy life and work to a level which promises them security. It might be, however, that a manager's orientation changes because a new circumstance in the manager's non-work life, such as parenthood, leads them to prioritise differently in their working life.

The possibilities are vast. The orientation adopted will be part of the overall way that an individual shapes their life in the light of underlying values, non-work circumstances and what is happening in the organisation. We are back to the basic notion of strategic exchange again. And, although every manager's personal orientation to work – the way their perception of the implicit contract between themselves and the organisation influences their thoughts and behaviour – is unique, it is possible to look for broad patterns which may prevail at a particular time within a given organisation, or even within a country or countries.

THE WORK ORIENTATIONS OF BRITISH MANAGERS: SOME CONFLICTING EVIDENCE

Various existing pieces of research on managers have attempted to generalise about what we might call the current 'state of mind' of managers, and I will look at just two studies which have attempted to generalise about managers in British organisations.

These two studies provided me with some of my own research questions.

I was intrigued about what they had to say about contemporary British managers and was anxious to see what light might be thrown on their findings by looking at similar matters in depth in just one organisation.

A recent major British study of managers, that by Richard Scase and Robert Goffee (1989), painted a very gloomy picture of what they called 'reluctant managers'. The study surveyed 374 managers (eighty of whom were interviewed) employed in six large organisations chosen 'so as to reflect different sectors of the economy and within which substantial numbers of managers are employed' (ibid.: 192). Interestingly, for present purposes, this included ' "high" electronic technology engineering' – a category into which ZTC would fit. The authors concluded that many of those looked at in the study could be described as 'reluctant managers'. They are people

> who are less than fully committed to their jobs and who have great reservations about giving priority to their work, their careers and, indeed, their employing organisations. They are more careful, perhaps, than in the past about becoming completely 'psychologically' immersed in their occupations and seek, instead, to obtain a balance between their work and private lives. They are reluctant to strive for career success if this can be gained only at the expense of personal and family relationships.
>
> (ibid.: 179)

Scase and Goffee use a concept very similar to my notion of implicit contract in relating this state of affairs to a changing 'psychological contract between managers and their employing organisations' in which many feel they are 'subject to greater demands to work harder and under more tightly monitored circumstances' (ibid.: 179). Circumstances of increased work demands with decreased resources for meeting them and with decreasing opportunities for advancement mean that 'large numbers of managers feel that they are subject to "excessive" pressures and query whether the rewards are worth the effort' (ibid.: 180).

Contrasting findings are reported by Sue Dopson and Rosemary Stewart (1990) as a result of interviews with twenty managers (and the personnel and training managers) in each of eight organisations of varying types. Similar environmental pressures to those observed by Scase and Goffee were seen in these organisations, but different outcomes were reported by the managers affected. In contrast, say the authors, to 'many of the studies and commentaries we had read', most of the managers in both the public and private sectors 'were positive about the changes and the ways in which they had affected their jobs'. The majority of managers felt that many of the frustrations of their jobs had been reduced, first, because

> the shorter hierarchy in most organisations meant that middle managers were closer to top management and the strategic and policy area
>
> (1990: 13)

and, second,

> more middle managers have their own clear area of responsibility
> together with more control over the resources that they need if they are
> to be effectively in charge.

(ibid.: 14)

The result of all this was that 'most of our sample felt that their jobs had
become more challenging and enjoyed the additional responsibilities and
variety of their work' (ibid.: 14).

Dopson and Stewart are less willing than Scase and Goffee to generalise
broadly about British managers on the basis of their investigations, but
they valuably point out that the gloomy predictions about middle managers
made in many of the studies they review must to be treated with caution.
Their admittedly 'limited evidence' suggests that pessimistic predictions
are 'at least an exaggeration' in that they can be shown not to apply to
'some managers in some organisations' (ibid.: 15).

These two studies, as I have suggested, were in part a stimulus to my
own research. Two well-designed research projects were finding quite
different patterns in apparently similar contexts. This could well have been
simply a matter of difference in the organisations sampled. By looking, in
depth, at managers in just one organisation and by working alongside these
managers I might be able to throw light on the issues raised by these two
preceding investigations.

MANAGERS' ORIENTATIONS IN ZTC RYLAND: A SHIFTING AND AMBIGUOUS PATTERN

My brief review of just two studies of British managers shows the range
of possibilities which may be found in different circumstances. My own
experience of studying and working with managers in ZTC suggests to me
that the contrasting situations described in these two studies are both
possibilities which can come about within British work organisations. The
ZTC evidence is helpful, I feel, because it shows a group of managers in
an organisation in a confused state of transition which could lead to
outcomes similar to either of the two patterns seen in the two studies. The
general message which can be derived from this observation is that we
should not too readily generalise about the attitudes or state of mind of
British managers. The situation is an open one, in the sense that a variety
of possible patterns are available. The actual pattern prevailing in any one
organisation will depend on how the organisation as a whole is managed,
as well as on the predispositions of the actual managers it employs. This,
in turn, means that there are choices to be made in any organisation about
how it treats its managers. The present research, it is hoped, can help us
understand the sorts of choice which need to be made.

My early analysis of what was happening to managers' orientations in ZTC Ryland left me puzzled. I heard constant complaints about the way the company was being managed at a senior level; about bullying and lack of clear direction on the Ryland site, and remoteness and callousness at corporate level. I heard complaints about an organisational structure which was divisive and fostered conflict rather than cooperation, and I heard regular statements of regret that ZTC under its current ownership was becoming an increasingly uncaring employer (of people at all levels, including senior managers themselves). In addition to this, there was distress about the fact that a regular part of many managers' jobs in ZTC was one of making members of their departments redundant. The security of managers themselves was limited: nobody was too sure what direction the company was going to take and doubts were growing all the time about whether the Ryland site would survive at all for more than a limited amount of time. Yet at the same time I found managers talking about how much they *loved* their jobs.

At times I found it almost bizarre to hear the very same managers, who would bitterly complain about their lot and attack various trends and developments in the company with passion and venom, later talk about their devotion to their work and how rewarding they found doing it. In this chapter we will mainly see the evidence for the positive side of the managers' work orientations. The negative side will become more central when the level of the focus moves upwards in the next two chapters, away from the individual in their immediate location towards their views and feelings about the organisation as a whole. To see the accounts presented in this chapter in context, however, it is necessary to recognise that a contrasting tone will emerge later.

How is this contrast to be understood? There are two possible factors operating. The first is what might be called a triumph of hope over emerging experience. Many of the managers had been with the organisation for a long time and had developed a strong psychological contract with an organisation which, in many ways, was run paternalistically. The current ownership, it was widely felt, was rapidly moving away from this but managers can be seen as feeling that the considerable investment of self in the company that they had made could not be readily abandoned. One manager who had 'grown up man and boy at Ryland' put it this way:

'I put everything I had got into the company and was happy to do it. They thought a lot of us then and looked after us – not that there was anything for nothing, don't get me wrong. I just find it hard to believe that what I put in in my twenties, thirties and forties is not going to pay off for me now. I've a lot to give. I want to give a lot. But do they want it? I'd like to believe they do.'

For a number of managers, their age and lack of prospects elsewhere in the context of an economic recession and a decline in manufacturing employment, helped shape their optimism or 'wishful thinking'. But in spite of the fact that there was a growing proportion of 'marketable' younger managers voluntarily leaving ZTC Ryland during my year with the company, there was a significant proportion of such individuals who continued to give commitment to an organisation which they felt was equivocal in its commitment to them.

In addition to this possible phenomenon of 'investment of self' in a formerly paternalistic organisation, there is a second factor which may help explain the contrasting patterns of accounts to be seen in this and in the next chapter. In the accounts presented in the present chapter, this relates to the extent to which managers are focusing on their personal and local situation, as opposed to their involvement in ZTC at the level of the business as a whole.

It is a basic assumption of this book that human beings, by their very nature, need to maintain a certain level of self-esteem. Their concept of self can only exist by being seen in the 'looking glass' of the perceptions of others (Cooley 1922). And to maintain a sense of internal integrity and a level of perceived worth in the eyes of others sufficient to facilitate interpersonal strategic exchange, individuals will tend to present themselves in a potentially positive rather than a negative light (cf. Goffman 1958). Thus, although a person may find themselves in what they perceive as an 'unhappy' situation, they will tend to emphasise the positive elements of their condition when focusing on themselves and their immediate locus (which they are more likely to be expected to control), whilst the negative evaluations within their accounts will be focused on factors more remote from themselves (circumstances, or 'others', are 'to blame' rather than ourselves). The following conversation which occurred after a management meeting (and which was written down immediately after its occurrence) illustrates this. I commented to Don Littleover:

> 'I've been listening to you belly-aching all morning, Don, about Ted, about Harrison, about the company, about the failure of marketing. But you were telling me yesterday about how great your job is; about how you are reluctant to go home at night. It doesn't make sense to me. Is your home life so bloody awful?'
> 'No it's not.'
> 'What is it then – go on, explain it to me.'
> 'I do get great kicks from what I do here every day.'
> 'That's hilarious: "kicks"! One of your biggest complaints earlier was about how Ted goes around kicking the shit out of everyone. You said the way this whole place is run is all wrong. Perhaps you like getting kicked?'
> 'You're playing with words again, Tony. Ted doesn't actually kick me that much. It's his blokes that really get it. But yes, I stand by what I was saying. I think the truth of it is this: I get great kicks, sorry, yes kicks, from the operation I run. It's great. But, to be honest, I fear that it will be all for nothing unless someone begins to pull everything together a bit better. I wouldn't be surprised if every one of us in that room would show commitment and excitement about our jobs – you know, our own bits of the action. But you heard how we talk about the way the company is going. Quite a different story.'

To risk a very broad generalisation at this stage of the analysis, I would say that there was something of an ambivalence about the work orientations of the managers in ZTC Ryland, a type of ambivalence which may well be replicated elsewhere as other organisations go through the sorts of transition occurring in ZTC. Many managers felt rewarded by the opportunities they had in their immediate jobs to achieve tasks, to be 'in control', to have the respect of the people they worked with and the people they managed. But they were increasingly becoming concerned about whether their energies were being directed towards the sort of overall business success that would give them the security (the psychological security of being in a 'good' company, as well as employment security) that they had once experienced. To put this more simply: they were positive quite often about what they were doing day to day, but becoming increasingly negative about what they believed they were doing it for. These growing doubts, which will become clearer in the next two chapters, were partly the result of recognising the extent to which traditional ways of operating in the company would not be sufficiently competitive in the increasingly difficult market environment. And they were partly the outcome of doubts engendered by a growing awareness of newer management ideas stressing strong cultures, focus on customers, continuous improvement and the rest. As we shall see, this awareness had been heightened by certain organisation development activities in the company. And this was the same company which many felt was preventing them from operating in such terms.

In this chapter I shall focus on managers' perception of their lives in ZTC Ryland and try to bring out patterns in the accounts given to me by managers about their work orientation. This will not, however, exhaust the theme of 'managers in search of themselves'. The idea of people 'shaping' themselves through their work and the way their work links with their personal idiosyncrasies and values will be taken up in Chapter 7 when we consider how individuals 'manage to manage'.

VARIETY, CONTROL, CHALLENGE AND THE BUZZ

I have been arguing throughout that to understand any particular manager's work orientation, we need to relate it to the way they 'manage' their own identity; the way they maintain a notion of the 'sort of person' they are. This expression was used by Jeremy Sneinton at the beginning of this chapter, and his use of the term was partly what led me to open with his words. However, he says something in connection with this notion which is equally significant and which is very close to the spirit of a lot of what was said to me by managers. Sneinton related the sort of person he is to the fact that 'I like to be on the move, dealing with all sorts of things, having an influence on what's around me.'

When managers were asked what it was they liked about being a manager, both in general and with regard to their current job, they frequently alluded to the idea of being in control rather than being controlled, leading rather than being led, 'having an influence' on things. Terry Carlton, for example, answered my question about what was the most important thing in life to him, after thinking carefully about it, with these words:

'I am trying to think of something where I wouldn't survive if it was not there [long pause]. I don't know if I can tell you what it is. It's a value-laden thing. It is to do with having the freedom to operate. It's about being able to control, not being controlled.'

When asked later what he liked best about being a manager, he replied:

'The need for control again. Although I am quite a shy person I like to get involved with people . . . understanding the way they work and the way they go about things. I think it's also being the child of teachers; I am a sucker for someone who says they "can't" or they are incapable. I tend to go out of my way to demonstrate that they can do things they have convinced themselves they couldn't do. I think being a manager is a fabulous place to be for that. There are three people out here for example. People outside the department will think they're "just admin", but the best bit about it is that they can learn all the roles that their superiors out there are doing and become one of them later.'
    'I was asking about being a manager in general terms, but what about this specific job?'
    'Yes, it's being responsible for achieving results through the team.'

The notion of being 'in control', then, has been related to Terry Carlton's upbringing, his having teachers for parents, but is also related to his conception of the line-management side of his job. Controlling is a concept Terry can relate to values, and these are clearly to do with helping develop others.

Geoff Clifton related the control theme more to strategic business issues, saying that what being a manager 'meant' to him was

'Being in a position to influence and direct the nature of the business we are in and then applying the same sort of interest to what is happening now, to support that . . . There is a degree of being close to the centre of things so that one knows what is happening – so that you get a broader view of the business rather than sitting in a compartment.'

Later when asked about what he liked about his job, he used the words 'it is influencing things – I really can'.

In a similar vein, we hear managers saying:

'I have always never been satisfied by being led, so I suppose that means that I am a leader. I am not saying I am a successful leader. I tend to want to lead.'

Which is similar to:

'I just like being the leader of people – I don't know why; it is just something that is there in me, I don't know why. I like to be the leader rather than being led.'

And:

> 'It's not that I am driven, that I absolutely have to be in charge. It's that I would rather be in charge than have someone else in charge of me.'

Control relates not only to people but to tasks:

> 'Being able to influence things, to say: "I had a say in that, I did that".'

And making a difference, where one is able to:

> 'What I like, though, is the feeling that you are controlling something – it is in your destiny, if you like, whether you make a go of it or you fail. The only problem we have is you may fail for something out of your control – where you have something like a shortage of materials. But if you have done everything you can to get that job out and at the end of the day you say you have done everything you can; then that is the satisfaction.'

Successful achievement of tasks is often related to the notion of leadership:

> 'When I am successful – you get a tremendous amount of satisfaction out of it, you know. It also feeds your personal ego – that all managers have. You tend to have wanted to be a leader to have wanted to do the job in the first place.'

And, of course, leadership takes us back to the people side of the job, which is also frequently related to the notion of task achievement:

> 'There is the reward of excellence and there is a reward in a sense of improvement, even if you are not there yet. There is also the reward of accomplishing things as a group of people. At the end of something you feel that you have pulled together and there is a sense of identity around that accomplishment. That is fantastic really. People feel they were part of a group that brought that about – it is super really.'

This notion of being in control is clearly related to a theme of the previous chapter, where it was argued that a popular conception of management among ZTC Ryland managers was one of 'achieving things through people'. But this sense of control, or perhaps we should say the autonomy which produces such a sense, is frequently recognised as being a relative matter. This is seen in the idea of leading, not so much as an end in itself but as something to be preferred to being led and it is seen in the reference to things which are beyond one's control:

> 'There are others above me, of course, who you could say are controlling me. Although I know they are there and they are often a pain to me, the freedom I have most of the day more than makes up for the pushing around I get every two or three days.'

Control is related to personal achievement as well as to task achievement by a department or team. Managers often spoke of challenges:

> 'It is the opportunity to use new skills and utilise ones I have already got – to bring about what I feel is a substantial achievement. If I could achieve an

effective board shop – and I will – where the quality is acceptable and the quantity is acceptable and the costs are better than they have been – I would see that as a considerable achievement.'

This challenge is frequently related to novelty, variety and mobility;

'What do you like most about being a manager?'
'It is the fresh challenges. There is always something new to take on.'
'And what do you like best about your particular job?'
'The challenges again, and the fact that in this job I get out and about a lot, around the country, around the company.'

Managers mentioned things like:

'There is always something new.'

'There are always new challenges.'

'No two days are alike.'

'What I love most of all is the variety.'

Managers at various levels used terms like 'love': 'I absolutely love being here – always on the go with one thing or another.' And one of the 'toughest' shop floor managers spoke of 'loving the people here'. The terms 'tickled pink' was used about the pleasure of 'bringing out the best in people' and the term 'buzz' was used both to describe the social or 'leadership' side of the job as well as the satisfaction to be gained from being in a position to direct events:

'I like being in a key position in the business as a director. You get a buzz from knowing that you make a difference to so much.'

There is a pattern, then, in what might be called the 'intrinsic rewards' making up the implicit (or psychological) contracts of the managers in ZTC. They didn't fail to mention more extrinsic rewards like 'a comfortable standard of living', 'the wherewithall to give my family a good life', 'the level of income making it possible to buy my kids a good education' or 'the company car and all that', but these were always stated as background matters, as things which, as one man said, 'go without saying'. There is also mention of status, as in 'the satisfaction of being seen as having got to the top of the pile'. The central theme of managers' accounts seemed to be one of being free to control their daily lives (which it was implied was less so among the 'led', those who were not managers).

All the managers in the core group of interviewees were asked, 'How free are you to do your job as you wish?', and it is striking how positively managers responded. Typical comments were, 'Not being glib, as free as I want to be', 'So far, very free', 'Totally', '99 per cent', 'Wonderfully', 'I fight to make sure I am'. The strength of positive comments here can be related to my earlier point about positive comments being associated with a focus on the immediate job. They can also possibly be related to an element of personal pride coming in dealing with a personally directed question – 'How free are *you* . . .?'. We see a less positive picture coming into focus when individuals choose here to look beyond their immediate context, as in:

'I am free to do it the way I like in terms of actually getting it done. But then there are all those restrictions which come from the corporate culture.'

'I am free – within the constraints imposed by the company. It is not as though my boss is very rigid, though.'

'I am totally free to succeed – within the rules of the site.'

These constraints, rules and cultural limits are to be the key concern of a later chapter and, indeed, they more typically emerged within my interviews at a later stage of the conversation, when I switched the level of discussion away from the manager's own job to the level of the business. But the issues were identified in relation to managers' own jobs to a limited extent when they were asked what they disliked about being a manager. Generally, however, the dislikes were specific ones which were taken to be 'part of the job' and were a matter of 'swings and roundabouts – you've got to take the rough as well as the smooth':

'Having to do boring things like paperwork.'

'Figures, admin, dealing with Personnel.'

'Telling people bad news.'

'Disciplining people, sacking people.'

'Meetings, meetings, meetings.'

'Aggro, rows.'

'The most uncomfortable thing is adopting edicts from on high that I disagree with.'

'Politics and back-stabbing.'

'Putting up with bloody Ted and his foul mouth.'

However, some evidence of concern about more structural worries did emerge with reference to dislikes associated with the specific job (as opposed to those associated with being a manager in general). There was a clear pattern of complaints coming from people who tended to identify themselves as innovators. Sometimes they related their frustration to particular individuals, often focusing on Ted Meadows who, as we shall see later, was often taken to epitomise the culture of ZTC Ryland. Phil Wollaton said:

'What I most dislike is seeing opportunities and not being able – perhaps smart enough – to share my enthusiasms with my peers. I can't talk to Ted Meadows about it. This part of the business is owned by me, not by Ted Meadows. But if I see opportunities I have to go to Ted Meadows and I go through seventeen types of torture: "Can you cut this, can you stop that". I wonder why I bother – I face this on a daily basis. There are lots of opportunities for the proper support of product. But there is a thought that if you can't make money from it, don't do it. But it is about the customer. If the customer sees you being responsive, you'll make money in the longer term. You have to make a trade between making money in the short term, and serving customers. I like the entrepreneurial part of my work, but I am stifled on this. I've nobody to talk to – fellow spirits to talk to saying, "Is this or that a good idea or not?".'

There is a suggestion of a cultural pattern, going beyond the influence of Ted Meadows alone here, with the suggestion that innovative suggestions are not valued by Phil Wollaton's peers. And the notion of cultural norms is suggested by the words of Carol Rowsley, a business development manager:

'It's the sheer frustration of not being able to get things done fast enough. Being constrained by "We've always done it this way"; having to justify everything "n" times. Everyone's sitting there saying, "We know you're right *but . . .*".'

We must not forget here that a person's orientation, and the accounts they give of the positive and negative aspects of their implicit contract with the organisation, arises from the interplay of their personal priorities or meanings and the structural contexts in which they find themselves. Both Phil Wollaton and Carol Rowsley are people whose roles involve an identification with the entrepreneurial side of business. Their frustrations at having to operate in a context they perceived as over-cautious and 'short-termist' (they both used this term at various times) clearly related both to their personal conceptions of who they were, as well as conceptions of what a business should be like. But perhaps the most powerful example of an individual who had invested a considerable degree of 'self' in the achievement of change was Charles Bunny, whose job was focused on bringing about major changes in operating style across the plant. His self-image at times resembled that of a prophet and at other times a revolutionary. He spoke of the frustration of his job being 'so developmental':

'You are going at such a rate of knots you are always having to drag people from the Dark Ages. It's the speed that the general organisation takes to get there. You know it will get there: six months on, you see people doing things they once pooh-poohed. You know time and again that this is going to be the case. That really upsets me. When we started ABC, people said, "You'll never do that; they won't let us have it; we'll never do this; we'll never get the other". But when you break it down and ask, "Why can't this happen; what are the influencing factors here? You can change this". Then you put a plan together and they begin to do things. It goes like that for a while, but then they regress again. You say you know its going to happen. Its like that beer advert on the telly – all these people pushing bloody great balls up a hill. It rolls back down the hill and . . . it's very big boulders up very big hills. It's not that that bothers me though. That's a challenge. It's back to this "You've seen it before, why can't you believe now?". I feel like Christ, sometimes, you know. He was there working miracles and people still didn't believe him.'

The notion of people's general tendency to resist change, and the idea that such a tendency was reinforced by the culture at ZTC (or at ZTC Ryland) was referred to by a good proportion of managers whose jobs could be understood as being especially focused on external business matters involving an entrepreneurial element or involving formal targets of establishing new structures or procedures. Charles Bunny was perhaps an extreme case, since he was both charged with bringing about some major changes in the systems operating in Rylands and because he was immensely concerned to advance his own career at speed. He left the company some six months after the above words were spoken. But he was not the only person to have been considering leaving the organisation to increase what one of the directors called his 'freedom to operate':

> 'You could say I'm leaving ZTC because I've had a damn good offer. It's an excellent career move. But the truth is I just had to go anyway. I am supposed to be a director of a business here in Ryland. But every creative move you try to make is hemmed in from one side or another. In this new job I'll be fully in charge of my patch. You can be sure of that. I've made damn sure of it before accepting.'

Another director, who also left some months later, said: 'I am on the board here, they make me responsible. But there are directors above me at corporate, and directors above them. I've got no autonomy, really.'

In spite of this evidence of negative orientations among those especially concerned with innovation, there was a generally positive response to questions which invited people to sum up their implicit contract with ZTC. I asked managers to tell me how they saw the overall balance between what they put into their jobs and what they 'got out of it'. This tended to elicit comments like 'I've had a good deal', 'It's pretty fair all in all', 'ZTC have looked after me'. The accounts had a tone, however, of looking backwards and taking into account the way the company had given individuals opportunities in the past. It seemed that a rewarding past was being used to balance up a less positive present and a potentially worrying future. Thus we get: 'Yeah, it's OK but we are getting increasingly strait-jacketed' and 'Yes, a good balance. But I am worried about erosion'.

The study by Scase and Goffee (1989) painted a picture of 'reluctant managers' who were less than fully committed to their work and organisations. This was anything but the case at ZTC Ryland, in spite of frustrations which were expressed. I asked managers about 'how happy' they were with 'the degree of commitment sought' by the company. The general response was that this was 'high but not unreasonable', 'not different from in other companies', 'quite a lot but we get well paid for it', 'you have to tailor your life'. I heard no complaints that could be interpreted as indicating that too much commitment was sought. The existence, elsewhere, of such a possibility was recognised, however, when individuals referred to people they knew who worked in US-owned companies where 'they own you body and soul', as one person put it. There were several references to this phenomenon and it arose on one occasion in a discussion involving several managers. The theme of the discussion was that most of those present would dislike what they saw as being over-identified with a company but (and this, I think, is significant) they felt that ZTC could, if anything, look for 'a bit more from us'. It was agreed, in the words of one of those present: 'We are a pretty committed bunch but I don't think ZTC know what to do with that commitment'. This point emerged in some of the interviews but it was, perhaps inevitably, rather vague. Ray Tollerton commented:

> 'They look for a lot, but whether it is the right sort all the time I don't know. This culture of putting in the hours is not really getting the sort of commitment you really need to succeed well as a business.'

Ray Tollerton was referring here to the practice of managers demonstrating their commitment and status within the organisation by staying at work late into the evening. This is a theme which will be returned to at later stage. For now I turn to a consideration of several individual ZTC managers to balance the preceding analysis of general patterns in work orientation with attention to the way the themes of individuals shaping their lives and the idea of *control* in managers' lives arise in a unique way in the life of each individual and can be related to the values they hold.

PERSONAL VALUES, IDENTITY AND WORK ORIENTATION

In the earlier explanation of the idea of an implicit or psychological contract identifiable at the core of a person's work orientation, I suggested that one of the 'wants' or 'rewards' which can be part of the trade between the individual and the organisation is that of an opportunity to fulfil one's personal values. A very clear case of this being central to a person's work orientation might be their choosing to enter a religious or charitable form of work, where the opportunity to fulfil deeply held personal values would compensate for the sacrifice of the greater material rewards which might be available in more 'mainstream' careers. But even within the more pragmatic kinds of work entered by most people there is likely, at the minimum, to be an avoidance of undertaking tasks which clash fundamentally with personal values.

The notion of values in social life is a valuable but subtle one. I define values in a relatively simple way as 'ideas about what is good and bad, right and wrong', and would stress that although they are social phenomena, in the sense that they are developed and transmitted through social and cultural processes, they are adopted in a particular form or with a particular emphasis by each separate individual. The combination of values held, and the various strengths with which each is held, is a matter of the way each person is shaping their identity at that time. Personal values amount to those assessments of what is 'right and wrong for me', what is 'good and bad for me', given my notion of who and what I am in my own eyes and in the eyes of others.

For any individual to give an account of themselves and their life, they are bound to give some indications of what values they hold or, in so far as these may differ, what values they wish to be seen as holding by those they are addressing. To say who you are is closely related to saying what it is you 'believe in'. The researcher, using the sort of detailed personal accounts which I collected during my research, should readily be able to infer value positions on the part of those studied. But some questions are more likely to elicit insights about values than others.

The most direct questions I asked in my core interviews were those of 'What is the most important thing in life to you?' and 'Can you identify any personal values or beliefs which you think are relevant to the way you work?'. The former question can produce revealing answers but, equally, can elicit what we might call the 'standard respectable' answer, typically alluding to spouse and offspring, or the platitudinous answer referring perhaps to 'happiness'. A valuable way to get insights into values, in addition to these more direct questions, is to ask people what they would name as their ideal job, if they could have 'any job in the world'. I draw on words spoken to me in response to these questions and various others in the following discussion of three ZTC Ryland managers, selected to illustrate the importance of notions of values and control in understanding the ways managers shape their lives and relate to their work. Mary Southwell is a manager of an administrative function which deals with organisations outside ZTC, Jim Somercotes is a production manager, Tommy Bulwell is a planning executive and Martin Hillside is in Personnel.

Mary Southwell: peeping inside the rain forest

Mary Southwell first spoke in terms which suggest a particular value position with regard to managerial work when she was differentiating her position as a manager from that of her own staff. She used the word 'dedication' as the key factor:

> 'I am not saying that my staff are not dedicated people, but I feel they have not got the same dedication and edge that I feel I give to the job. It is not a love for the company – if you are that sort of person you will apply yourself wherever you work. This dedication is a matter of what you are.'

Here again is use of the notion introduced at the beginning of this chapter, the 'sort of person you are'. Mary connects this notion of dedication to the idea of being a 'good manager', something she strongly relates to the way they 'deal with people'. She believes that people worthy of the title of manager are those who operate with 'feelings or thoughts for people'. Bad managers lack this: 'they don't get the work done for the business because people don't respond to them'. Mary reveals that this position is very much being worked out in her own mind and that it emerged from some of her own doubts about the way she handled problems. She told me about her having to tell one of her staff that he was not performing well. She had worried greatly beforehand, but

> 'When it came to the morning I had not formulated anything in my mind, so I thought I will just have to go through with it. And it worked out fine. It was someone in the department who was failing quite miserably and I had to explain that I was having to pull them away from the job – to do something less critical.'

Mary was concerned about the agonising she had gone through:

> 'I think that I think too personally and emotionally about people. I did not want to upset them and I worried about how sad they would feel – losing a job that they thought they were doing well on. I was feeling for them. I thought, "Is that a failure because that is what females feel and not males?". But, again, is that a good or a bad thing? All this is put in context though by the fact that at the end of it all I am always concerned for the business. I would say that is the most important factor; the business has got to be right and if you can't put the right people in the right job it is not going to be OK. I know that I must not be afraid of making people do the job well. Everybody's job depends on this.'

Mary Southwell here brings together her own doubts about her sensitivity to people's feelings with the basic responsibility of the manager. In line with the argument developed in Chapter 1 about thought being rhetorical, she is 'arguing with herself'. And she resolves the argument and the worry about whether she is being over-sensitive ('as a female') by taking the position that managers *need*, as people with a responsibility to help maintain the viability of the 'business', to be sensitive and thoughtful about their staff. Some of the background to the values operating here was indicated in the following dialogue. Mary gives an account of herself and her past which makes sense of her present interest in combining control, caring and dedication in her business career with earlier, and quite different career interests. But, first, she switched surprisingly from talking about people to reporting a seemingly greater interest in animals:

> 'Tell me, Mary, if you could have any job at all in the whole world, what would it be? What would be the ideal for you?'
> 'To work on a farm or in a zoo.'
> 'That's interesting. Why is it that after everything you've said about working with people that you now tell me that it's animals you are really interested in?'
> 'I just like animals and sometimes I do feel that I like them more than people.'
> 'Really?'
> 'Well, until I am with people anyway. But don't think that I go about thinking "you are like a giraffe" and "you are like an elephant". But maybe I do see people as animals in the sense that they are my herd, my flock, I suppose. The appeal of the farm or the zoo is looking after the animals. And it is the same

thing as here – they, my staff, are looking to me to look after them and I am going to be responsible and get that satisfaction from keeping them well and healthy.'

'That is really fascinating. Can I take it that what you are saying is that you like to have a sense of being in charge of situations and that being in charge involves caring for those you are in charge of?'

'Yes. If I go back to being a girl, I firstly I wanted to be a nurse. My grandmother said "you should be a nurse". When I was twelve my mother had a spastic baby and I fell into all the baby-sitting and taking for walks. I really loved him and I had the most fantastic contact with him. I think from that perhaps I would like nursing. But for some reason I changed my mind when I was fifteen. Yet I have ended up in some ways doing the sort of things which come into that; things which are, I suppose you could say, me.'

Here we have a very direct relating of managerial tasks to personal identity with the notion of 'things which are . . . me'. And Mary Southwell was able to express particularly clearly some of the ways in which she defends her notion of herself as a distinctive and unique 'me'. When, prior to the above conversation, I asked her about personal values or beliefs, she spoke of how she hated 'the telling of lies' and would 'be hurt if people were lying to me'. But she then went immediately on to say that:

'I have got quite a lot of disciplines – some strange ones as far as some people are concerned. It's things like I wouldn't eat in McDonald's and I wouldn't watch "Dallas".'

Mary, laughing, continued: 'I just feel I won't do it because people are so brainwashed to do it. It is like a principle to me now . . . perhaps I might quite like "Dallas" if I watched it.'

'So what are these "disciplines" about?'

'I like to feel a little bit different perhaps. I just don't like people to be brainwashed into being the same and into believing that "this or that is the best thing since sliced bread: you *will* watch it".'

'So it is to do with being yourself, and with being independent, is it?'

'Yes. We have a caravan and tour a lot and go away at weekends and I feel if I wasn't married I would be very much one of those people who travel the world and get involved. I would love to be more involved with everything in the world than I am. I would like to have peeped inside the rain forests.'

In spite of this interest in extending her horizons, Mary Southwell was not ambitious in career terms. She said in fact that 'I could not do a more complex job because I have not really got the brains to do that', but she clearly values taking up challenges and being in a position to understand the business situation beyond her immediate job. Her answer to a query about what her ideal job in ZTC would be is revealing, in that it indicates her interest in people, her concern about the business as a whole and her curiosity about how senior management operates. There is also perhaps the suggestion of a deeper desire to enter such a realm if that were a realistic possibility for a woman in her mid-forties with, as she put it 'zero qualifications'. She said:

> 'Perhaps this is my ideal job. Sometimes I think it could be in Personnel. I like the contact with the business in this job but I do a lot of personnel work. Then again I wouldn't mind Mr Meadow's job – if I could have his Jaguar to go with it. It would be nice to know why, when he is saying no, he is saying no. We never know that. I would like to know the why.'

Perhaps this is another aspect of 'peeping inside the rain forest'.

From these small excerpts from my conversations with Mary Southwell we gain insight into the way just one person makes sense of their life, their past, their interests, their values and their job. All these various elements can be seen as forming part of a picture Mary paints for us and for herself. In painting this portrait she is shaping her concept of self, exerting control over her identity and the ways she orients herself to her work.

Jim Somercotes: flying, farming and controlling

Like Mary Southwell, Jim Somercotes, a production manager in his late forties, spoke of 'dedication' when considering the qualities to be found in a good manager. Like Mary again, he spoke of values of honesty:

> 'To talk of good managers you have to use all the clichés like "dedication", like having to be honest and fair.'

In the same way that Mary said that she 'liked to be the leader rather than being led', Jim said that he had never been satisfied by being led and that he would always 'tend to want to lead'. Like Mary he related the way he was to his earlier life; as a member of the Royal Marines he had quickly risen to the rank of sergeant. In saying this, however, Jim was not suggesting that he was 'a successful leader', and pointed out that his military rank was less than that of his father and brother: 'You could say I was the drop-out of the family, if you like.'

The process of shaping identity involves elements of what we might call repair work where there are felt inadequacies and aspects of self which, it is feared, will not be seen positively by others. Jim spoke of his own insecurities and handled these by playing something of the role of a ruthless self-critic. At the beginning of my formal interview with him (and I was by no means any kind of stranger to him by this time) he apologised for his 'broad Brummagem accent' and, later, when speaking of early career choices said:

> 'I had a hang-up about my background and my accent which I have carried round until now (you've heard me apologise for it already). It is something I am very aware of; it is a bit of inferiority.'

He went on to speak of how 'nasty' he could be when he 'got a failure'. Although he felt that a democratic style of management was the correct one, he noted that 'if I analyse myself I suppose I am more autocratic than democratic' and this would become apparent when he faced failure:

'Then I totally switch over and become totally autocratic. That is when you see the nasty side. I am a pure-bred bastard then; which I often am to be honest – when I feel things are not going the way they should go, I am then known for putting my boot in.'

Jim related this to what he called his 'two failings'. First, he tries to be a perfectionist (which he commented was 'dangerous'):

'The second thing is – and this is a real failing on my part – I cannot stand failure. If I believe I am failing I just drive myself to achieve the objective.'

But Jim's self-analysis was that this was not a facet of his particular approach to managerial work, but was something in his 'basic make-up', something, in turn, which could be related to his earlier biography:

'This was not brought about by my desire as a manager to be a total winner. It is just something within me on basic make-up really. I think it came from joining the services at seventeen. You are very susceptible to being brainwashed. I totally accept that I was brainwashed because the Marines are trained to be totally independent; to be individuals and to be winners. They never accept failure. I have never been able to shrug that off.'

The idea of 'brainwashing' here is not unusual as a device of lay theorising used by the people I interviewed when they were talking about issues of personal identity. Jim used the idea to account for his present approach to his work, whereas Mary Southwell had used the idea to explain her personal resistance to manipulation. Jim partly used the concept, it seemed, to help deflect 'blame' for what he saw as some of his 'well-known bad ways' from the company:

'My bosses wind me up. They know that I cannot sort of live with myself if I don't succeed. Is that bit on tape? Oh shit. Look: this is all down to my personal ego. You can't put it down to the company if it is the way *you* act.'

Jim Somerville observed that he was 'a fairly complicated person, to be honest' and he made this point when speaking of his 'ideal job'. Twenty years ago, he said, he would have spoken of being a pilot. But his 'other side' meant that he would 'have loved to have been a smallholding farmer'. The latter would not have been a possibility, however, because 'you need capital' and the former was ruled out because Jim's 'hang-up' about his 'background' meant that 'I imagined that I could not have got into the Air Force'. His entry into the Marines was related to two things: the 'privations of post-war food-rationing' gave one a 'natural inclination to go into the services' and the 'Marines were the best and the Marines would get me about the world – perhaps even into the air'.

My inevitable question to Jim Somerville about these two seemingly contrasting 'ideal jobs', flying and farming, was whether there was a 'common thread' between the two. He explained:

'Once I left Birmingham and was training in the open air I developed a love of the countryside and for animals. I began to appreciate the ecology and how things fit together – trees, plants . . . On reflection I think I would have been a happier man on a smallholding, running it myself. I'd be my own man if you like – "I am doing this because it is the way I want to do it". It's the same with the pilot. He does it himself and he is responsible. I have got that hang up: if I am in control of something and doing it myself I will take all the stick and I will take all the responsibility. I am not afraid of doing it wrong, because I know I will do it right, maybe not the first time but I will get it right eventually. The trouble is today you are not in control; too many people are sticking their oar in and destroying what you are doing.'

Here, we are back to our key notion of *control*, and a link between 'what sort of person' the manager is and how they approach their work. Jim Somerville saw himself as in a very difficult situation, caught between the 'demands of the job and my own personality'. The pressures to achieve monthly output targets in a context where he was not as free as he would like to have been, together with the internal psychological pressures to succeed, led him to act as a manager in a way he disapproved of. He therefore struggled to keep his 'autocratic tendency in check':

'If I let it run riot I can be extremely autocratic and I accept that that is totally false as a way to go on.'

However, Jim was not discouraged by this and was very anxious for the company to stop treating him as a 'work-horse' and to give him a real challenge. His ideal job in ZTC would be to set up a new factory overseas. This would

'. . . give the opportunity to develop myself. I have got all these latent skills I am dying to develop. I know I could do a really good job. It would be training of managers, of operators, machine techniques, lay-outs, material control. It is all there – I am dying to go and dying to have a crack – I want to develop myself.'

This notion of it being 'all there', about being in overall control of an operation (like the pilot of the aircraft or the farmer of the smallholding) arises again in the case of Tommy Bulwell.

Tommy Bulwell: planning, exploring and putting it all together

When asked about his ideal job, Tommy Bulwell suggested:

'I would either be a travel writer or involved with developing the television travel programmes. I like exploring and I would like putting it all together. I have wondered about consultancy too; using the skills I have developed here to help small companies. I could put my managerial and planning skills alongside their entrepreneurial strengths.'

Rather like Mary Southwell and her desire to 'peep into the rain forests', Tommy spoke of the 'really memorable' things in his life. These occurred when on holiday and when

'I have been able to creep off and look at the things I wanted to do; to look at Knossos and drive around the island to explore the place and walk part of the Sumerian Gorge.'

This interest in travel is related to Tommy's love of 'putting all the pieces' together in his world; hence the idea of translating the holiday pleasures into a fantasy type of work which would produce books or television travel programmes. Throughout a very long interview with him there was repeated reference to 'planning'. An early appointment as an industrial engineering manager followed an approach which said, 'Well, you've done a lot of planning so would you go for an interview?' When asked what part of his job he was best at, he said 'planning'.

Planning was central to Tommy's work identity. He saw it as something which took him into management in the first place and he recognised that he was happiest when he was doing it:

'I enjoy being a manager when I get on to projects like bringing new products on stream I suppose – when I am planning. There is a saying somewhere that you are living life at its best when you are planning.'

His 'ideal job in ZTC' would be to take charge of bringing the next new product into the plant, but this was stated with the important qualification: 'as long as I had the freedom not to have to get approvals on every little detail.'

Control for Tommy Bulwell was not a matter of being 'in charge' in the sense that a chief executive or entrepreneur might be. It was similar, in that the ideal job would have a 'holistic' nature and that one would not be too constrained in the way one helped bring things about; whether one was acting as a consultant to a small business entrepreneur or establishing new systems and procedures for a product.

The idea of there being a manufactured product was very important to Tommy. This was something he often spoke about, and it arose when he was talking about his personal values. He spoke first, however, and in a way reminiscent of many others (including Mary Southwell and Jim Somercotes) of honesty. He spoke with passion about how he believed 'everybody should be honest and truthful with each other' and that 'career politics should be banned out of the place'. He explained:

'I am not really a religious guy any more and some church people I know are not religious at all. But at the end of the day I don't think you should ever dump on anybody. I will tell lies to support my colleagues, especially if I believe those colleagues have tried their hardest and are of value to protect.'

He went on, though:

'I have a more fundamental hang-up though: people have got to get to grips with making things.'

Tommy felt that manufacturing was a vital part of any economy and that people were dignified by being involved in production. He reported that he was seriously worried about whether his own company would survive and continue to give him the opportunity to fulfil his values through his own contribution to this vital activity. For ZTC to succeed, however, there needed to be more openness and less time spent fighting 'political battles'. Tommy quoted to me two of the aphorisms he had written in his 'time manager' (his diary or personal organiser). The first was 'arguments thrive when facts are scarce'. He had the skills to gather facts and to deploy his knowledge to productive effect. To be in control is to be able to handle the unexpected; wisdom and mastery can be in the hands of the planner. As the words inscribed in his 'time manager' said: 'True wisdom lies in the masterful administration of the unforeseen.'

Martin Hillside: watching, questioning and influencing people

Like Tommy Bulwell, Martin Hillside felt deeply about the importance of manufacturing industry and the dependence of the supply of necessary welfare services like those of health and education on 'the wealth-producing sector'. His personal values were consciously thought out within a Christian framework and we are reminded of Mary Southwell's rationalising of the need to discipline staff by relating discipline to the need to keep the business viable, by Martin's response to his vicar:

> 'My vicar always, no often, asks me, how can I do it; how can I make two or three hundred people redundant and call myself a Christian? How can I live with that? I tell him I don't have any difficulty whatsoever. If they don't go through that door, the company folds and two or three thousand lose their jobs. It does cause me personal anguish, but in managerial terms not at all.'

Martin relates this to a principle of having a responsibility 'to the job' and of being 'loyal'. This is highly reminiscent of Mary Southwell's words about dedication. Where Mary spoke of it being part of what she was like, Martin noted that 'I have felt this at whatever level I have worked, and it was the same in my previous organisation'. However, there was, it seemed to me, a possible tension in Martin's position about the company, arising from his ambivalence towards entrepreneurial activity. He spoke of the vital importance to society of trade and of 'selling things'. He found 'being involved in running a business . . . fascinating':

> 'I think in trade there are so may aspects to it, because business is essentially about having something somebody else wants and is prepared to pay for. And in any business – a bookshop or a billion-pound operation like this – um there is marketing, there is people, there is accounting, there is the whole gamut of human life if you like [laughs] and there is the opportunity to influence that sale. It is exciting. Some people will argue that I am the person on the board furthest away from that sale, but I say there is a buzz about it.'

This prompted me to ask,

'You like the idea of selling things?'

'Heavens, no. I am no salesman. I know, I know what it is: I'm doing it vicariously. I see selling as important. I can't do it, so I get involved in it indirectly. It's like you watch rugby but you don't play.'

'Martin, you'd no more get me to watch rugby than . . .'

'But you know what I am saying; can't you relate to the point?'

'Yes I think so. Of course I can. Yeah, I watch plays, films and read books about all the things I don't do: have affairs, commit crimes, solve crimes, fly aeroplanes and so on. I'm just a voyeur rather than a doer. Perhaps that is why I am an academic. Does that fit you: you do personnel work because you keep safely on the sidelines?'

'It's great, yes, one is a voyeur [laughing]; I like it. I think there is something in this, academics and personnel directors being people who stand back from the action. But we mustn't be unfair to ourselves and our colleagues here; it is this standing back that might make us good at what we do. Um.'

'How?'

'Helping us see things more clearly. The same could apply to the law – my other great love you could say. But, but, to be fair again, having the insights is not enough. For personnel work anyway, you have got to do something about what you see.'

'So you are not reluctant to move onto your rugby field when your spectator's viewpoint has suggested to you what needs to be done?'

'No, you know damn well you're there to act. It is just a matter of exploiting your voyeuristic leanings to help you act better, more effectively.'

'But let me go back to what you were saying about selling. You see it as important but feel unable to do it yourself. You couldn't be a salesman but you could – what was the word you used – do it vicariously?'

'Yes I do have doubts about selling and that – you know, moral problems.'

'Like the old Christians and usury?'

'Yes, that's right. But I know it has to be done. There has to be trading to create, you know, the "good things" people want, the things they need. I can't do it myself. So I'll recruit the salesmen, I'll train the buggers. Just don't ask me to do it.'

'Are we getting there? Do you think you are getting to the roots of what it is makes you tick?'

'I don't know. Yes, it's plausible.'

This dialogue was in some ways a joint process of self-exploration. There was much in what Martin Hillside was saying that I could identify with and which, I suspect, had been a part of my own value orientation when working in personnel and industrial relations management. And, like myself, Martin enjoyed analysing and reflecting on what was going on around him. He explained that one of the greatest sources of pleasure in life for him was in

'. . . just passing through life, observing and working things out. People often say to me when they see me sitting back and reflecting, "a penny for them".'

But, at the same time, Martin was wary of being pretentious and was concerned that he was not 'well read enough to be able to articulate my ideas'. He put this down to laziness, a notion which at first astonished me (knowing how much harder than me he worked!) but then enabled me to return to the Christian roots of his values. The conversation went:

> 'Maybe I suffer from laziness.'
> 'What? [incredulously]'
> 'I could do so much better if I applied myself. I've done two degrees and the second with a crying baby in one room and the wife studying as well . . . and the sun shining outside. You do all that and . . . and . . . and I could have done a lot more with it, I could have done a lot better.'
> 'Isn't this the old Protestant ethic again: you are letting down your God because you are not using all the talents he gave you? What would you have been, for goodness sake?'
> 'Exactly, I don't know.'

This prompted me to raise the question about Martin's ideal job:

> 'Let me ask you this, then: if you could have any job in the world, what would it be?'
> 'A politician or the Archbishop of Canterbury. I like the idea of the politics but I feel that it's a bit shallow. It's all the glib stuff I don't want.'
> 'It bothers you in the same way as the idea of being a salesman?'
> 'Yes . . . kissing babies and all that. That's why I'd go for Archbishop. He doesn't have to do all that. He does it through the hierarchy.'
> 'He delegates the baby-kissing you mean?' [laughter all round].

It seems that Martin is somebody who likes to be 'in charge'; to be influencing action whilst staying clear of the uncomfortable or morally doubtful aspects of it. I asked what it was that attracted him to these two occupations, and he replied:

> 'It has got to do with people – influencing people's behaviour really . . . so that they are more constructive and creative . . . making a [laughs] a better society and all that stuff.'

MANAGING, SHAPING AND CONTROLLING

Throughout all this material on both the broader patterns in the work orientations of managers in ZTC Ryland and that giving us glimpses into the lives of four particular individuals, there is a theme of people in the process of making sense of their biographies, of their significance in the world and of what they are doing as managers in a telecommunications company. In their managerial work, they are helping (however effectively or ineffectively) to shape the organisation which employs them whilst trying to make sense of the 'sort of person' they are and the 'rightness', in moral terms, of what they do from day to day.

Time and again, the managers I spoke to identified themselves as people who needed to be in control rather than be controlled (leaders rather than led). Often implicit in this, but also explicit on occasions, was the idea that they were different from those who were not managers. But there was little suggestion, it seemed to me, that this desire for control could be understood as a desire to control other people, as such. A powerful Marxist or *labour process* view of managerial work sees its rationale in managers' control over those who supply labour power in order to deliver surplus value to the owners of capital (Braverman 1974). Such a view can be defended on the grounds of how management functions in the capitalist 'mode of production', as long as you see the economic system as operating in these basic class terms. However, I would argue that there is little evidence that any of the managers I looked at conceived of their work in terms anything like this. They were indeed interested in 'control', but it was control of their own circumstances. They wanted control over events so that they could fulfil their employment contract in a way which would allow them to meet their personal requirements for satisfaction, at the same time as enabling the organisation to continue in business (an issue I shall return to in Chapter 9).

Poole, Mansfield, Blyton and Frost (1981), after a survey of managers' attitudes to factors at a societal as well as an organisational level, came to a corresponding conclusion. Managers were not seeking control on the behalf of other groups, neither were they seeking to further what James Burnham (1945) called the 'managerial revolution', whereby managers would displace other groups in society in order to be members of the ruling caste of a bureaucratic world. Michael Poole and his colleagues noted that managers' 'strongest attitudes seem to relate to the nature of the job itself rather than to issues affecting the development of the wider society' (1981: 154). They were 'interested in control in terms of freedom to perform their own jobs unconstrained by intervention from the state, trade unions and other pressure groups' (ibid.). The managers at ZTC Ryland were not 'reluctant managers' like those reported by Scase and Goffee (1989) (see p. 63), but neither were they as sure of their capacity to influence events as were the majority of the managers interviewed by Dopson and Stewart (1990) (see pp. 63–4). The enthusiasm shown by many of the ZTC Ryland managers for their jobs and their commitment to ZTC was becoming increasingly threatened by the constraints being put on their freedom to operate by the company itself. The nature of these constraints will be a key concern of Chapter 6. First, however, we consider in the next chapter the way ZTC can be seen as an 'organisation in search of itself'.

Chapter 4

The organisation in search of itself

'The company has got to sort itself out. I don't think we yet really know what sort of outfit we are. A year and a half ago I thought we were getting there – coming out of the merger and defining what we wanted to be; what we needed to be. I am not so sure now. We are just part of a much bigger set-up and our fate is just one little bit of all that.'

'"All that" being . . .?'

'Well you could say the whole thing about business in this country – no, in the world. But let's just keep it to telecoms. The big sort-out has been going on for years – and it is a world thing, a global picture with fewer but bigger and bigger players. There's liberalisation (but that's uneven) and the shift from hardware to services, you know, to solutions rather than boxes. I . . .'

'You . . .?'

'Yes, I was going to say that I have to fit myself into all this. Putting it crudely I have got to work out whether there is a place for me in this game. I think I could move out of telecoms if I move now. My age – well, I'll be stuck here if I let myself get too much older. So, looking at ZTC, Ryland I mean, I want to know what's going to happen to it. I'm watching how it's going to sort itself out. What is it going to do? Will it get the chop?'

'Hang on though, Peter. What do you mean, how is it going to sort itself out? What's the "it"?'

'Sorry, I don't follow. Do you mean how much of Ryland will survive?'

'No, I mean, you are talking about ZTC at Ryland as if it existed separately from you and me and everybody else and as if decisions made themselves.'

'Got you, got you. I know exactly what you mean. It's what we were saying the other day in my control meeting. We are the managers here, even if there are bigger managers elsewhere, and we must take responsibility . . . I mean we have to believe . . . well try to believe anyway that we can . . . we can . . . come on, help me.'

'Shape our own destiny?'

'I'm not sure. Yes, that is it. I must control my pessimism.'

'Are you sure it isn't fatalism, rather than pessimism?'

'Oh I suppose so. It's just me at the moment. You know what I was saying just now. I have got to look at my own life and decide whether to put all my effort into this operation, into this fight I suppose, or whether I am going to look at making my life elsewhere.'

SHAPING AND BEING SHAPED: THE EMERGENCE OF STRATEGY

Peter Manthorpe touches on a theme common to many of his fellow managers; that of a confusion about the extent to which managers can shape their own life in, or outside, the company and the extent to which other people, or circumstances, decide it for them. As we shall see in this chapter, ZTC can be seen as a company striving to find an identity and a position in the world – a process begun two years before my involvement, when the company was created by a merger of activities from two pre-existing companies. In a sense, then, ZTC was from its inception an organisation 'in search of itself'. But, of course, an organisation cannot literally search for anything. As was recognised in my conversation with Peter Manthorpe, an organisation is not really an 'it' which thinks, decides and acts as such. It is the people who make up the organisation, together with all of those with whom, in the broadest sense of the term, it 'trades with', who think and act.

Those formally charged with shaping ZTC were its managers (with some, of course, doing more shaping than others) and we shall here consider some of the ways in which ZTC top managers went about establishing an organisation to take a significant place in the world telecommunications markets. We rarely get an opportunity such as this to look at an organisation in which there has been such a deliberate attempt at 'shaping' an organisation, in the sense of explicitly setting out to develop a *strategic intent* and what was hoped would be a *winning culture*. Once we have looked at this initiative by the top management, the parts being played in following it up by the managers at ZTC Ryland can be examined; this all contributing to our key concern with understanding the links between the ways in which managers shape their own lives at the same time as they work towards shaping the work territory they manage. This was something Peter Manthorpe was concerned with in his conversation with me and which he recognised as taking place in a world which can very much feel as if it is shaping you more than you are shaping it.

A view of the nature of organisations and of the work of managing them was set out in Chapter 2. This sees the organisation as a set of relationships and understandings in which its management have the responsibility of orchestrating a series of exchanges, material and symbolic, with parties internal and external to the organisation in order to achieve long-term organisational survival. Following the view particularly associated with Henry Mintzberg that the strategy of an organisation can usefully be seen as 'a pattern in a stream of actions' (see p. 27), we can conceptualise an organisation's strategy as *the pattern to be seen emerging over time as actions are taken to enable the organisation to continue into the future*. To an extent, such a pattern follows what was intended by the management of the organisation. Mintzberg calls this the 'intended strategy' but, given the great complexity and unpredictability of the world, there is unlikely to be a close match between this and the 'realised strategy'. It is therefore most worthwhile to focus first and foremost on the realised strategy of an organisation. Consideration of the part played by what we can most usefully see as a contributory element of strategy – the deliberate and explicit strategic plan – would then follow from this.

Strategic management is very much a matter of the interpretations made by a management of the circumstances in which it finds itself. Managers do not simply react to their environment, but act in the light of their perceptions of it. As Karl Weick (1979) puts it, they *enact* the environment: act within and towards it in the light of the particular sense they are able to make of it. That sense is always going to be partial, given the inevitably limited capacity that managers have for selecting and organising the vast quantity of information theoretically available to them. They have to work within the 'bounded rationality' which characterises the human animal (see p. 20). To help us understand the attempts of the ZTC Ryland managers to make sense of the business direction and strategic context of ZTC (something they are both influenced by and contribute to), we need to establish our own understanding of the context of the telecommunications industry.

TELECOMMUNICATIONS: INTO THE MARKET

Reference was made by Peter Manthorpe to a 'big sort-out' in telecommunications. This was occurring on a global scale and he spoke of there being a falling number of 'players', which he said were ones of increasing size. He also mentioned 'liberalisation' and implied some significant technological change with his reference to a switch from an emphasis on hardware to one on services. This latter issue is just one aspect of the technological trends which are unfolding and which I shall now briefly sketch. This will establish what it is that the industry does in the world, as well as indicate some of the specific pressures on ZTC. And these matters can then be set within the close interrelationship of market and state political factors which characterise the telecommunications industry.

Telecommunications is concerned with the movement of information and has its roots in the telegraph and telephone systems with which most of the world is familiar. Current innovations are enabling vastly greater amounts of information to be transmitted by using optic fibre cables, and a greater flexibility of operation is being created by the increasing incorporation of radio into systems (portable telephones being an obvious example). Information in the typical form of voice (increasingly digitised) is being joined by computer data and image material, and these can all be linked together in multimedia systems. The managing of all this traffic is increasingly involving the use of computers with software-based 'virtual networks' which move information about at the speed, cost and level of flexibility desired by users. It is this latter area which Peter Manthorpe had in mind when he spoke of the shift from hardware to services; a company like ZTC could well move away from producing telephone equipment for organisations, to taking on the managing of their communication traffic, moving it for them through paths within the public systems.

These technological factors can be seen as a pressure towards the globalisation of the telecommunications business. They produce some of the key links which will tie together the various parts of the world. And the considerable cost of developing the technologies implies a need to merge producers into units bigger than are likely to be contained in any one nation state. However, technological pressures only become pressures once they are related to social, political and economic factors. Alan Cawson *et al.* (1990), in an important book on the European electronics industry, stress the centrality to understanding changes in telecommunications of what they call 'social factors'. By social factors they mean the nature of interactions between people, groups and institutions across societies. They draw on the sociological analyses of Max Weber and his notion of *social closure*. This is the process whereby human groups or organisations seek advantages and then erect barriers around themselves to protect that advantage. The context in which businesses operate is characterised by a constant tension between competition and closure, and Cawson *et al.* examine the changing pattern of European telecommunications (as well as consumer electronics) in terms of the changing closure strategies being adopted by companies.

A closure strategy is followed by a firm once it is 'winning'. Three types of closure strategy are available to firms wishing to consolidate their advantageous positions:

1 *Market oriented*, where the firm competes head-on with competitors and defeats them by keeping ahead in the market-place.
2 *Cartel oriented*, involving firms getting together in trade associations, developing products at a modest pace and ensuring that markets are fairly shared out between them.
3 *State oriented* closure strategy, in which a firm may either seek protection from the state or be drawn by the state into a near partnership. This is typically seen in national defence industries.

Whilst the European consumer electronic industries largely were characterised until recently by cartel-oriented strategies, the telecommunications industries of France, Germany and the UK followed the state-oriented pattern. The typical pattern, say Cawson *et al.*, was one with the service side 'controlled by a public monopoly, usually a government department known as the Post, Telegraph and Telephone authority (PTT) or else a public corporation' whilst 'the equipment side had been dominated by a small ring of private manufacturers and these have been protected against both domestic and foreign competition by the chauvinistic purchasing policies of the public service monopoly, their chief customer' (1990: 77).

A combination of technological developments, ideological pressures towards market systems and 'liberalisation' (especially in the UK, where the greatest ideological fervour in this direction led to the privatisation of the public telephone system as well) and political change such as the growth of the European Community have led to a decline in this strategy. To develop technologically and to compete in the world market (many customer organisations being multinational or global), telecommunications firms have sought mergers, strategic alliances and joint ventures which take them beyond the embrace of any nation state. The closure strategies of telecommunications companies are now market-oriented ones. ZTC is the product of this kind of process. The Ryland plant once belonged to Parry, one of the members of the 'ring' or 'telecom club' which was tied into the British Post Office. It is now part-owned and managed by ZEC, another former member of the circle, but ZEC shares its ownership of ZTC with a European electronic 'giant', Siegfried. Let us now look at how this came about.

KICKING AND SCREAMING: THE BIRTH OF AN ORGANISATION

It would be difficult for anyone trying to make sense of the issues engaging the managers of ZTC Ryland without knowing the fraught circumstances of the company's birth. The Ryland site had been involved in the production of telephone equipment since 1903, when it was part of a Swedish company. The British part of that company then became independent and in 1961 it became part of Parry, which combined it with another telecommunication business to form Parry Telecommunications with plants in various parts of Britain. Most of the ZTC Ryland managers involved in this present study had worked for this organisation. Parry Telecommunications was just one part of a larger electrical and electronic organisation, and this was also the case with the telecommunications business of ZEC. During the 1980s both of these large organisations were reconsidering their telecommunications strategies in the light of the increasingly competitive situation both in Britain and abroad. The state-oriented closure strategies were clearly in need of replacing. Parry looked towards the USA and acquired an American telecommunications business in 1982. At the same time it looked towards the EC to participate in the collaborative research programmes which the Community was sponsoring. ZEC did this too but did not try to take on the US market. Its reputedly cautious style is reflected in its policy of licensing products from other firms. However,

ZEC's management also identified as a priority the establishment of a joint venture with Parry in the telecommunication field.

ZEC's approach to Parry was not welcome, and ZEC went on to the attack and attempted to take over the whole Parry business. This battle concerned a great deal more than telecommunications issues. As Cawson *et al.* put it, ZEC's 'core argument was that the merger would provide the economies of scale necessary for the new group to "fight off foreign competitors at home and abroad"', whilst Parry attempted to refute the size argument. They put forward an argument which appealed to an increasingly competition-oriented British government that the new business would massively dominate the UK market, especially in the defence sector. Also, they argued that, as Cawson *et al.* report, ZEC's 'philosophy of short-term accounting and cash accumulation was "fundamentally unsuited to running a high technology business"'. This notion, as we shall see later, is still highly relevant to thinking within ZTC.

The take-over of Parry by ZEC did not succeed. It had been opposed on many fronts, including by the state's Mergers and Monopolies Commission, whose decision killed it. In using the language of war to report these events, I am following the spirit of most accounts which are available, whether they be in academic books, in the financial press or on the lips of current employees of ZTC. It was a bitterly fought engagement which has left many wounds still unhealed. In spite of this, however, ZEC and Parry were very soon announcing the merging of the telecommunications operations. Press accounts imply a degree of terseness and doubt surrounding this decision, with one financial paper, for example, saying that neither company 'are saying anything more than the bald statement issued last week'. Another financial paper had reported that 'within 24 hours of announcing the joint venture agreement Parry's managing director had handed in his resignation'. It was commented that 'by departing at such a critical time' the managing director had 'focused negative attention on Parry and possibly opened the way for ZEC to gain a greater degree of control in the joint venture'. It was speculated that the business would be headed by Robert Arnold, who was currently the managing director of ZEC's telecommunications business.

The 'personality issues' involved in these business restructuring processes can only be inferred from hearsay and from press reports. The basic stance of this study, that the shaping of work organisations is intrinsically linked to the processes whereby human individuals and groups shape their lives, would lead us to expect them inevitably to play a part one way or another. However, the degree of acrimony involved in what is ostensibly a matter of entering a cooperative relationship appears to have been considerable. Press reports refer to the 'boorishness' and 'bombast' of Parry's chairman at the press conference where he was speaking as the chairman of the holding company which would establish the new company. One financial journal spoke of the 'the equivocal origins' of the new enterprise, going as far as to call it 'an abortion as far as significant players in the world telecommunications industry are concerned' and sarcastically calling it a brave decision to 'schedule its birthday for April Fools' day' (something echoed in the words of several ZTC managers during my research).

The same journal, partly taking a swipe at the Parry (and holding company) chairman, made a point, also made subsequently to me by managers in ZTC Ryland, that it was 'going to take managerial skills of a very high order to prevent it from becoming an embarrassing and costly mistake'. The Parry chairman appears to have been keen to reassure the press that the problems were not being underestimated. He spoke of past differences and claimed that the dangers of 'cultural clash' had been anticipated and taken into account in the way the new company was being structured. This was to a large extent a matter of the individuals being appointed. Conscious of the fact that the business press and many people in Parry were looking askance at the appointment of Robert Arnold, a ZEC man, as managing director, he pointed out that this individual had once worked for Parry, adding in his comments to journalists, 'once a Parry man, always a Parry man'. The chairman of the new company would be Arnold's opposite number from Parry.

ZTC thus began life on an April Fools' day as a joint venture between two previously competing telecommunications operations only three years after a bitter war had been entered into by their owning and controlling groups. The Ryland plant included elements of the four main business groups into which ZTC was grouped. The largest of these on the site were the Business Communications Group (BCG), which produced telephone systems for corporate organisations, and Mobile Products Group (MPG), covering portable telephones, payphones and the like. There were also departments of the businesses concerned with public telephone systems and with the transmission networks which link such systems. Although most of the directors of the BCG board were based at Ryland, its managing director was located at the corporate headquarters forty-five miles away. The 'operations director' of BCG, Ted Meadows, took responsibility for the Ryland site, thus having an overview of activities in business groups other than his own. All employees on the site were administered by the Ryland personnel director, who was also the personnel director of BCG.

I shall shortly take up the story of how the senior management of ZTC set about shaping the 'new' enterprise of ZTC which had to weld together these rather complex elements within Rylands as well as create a culture to bring together the various plants of ZEC and Parry located in various towns and cities around Britain. However, it is necessary first to explain a further development in the issue of the ownership of ZTC, one which we shall see later to have had an impact on this process of shaping the company. Less than two years after ZTC was established as a merger of the telecommunications operations of ZEC and Parry, ZEC had succeeded in its earlier plan to take over Parry, albeit this time with a partner, the German company Siegfried. The various Parry businesses were 'carved up' (as several papers put it) in different ways between the two 'victors' in this re-fought war. ZEC would manage ZTC and take 60 per cent ownership. Siegfried would own the remaining 40 per cent. As it was put to me by a ZTC Ryland manager:

> 'It was as if you'd been fighting for years with this kid from down the street who is your bitter enemy. You are then told you have got to play with him. But before you've worked out whether you are playing cops and robbers or cowboys and Indians he suddenly appears with a big lad from another street and tells you it's all his gang now.'

This was the ownership situation during the year in which the present study took place. However, a number of the more senior managers at Ryland did not feel that this was necessarily the end of the story. As we shall see, there was speculation about the possibility, and indeed the potential benefits, of 'the big German lad taking over the game completely', as my colleague put it.

The change in ownership, and a number of other problems which were besetting ZTC at the same time created difficulties for the broad approach which the senior management were taking towards its strategic development. What is necessary now, however, is to explain the distinctive approach which the senior management of ZTC initiated as the means of shaping the strategy, culture and style of the 'new' organisation.

STRATEGIC INTENT AND THE SEARCH FOR A CULTURE

One of the ZTC directors said to me:

> 'We knew from the start that we had not just got to weld two old, different and indeed competing cultures together to create ZTC. We had to make a new culture to put in the place of the old ones. How the hell could we do that? One thing that was absolutely clear was that there was no way we were going to get away with inventing and then imposing a new culture on people. No way. We were going to have to involve people in building a culture – their culture. We could only work through our people. And, as it happens, we'd got the task, at the same time, of working out what our strategy was to be. You can look at DOC as the way we brought these things together.'

This statement about the Project DOC programme, ZTC's 'Developing Organisational Capability' programme, was made with hindsight. It introduces a style of rhetoric which was central to this initiative – 'working through people', for example – but it does seem to me to fit with my understanding of the way Robert Arnold and his colleagues sought at the same time to establish a strategic direction for the business and a style through which the organisation might be enabled to fulfil it. In his 'welcome' message issued to all employees as the company was launched, Arnold referred to the 'difficult period' through which 'we all had to live'. He claimed that this was 'largely out of the way' but that there would inevitably be frustrations and disappointments. The tone-setting notion of 'we' is repeatedly used in the message, together with an appeal to patriotism and a team spirit, but there is also an explicit recognition of the problems of human relationships which could arise, given the difficult history of recent years:

> 'We are engaged on a tremendous task that is important for us and for the nation – nothing less than ensuring that ZTC can prosper amongst the world giants in telecommunications. We must not underestimate the difficulties, nor can we afford avoidable problems such as personality clashes, personal prejudices or divisive misplaced loyalties. We are now one Company – we need each other's help in every way.'

Arnold openly recognises the inappropriateness of the senior management deciding for others for all time how the firm is to be shaped: 'What is thought best is not necessarily the shape of things for all time, and experience may require changes in some of the early decisions.' This turned out to be truer than he might have imagined. But how was the shaping to be begun? The same document gave some indication in the section written by the personnel director. He said that one of his major tasks was to 'help weld the constituent parts of the organisation together' and revealed that the Board had 'obtained the assistance of a group of Business School teachers and consultants' to run workshops for 'our management' to help study 'major competitors across the world' and to assist in 'the development of our competitive strategy'.

The involvement of business academics in this process of strategy development is significant and helpful to us in research terms, because it enables us to learn about the concepts being used from the published writings of those academics. The first key idea used was that of *strategic intent* (Hamel and Prahalad 1989) which suggests that organisations should not seek a fit between existing resources and emerging opportunities, but should deliberately create a mismatch between resources and objectives so that the organisation can be 'challenged' to close the gap. The other key concept was that of corporate *core competences* (Prahalad and Hamel 1990) and this refers to the elements of 'collective learning' which exists in an organisation about how to 'coordinate diverse production skills and integrate multiple streams of technologies' (1990: 82). An organisation should be seen as a portfolio of these competences, rather than a bundle of strategic business units. Examples of these competences would be Sony's with miniaturisation, or 3M's with sticky tape. A third notion of these authors is that of a *strategic architecture*, 'a road map of the future that identifies which core competencies to build and their constituent technologies' (1990: 89). All of these were deployed in the development of ZTC's 'strategic intent' and the DOC programme which was to help bring it about.

A company document which explained the DOC process as part of an application for a national training award gave the rationale for the programme as that of overcoming the difficulties of merging the ZEC and Parry telecommunications businesses into one:

> Similar mergers in the past failed to fulfil their theoretical commercial potential by failing to manage effectively the human process. The new enterprise has to give people a new focal point for their loyalty, commitment and enthusiasm.

ZTC needed a vehicle to give its '24,000 employees worldwide a sense of identity and a vision of the future as members of the ZTC team'. Initially, the ZTC Board worked with the consultants to build themselves into a team, spending time 'learning, speculating and planning some possible options'. This was followed by what became known as DOC I, involving the company's 200 most senior managers in ten three-day workshops which ended in a two-day conference. This produced a 'strategic intent' and a concept of a 'winning culture'. These were taken back to the Board for refinement, and a task force of twenty 'change champions' and seventy 'change agents' was created to 'cascade' this thinking through the organisation. DOC II did this through the managerial population via workshops run by the change agents and 400 further change agents were selected from this population and trained to run workshops for the whole workforce who were then, in DOC III, invited to workshops of twenty to twenty-five people. This was followed up by an 'effectiveness survey' to all employees, the results of which were considered by the Board and used to devise an 'action plan' on such matters as improving team briefing processes, implementing appraisals processes and the like.

What then was the strategic intent devised in the first stage of this process? It was to move from the start of ZTC as a £1.28 billion company, to a £5 billion company six to seven years later. It would move from being a 'PTT and voice-dominated' business with a 'UK orientation' and a 'US foothold' to a balance between PTT, business systems and 'lifestyle' markets on a global scale. The summary statement of this, issued to all employees on a credit-card style piece of plastic, referred to ZTC being a global force in telecommunications, symbolised by the formula $1 + 2 + 3 + 4 = 5$. This represented being placed first in Britain, second in Europe, third in the US and fourth in the Far East. And it added up to an intent to be ranked as fifth among telecommunications companies world-wide. On the reverse side of the card was a statement of the winning culture in the form of a series of slogans:

Bringing people together
Responsive to customers
Commitment to excellence
Recognition of individual contribution
Willingness to change
Profitability, technology, growth

The strategic architecture, or 'road map', accompanying this was explained as involving a move away from a style of 'strategic planning' to using the strategic intent to guide responses to opportunities as they arise. And instead of viewing the company as a 'collection of businesses', there was to be a 'move to behaviour which comes from a view of ZTC as a portfolio of skills and competences which are shared across businesses'.

As these messages are recorded here, they sound more glib than they were generally taken to be by participants in the workshops. These events provided case studies on film of companies like Honda and involved employees in considering the practical and organisational implications of the 'slogans'.

Perhaps the greatest sociological significance of DOC, as I have come to understand its role in ZTC Ryland, is that it created some very large expectations. The expectations for growth were enormous, in the spirit of Prahalad and Hamel's concept of strategic intent. The script used by the change agents summarised the strategy at one point by stressing three 'key points': 'ZTC has chosen aggressive growth; it implies a major stretch; it will require commitment from all'. This is clear, but the scale of the growth ambition courted the danger of disillusionment should the economic and ownership context, or any impediment to meeting such a vast challenge, make these ambitions unrealisable. But a further danger of creating cynicism was risked by the equally considerable expectations created about how the company was to be managed.

One of the slides shown to workshop participants stated: 'If we conclude that the intelligence of a few, however brilliant, top managers is insufficient to meet today's technological and economic challenges, then we must question *the role of management*'. A management should not be committed to a strategy, the change agents explained. This would cause them to 'lack humility, take themselves too seriously, become rigid'. Corporate direction would evolve from 'unfolding events' which the management would assist through encouraging 'adaptive persistence'. Whilst showing a slide which indicated a replacement of an organisational pyramid with 'thinkers' at the top and 'executers' at the bottom with an inverted pyramid showing the inverted base directed towards 'customers', the change agents stated:

'We must question the conventional wisdom which can be expressed as "the bosses do the thinking and the rest of the organisation the executing".'

'The winning organisations will be those who can mobilise the intelligence, skills and energy of everyone.'

'This requires managers which support their people in the endeavour to reach and satisfy customers.'

A further slide stated that the 'fundamental condition' for success would be 'The ability of the organisation to move information and ideas from the bottom to the top and back again in continuous dialogue.'

A company document describing the benefits to be derived from DOC included 'the establishment of a participative style of management with consistent values and beliefs across a dispersed and previously fragmented organisation'. It also referred to a 'notion of employees as "empowered" rather than "obedient" people'. These were indeed radical departures for both ZEC and Parry managers and employees. But the workshops were run with enthusiasm, I was generally informed, and I developed the impression that although many people received the messages with a degree of scepticism, there was a general willingness among a large proportion of the managers and the workforce at Rylands to 'give it a chance', as it was put to me by several people. How well it was given this chance in the event is a question we have to consider. First, however, we have to look at another major initiative in the Ryland plant of ZTC, one started under the aegis of the employee relations function of the plant whilst it was still part of Parry. This was BIP: the Business Improvement Programme, an initiative which metamorphosed into the PDP, or Personal Development Programme.

PERSONAL DEVELOPMENT AND THE SEARCH FOR GROWTH

'The success of this business is wholly dependent on people. If we are going to grow the business we have got to offer people more than pay and good working conditions. We have got to offer them opportunities for personal growth.'

This statement was made to me by one of the line managers who told me he was an 'upholder of the faith of BIP and PDP'. I had laughed at what always seemed to me to be an incongruous mixing of the language of religious belief with the bureaucratic jargon of three-letter abbreviations. But, having been admonished for my levity, I shifted to a more serious tone of voice and asked Des Plumtree how he would summarise this faith. It was in response to this question that the above words were carefully enunciated. What then were the programmes which made this faith manifest?

The Business Improvement Programme was initiated at Ryland by the Parry employee relations staff two or three years before ZTC came into being. It came to be seen by its advocates as entirely compatible with the DOC programme which was launched following the formation of ZTC.

As I heard it stated: 'It came before DOC but could nevertheless be seen as DOC in practice'. The original initiative came from Derek Draycott who put the argument to the plant's management that a significant shift needed to be made away from the traditional pay and productivity scheme which had been in existence for fifteen years. The scheme had involved seven collective bargaining groups and each of these had its own terms and conditions attached to it as well as its own pay levels and gradings. This meant that there were three thousand job descriptions and more than fifty separate grades. Some people were paid on piecework schemes, others on measured daywork schemes, whilst others were paid salaries. The decay of the incentive effect of the bonus schemes was seen to have been considerable, with the bulk of bonuses being paid as averages, rather than as an outcome of actual work done. As in many other manufacturing organisations of this time, it was felt that the necessary speed of change for the plant (in which there was considerable investment being made) could be fatally hampered by the need to engage in lengthy negotiations over every proposed change in the factory and by the need to haggle over what Draycott called the '"what's-it-worth?" price tag'.

Derek Draycott persuaded the management that it would not only be beneficial to remove this kind of impediment to change but that there was a great deal of talent and potential commitment within the workforce which could be unlocked to the advantage of both the company and the individual. In a statement to the press, Draycott claimed:

'This is not a selfish project. We want the best for our employees and ourselves so we can become more efficient.'

He also claimed that:

'If this works we are going to be state of the art in terms of employment practices. Success breeds success.'

This state of the art, developed with a firm of consultants who became closely involved in the scheme, would involve the establishing of a skills-based grading structure, with all staff up to and including junior managers being located in one of a dozen grades. There would be 'harmonisation' of terms and conditions of employment and the pay system would be based partly on the skills which the individual possessed (putting them in a grade) and partly on how effectively they applied those skills (performance-related pay). The style of management to accompany this would be one emphasising people's 'personal development'; enabling them through the way they were deployed and the provision of training or 'skill modules' to increase their skills. The formal element of this would be regular appraisals and individual performance reviews. And in addition to all this there would be the setting up of team-working groups to engage in problem-solving across the business, building on efforts already started under a 'total quality management' initiative. These 'Business Action Teams', each tackling a specific problem, would be coordinated by 'Business Improvement Teams' who would cover broad areas like production, personnel or purchasing. To the plethora of three-word abbreviations were thus added the three-word acronyms of BITs and BATs.

When I joined ZTC Ryland I immediately became involved in discussions about implementing what was called 'BIP stage II'. This would cover the implementation of the appraisal process across the grading structure, the introduction of skill modules and other training measures to develop individuals' skills along lines negotiated in their appraisal event, and the implementing of performance-related pay. The package was grandly named the Personal Development Programme, thus adding another trio of letters, PDP, to the ever-growing alphabetic inventory. This was a further extension of what amounted to quite large-scale changes that were being attempted by ZTC Ryland in its search for an identity and a future. The BIP and PDP initiatives were particular to the three thousand plus employees at Ryland, but it was tentatively recognised corporately that they might later be taken up by the other ZTC plants in other parts of the country. There was a clear fit between the ZTC-wide DOC project and the Ryland employee relations initiatives. The main glossy brochure which ZTC used to explain itself to the world and present a corporate image to customers, employees and others not only put DOC and its associated concepts of strategic intent and winning culture on the first page under the heading 'This is ZTC' but pointed out that annually the company spent over £800 on average per employee on training its employees:

> The company sees training and career development as a partnership between the company and the individual and as an essential element in the achievement of its growth ambitions.

TOWARDS THE NEW CENTURY: DARING AND RISKING THE ORGANISATION

The scale and daring of all these initiatives was considerable. And it was an important element of top management rhetoric to argue that such a wholesale shift of emphasis was vital to survival. An attempt was being made to shape the organisation to achieve long-term survival. It is this that I have been suggesting represents the basic logic of all managerial work.

An example of the articulation of the view that the way people were treated in ZTC would be vital to its survival is seen in the introduction to an internal document, 'agreed and issued by the Managing Director and Management Board of ZTC', setting out ZTC's initial Personnel Policies:

> Each year, commercial competition intensifies. The companies which will survive and prosper into the next century will be those which find

ways of drawing upon the energy and imagination of their employees. Both acute sensitivity to market needs and a passion for innovation and improvement will characterise the labour forces of tomorrow's successful companies.

The considerable investments of resource and effort which were put into the DOC and BIP schemes suggest that this aspiration to create a workforce which was highly business-conscious as well as passionately innovative was a real aspiration, and not simply a matter of empty rhetoric. We may judge later whether it was *effective* rhetoric or not, but it was a rhetoric passionately asserted by a number of the originally influential top managers. Earlier, I pointed to the implications for managerial styles of the DOC project; it directly encouraged employees to believe that there would be a generally participative style of management and, more specifically, it staked the senior management's credibility on the achievement of an utterly massive and exceedingly fast growth in the size and reputation of the company. The whole project was based upon the research and the prescriptions of Gary Hamel and C.K. Prahalad, and we must return to their work at this stage to note the profound implications of the position they take about the strategic management of companies. The question we then have to raise was one of whether it was ever feasible for this particular company to embark on the daring journey which they encouraged ZTC to take. We can also ask about how well the conceptual analysis of these authors was ever understood within ZTC.

The scale of the challenge Hamel and Prahalad were making to traditional assumptions about strategic management was certainly clearly stated in their articles in the *Harvard Business Review*. They say, for example, that the 'new global competitors' (upon which ZTC were to model themselves) 'approach strategy from a perspective that is fundamentally different from that which underpins Western Management thought' (1989: 63). The traditional Western model of strategy emphasises 'trimming ambitions to match available resources' whilst that followed by the typical Japanese 'new global competitor' emphasises 'leveraging resources to reach seemingly unattainable goals' (1989: 65). This leveraging process involves the simultaneous top-down and bottom-up approach which allows strategy to emerge from dialogues between those 'higher up' and those 'lower down'. This fits with the kind of 'crafted' emergent strategy advocated by Henry Mintzberg in the same journal two years earlier (1987) as well as with what Peters and Waterman (1982) call 'purposive evolution'. It is an approach most fully analysed by James Quinn (1980), who argues that successful strategies are ones which develop incrementally through management processes which allow an open-minded approach to solving specific problems as they come along. From the outcomes of the way these problems are tackled emerges a strategic direction. Hamel and Prahalad add to this the bold and daring growth aspiration of the 'strategic intent', something which frames this participative adaptive effort.

ZTC top managers had followed Hamel and Prahalad's challenge to commit themselves to 'heroic goals' which 'lay beyond the reach of planning and existing resources' (1989: 76). But had they noted the dangers which these authors had observed in their research as arising in many decentralised organisations in which business unit managers are 'rewarded solely on the basis of their performance against return on investment targets'? This is a danger; it

> often leads to denominator management because executives soon discover that reductions in investment and head count – the denominator – 'improve' the financial actions by which they are measured more easily than growth in the numerator – revenues. It also fosters a hair trigger sensitivity to industry downturns that can be very costly. Managers who are quick to reduce investment and dismiss workers find it takes much longer to regain lost skills and catch up on investment when the industry turns upward again. As a result, they lose market share in every business cycle. Particularly in industries where there is fierce competition for the best people, and where competitors invest relentlessly, denominator management creates a retrenchment ratchet.
>
> (1989: 74)

In many ways ZTC was such a business unit of ZEC, a company, which we noted earlier had at one time been attacked by Parry as having a philosophy of short-term accounting 'fundamentally unsuited to running a high-technology business'. When ZTC was set up it was only half-owned by ZEC. But before long it was 60 per cent owned by ZEC and 'managed' on the behalf of themselves and Siegfried by ZEC. And in the press coverage of ZEC's response to a fall in profits in the year following the establishing of the arrangement with Siegfried, we read of the ZEC managing director 'targeting' ZTC where, he says, 'cost cutting has not gone far enough' and 'rationalisation at ZTC will be dramatic, it will be very significant'. The industry paper which reported this made the inference that one of the ZTC sites might be completely closed, whilst measures would be taken 'to dramatically trim back operations at two of ZTC's three major sites'. One of these was Ryland. Yet it is apparent that the ZEC managing director was conscious that he could be inviting further attacks on the quality of his stewardship of a high-technology company like ZTC when he stated 'the reduction in expenses we are talking about does not apply to those parts of the business where technology is important'.

Whatever interpretation one makes of the impact of ZEC ownership, with its famous concern for cost control and managing business units through accounting ratios, there is clearly room to question the likely capacity of ZTC to live up to the bold aspirations resulting from its association with Hamel and Prahalad. The prescriptions which these authors and consultants had developed from their research were drawn to a large extent from Japanese companies whose styles were quite different from either of ZTC's two original parents, the cost-conscious decentralised ZEC and the hierarchical but paternalist Parry, or the new step-parent, Siegfried. This was a long-established giant with a reputation for long-term investment and a strong engineering orientation, but was hardly known for an inclination towards fleet-footed innovations and heroic leaps of strategy.

When ZTC originally set out upon its strategic route, its leadership was apparently unaware of the possibility of their becoming in part taken over by one of the existing world telecommunication giants – this event overnight invalidating the strategic intent of becoming 'second in Europe' and the rest – or of becoming more directly managed by ZEC. It would also appear that they underestimated the extent and persistence of the economic recession into which they were heading and the extent to which, as they were to discover, the markets for many of their existing products were approaching saturation (the British market for company telephone systems or 'switches', for example).

During the period of my research within ZTC Ryland, these issues were all coming to the fore. The difficulties flowing from them were exacerbated by what we might see as a deeper structural problem; the fact, noted by Cawson *et al.* (1990), that trends in telecommunications meant that even growth in business size would see a diminution in the size of the labour force. As a combined result of this and the cost-cutting measures required by ZEC, there were significant numbers of redundancies from all levels of the workforce. This hardly inspired confidence in the firm or an enthusiasm for innovation. The message of the DOC project was thus not only threatened by the disappearance of the strategic intent, it was undermined by the unilateral imposition on Ryland managers of stringent retrenchments and financial controls. The Business Improvement and Personal Development Programmes (BIP and PDP) were similarly challenged.

The difficulties of maintaining the impetus of these initiatives were further increased by the imposition by ZEC of what was perceived as a reduction in the quality of the pension scheme. And an even bigger threat came from ZEC's insistence that the terms of the existing redundancy agreement be significantly reduced. This not only had a negative effect on general morale, but took ZTC into a major legal wrangle with trade unions, one concomitant of which was a union ban on members taking part in the Personal Development Programme.

This was the context in which I studied the managers who are the key subjects of this book. At the time I entered ZTC a new managing director, Paul Syston, was appointed to manage ZTC by ZEC in the place of Robert Arnold, who moved to replace the former Parry man as chairman of ZTC.

RACING FOR THE NEW CENTURY: STARTING AGAIN

A popular view among Ryland managers was that Paul Syston was the personal choice to run ZTC of the managing director of ZEC. There was gloomy speculation that he might be an 'axeman', and managers who were among the first to meet him were eagerly sought out by others to learn about the man. I took part in a meeting of managers at the time this was occurring and the two individuals who had met Syston agreed that 'he is a difficult man to read'. The others sought clarification of this and received the vague information 'well he did seem a bit of a miserable sod' from one and 'Mr Charisma he isn't' from the other. The group was well aware that Syston was going to have a considerable influence over their lives, and there was a reluctance to be too pessimistic, as we see in the following conversation, involving several of these managers:

'So are we just going to put our heads on the block then, and feel the chill on our necks?'
'I don't think we should just assume he is the dreaded axeman.'
'The way he just looked at me when I told him about our stock problems really gave me the shits, I can tell you'.
'Everything puts the wind up you, Freddy. What did you think, John, when you saw him?'
'I know what Fred means. I got pretty rattled. He just sat there and I found myself going on and on and on. Eventually I just stopped and there was this horrible silence. "What the hell have I said?", I thought. So I asked him; I can't remember what I said. But he just looked at me for what seemed like for ever – it was probably only a fraction of a second – and then he said, "Go on, I am listening".'
'You think he was listening? I mean is he open, you know, to other views?'
'I think that is what we have got to hope. I prefer to think that whatever he does, and we all know it is going to be painful, it will be after proper consideration of what's best for the business.'

At this point I was asked to 'stop scribbling away in your sodding notebook and tell us what you've got on Syston in your files'. I reported that my 'research in the archives' suggested that in his previous job as the managing director of another British telecommunications firm, BTC, he had claimed to be creating an organisation 'focused on customer satisfaction'. This meant producing 'not just a new technical strategy' but a 'total rebirth' of the company. The *Financial Times* had referred to his 'contempt for the old regime' at BTC and had suggested that he was attempting to introduce the 'informal and dynamic style' of the computer industry, from which he had come, into telecommunications. Another report said he was going to end the idea of BTC standing for 'bugger the customer'.

'Well,' said John, 'There it is, chapter and verse. I think I did hear him mumbling something about "time to market". But, well, "dynamic" I am not sure. And from what I understand of BTC, they have all these ZEC-type financial controls, you know, ratios and that. I cannot see him getting rid of those here. We will just have to wait and see.'

I made a comment to the effect that 'waiting to see' was 'a bit pathetic' and that we should try to make 'our own inputs' to Paul Syston. 'Work on the assumption that he really is listening', I said. This was generally thought to be a reasonable point, especially when I added that:

'Just like all of you, [Syston] wants to build his career. Put yourselves in his position and ask yourself whether at his relatively young age you would want to be seen as an axeman put in to demolish a business. You would have a career incentive to make it work, wouldn't you?'
    'We'd better say yes to that or Tony will write us all down as wimps and pessimists in his book', Freddy concluded.

In reporting this conversation I am attempting to do more than continue my story of how one organisation was 'searching for itself'. I hope also to give some insight into the way interpretive processes are generally engaged in by managers trying to make sense of the changing context in which they have to act. Lynn Isabella (1990) looked at the processes whereby managers interpreted the appointment of a new organisational head in her research on managers' 'evolving interpretations' of change events. She questions the common approach to understanding change as a matter of overcoming 'resistance to change'. She shows that interpretations change through the stages of learning about unfolding events and that in change situations it is 'not so much that people want to hold on to what they have as that they are simply questioning what the change will mean to them' (1990: 34). The ZTC Ryland managers were worried about the implications of the appointment of Paul Syston for their jobs. This informed the interpretations of the limited knowledge which was brought to the informal managerial conversation I have reported. But there is also visible in that conversation a process whereby members of a group negotiate between them the interpretation to be made of events. This then helps shape a particular orientation to action – one involving working on the assumption that Syston is 'listening' for suggestions relevant to developing, as opposed to diminishing, the business of ZTC.

As time went by, several of these managers became more optimistic about Paul Syston's intentions, although they remained sceptical about whether he would be able to succeed, given the limitations commonly felt to be imposed on any senior management by the overall ZEC steward-ship of the company. His personal style continued to discomfort many managers and it is interesting, in the light of the conversation I have reported, that when I directly raised with Syston the issue of his 'personal style and manner' he simply commented:

'It is my style to look around a lot, and listen. I listen a lot, think things over very carefully. And then I act.'

'So when you appear to people to be somewhat remote, it is because you are thinking about what you have just heard, is it?', I then asked with a small laugh, implying that my question might be a rhetorical one.'

Syston presumably took it that way. He just looked at me. It was easy to see what made so many ZTC people uncomfortable.

Within months of joining ZTC, Paul Syston was unveiling the structures, style and strategy which he announced to the company under a heading 'The Way Ahead'. The statement closed with the inspiration: 'The race to the New Century has started – we are going for gold!' How was this to be achieved, whatever this gold medal might be? The focus to be given to the company was to be on the 'benefits and applications of our products rather than on their technology'. Syston wanted ZTC to be 'the world's most customer-focused telecommunications solutions provider – a company which delivers solutions to help organisations communicate for competitive advantage, and people communicate for personal convenience.' The 'driving force of everything we undertake' would be the 'New ZTC Mission'. The formal statement of this was:

> To deliver increasing value for money to a widening base of customers and our shareholders through the provision of telecommunications solutions to world class standards of quality, time and cost.

The component businesses would be restructured to give three 'core' businesses, based on the three existing product areas of public switches (exchanges), private switches and transmission. The mobile products group was to be dismantled and a number of its activities taken up by an 'enterprise' group of businesses 'characterised by an entrepreneurial start up style, low costs and low overheads, and less constrained by past custom and innovation'. The businesses were to be made 'fully accountable' and there was a significant reduction in the size and scope of the corporate headquarters functions.

There were many detailed changes throughout the organisation intended to fulfil the aim to become customer rather than technology-focused and to emphasise the idea of 'value added' rather than that of 'cost' as such. We will see something of these changes at a later stage. But, at this stage, we have to consider how far there could be a picking up again of the sort of ethos tentatively established through the Developing Organisational Capability programme for the company when it was going to implement the original heroic Strategic Intent of becoming fifth in the world. As we have already seen, these ambitions necessarily became irrelevant with the ownership involvement of Siegfried. And shortly before Paul Syston appeared on the scene, his predecessor had written in the company newsletter that the results for that year were 'disappointing, below budget in almost all areas, with the aggregate affect [*sic*] of ZTC falling short on our key financial objectives'. It was observed that a growth budget had been set for sales, orders and investment but that 'we failed to achieve the orders'. A large element of this, it was claimed, was the result of a 'sudden change in the UK ordering pattern, particularly from our major customer BT'. However, 'we also failed to achieve planned orders in many other sectors'.

This sorry news was followed with an implicit look back to the heroic strategic intent of two years earlier, with the statement that ZTC 'has not cast aside its ambitions for the longer term future – the aim is still to grow substantially – aided now by our partner Siegfried'. And this message was followed by a new statement of 'strategic intent'. Its tone contrasts significantly with that of the earlier daring one:

> The Strategic Intent is to establish profitable growth in selected markets for our systems and products; especially the protection of our dominant UK position, together with the establishment of leadership programmes for ZTC in growth markets both at home and selected overseas territories.

A director in one of the business groups said to me, having passed me this document across his desk:

> 'Who's going to remember that, let alone be inspired by it? It's a bit different from 1 + 2 + 3 + 4 = 5, isn't it? Instead of going out to win the West, we're circling our waggons. Just look at that language: "protecting our dominant UK position". What a turn on! Wasn't "strategic intent" meant to be all about ambitiousness, "stretch", big leaps and all that?'

And a technical manager spoke of another of the DOC principles, that of 'core competences'. He had seen the technical groups at corporate level as 'the key to locating and developing core competences across the various businesses' and now asked, with these having been cut,

> 'How are we going to get the vital linkages between people with complementary expertise in different corners of ZTC if there is no one pulling them away from the details of what they are doing in their own businesses?'

A similar comment was:

> 'Look, I see the logic of getting people to work in self-contained businesses with their own accountabilities. That's fine. But the way we were meant to be doing things was getting people together to develop what we are best at, regardless of whether they are located for the moment in payphones, multiplexer development, video or whatever. We are putting people back in the boxes DOC wanted us out of.
>
> 'I might not be too worried about all that – after all, DOC is dead, whatever they say about another phase – but I've got this suspicion that Syston just doesn't have a feel for the importance of the people and the team thing. Have you got one of the DOC cards in your pocket? OK, look at what it says. What

is the first statement of the "winning culture"? It's "Bringing People Together", right? Now look at this transparency that Syston showed at the management conference last week as his version of the "winning culture". Yes, there's the responsive to customers bit; there's the commitment to excellence; there's recognition of individual contribution and there's willingness to change. But what's missing? The line mentioning technology, growth and profitability has gone. And what else? Yes, there it is: gone – "Bringing People Together".'

Overall, ZTC was in a considerably more difficult position than it had been when it had set out. There had been unforseen circumstances in the market-place and in the change of ownership. But a view taken by a number of managers (with hindsight, of course) was that these should never have been as unforeseen as they appeared to have been. The loss of business with the now privatised national telecom service was regarded as something that, as one senior man put it 'should not only have been foreseen but not allowed to happen'. Whether or not it was naively conceived, enormous effort had gone into establishing a culture, a strategy and an operating style which had really never had an opportunity to take root. A new managing director had come in to consolidate matters and adapt the company to its new circumstances. But he had not just to overcome the defensiveness to be associated with the threats inherent in the new business context; he had to cope with the cynicism created by the failure of the expectations which had been established with such panache and energy by ZTC's change champions and change agents in the early months of ZTC's 'search for itself'.

During one of the bouts of speculation among managers about how Paul Syston would attempt to manage ZTC, a comment was made about his tendency to listen to what others say and to offer little by way of comment:

'He's an inscrutable bastard.'

This received various responses:

'I'm not worried about him not speaking. I'm worried about what he's thinking. What is going on behind that frosty face?'
'We'll know soon enough. He's got to say where he stands before too long.'
'It's not just what he's going to say, though, is it? What language does he speak? Is he going to speak our language?'
'What do you mean "our language"? What the hell is our language? Which language are we really speaking these days?'

Like so many such everyday conversations among managers which I listened to and struggled to make readable notes of, this one stopped at a point when I hoped it was about to lead to some fascinating insight or piece of lay theorising. I would have loved to have known what this individual was implying when he suggested that more than one language was being spoken in the land of ZTC's management. The conversation lurched on into some entirely separate issue, as informal conversations are wont to do, before I could intervene to get this observation clarified. But I found the allusion to the possible existence of alternative languages among the managers very encouraging. It was occurring to me that one could see managerial discourse in ZTC Ryland as drawing on two rival languages, or ways of talking and thinking about things, and that such an insight might be helpful in understanding how processes of strategy-making and cultural change were working out in practice in the company. Chapter 5 develops this idea.

Chapter 5

Strategy and culture in practice
A tale of two rhetorics

'I think that people are deeply confused about where we are going. For years they had worked away without a strategy. Then it was all "now we are ZTC and we must have a strategic intent". But now it's not clear whether we've got a strategy of any sort at all.'

'What did you mean by "working without a strategy"?'

'Oh I mean back in the Parry heyday. In the old days the telephone business was as safe as houses. You didn't need a strategy, you just produced what the Post Office was looking for and there was plenty of work producing switches for businesses. There would always be new businesses and old ones would build new buildings. Besides, if we kept developing new and fancy things that could be offered on the switches, people would queue up to get the latest box of tricks; "look what we can do with our phones now".'

'But wasn't there a strategy behind all this?'

'I suppose there was. But you didn't give it a lot of thought because you didn't really need to worry.'

'Why do you only think about strategy when you are worried, though?'

'If you are not worried you just get on with the job in hand. You don't pay attention to what you are doing it for – where you are going, like.'

'So a strategy is –?'

'You talk about "strategies for survival", don't you?'

'So why did ZTC consciously set about constructing a strategy, its "strategic intent"?'

'Well, that's exactly it. It was part of DOC, which they said was needed because the two very different companies had to be merged into one. So you had to have a shared strategy and a shared culture. A "winning culture" – my God.'

'Why "my God"?'

'Because we ain't winning, are we? You see the whole point of Parry and ZEC putting their telecoms operations together – as much as we fought like hell to prevent it at the time – was a matter of fighting for the survival of a significant British presence. That's the point of the "fifth in the world" bit of the strategic intent.'

'So a strategy was produced when it was recognised that there was a problem of survival?'

'Yep.'

'But there's no strategy now, you are saying. Does that mean – '.

'It means we're really in the crap. Survival's more the issue than ever now. There's no Post Office and British Telecom don't want to know us. Businesses are dying on their feet; nobody's building. And people don't want their phones to do fancy things – if they ever did.'

'So there's confusion, you say?'

'Yes. We are up shit creek without a paddle . . . no no. We are – wait for it – up shit creek without a strategy. My God, why am I laughing?'

SURVIVAL AND STRATEGIC EXCHANGE

Chris Wilford is here connecting the concept of strategy with the idea of organisational survival. Although there is, in Mintzberg's (1988) terms, a 'realised strategy' to be inferred about the way the firm was run in the 'Parry heyday' (when Wilford suggests there was no strategy), the associating of survival questions with strategic issues fits with the view of the underlying logic of all managerial work which I have been developing: a view that the management of an organisation functions through a process of exchange or trading with the multiplicity of constituencies or stakeholders inside and outside the organisation, in order to bring about the long-term survival of the organisation. This stress on long-term survival of organisations as the key to the logic of their functioning accords with some significant developments in modern organisation theory: the 'population ecology' ideas of people like Hannan and Freeman (1977), Hannen (1989) and the 'resource dependence' approach of Pfeffer and Salancik (1978) and Watson (1986). To see organisations as bodies which 'trade' with their environment to stay in existence avoids all the arguments about whether, say, a telecommunications company has as its main goal the making of profits, the provision of employment, the satisfying of customers, or whatever. Instead, we see it as doing these, and many more things, to the extent that profit, employment, desired goods and so on are demanded by owners, employees and customers to ensure that these constituencies continue to supply the organisation with those resources it needs to continue in existence: capital, work effort, revenue.

To say that the main strategic thrust of all organisations is one of strategic exchange to achieve long-term survival (with profitability, market share and all the other typical strategic concerns as means towards this) can be justified in various ways. We can point to the rarity with which organisations (once they have survived the early years of infancy) are simply allowed to die, even when their original focal task has been achieved. We can point to the fact that people in organisations invest a lot of meaning in their involvement and have a lot of what Howard Becker (1960) called 'side bets' associated with their involvement (owning a house in the neighbourhood, having children at a nearby school) which lead them to resist its demise. But more important than all of this is that the production of the very goods or services on which the organisation focuses – making telephone systems or teaching students, say – requires a degree of perceived security and confidence among workers, investors, customers or clients. To get the levels of commitment needed for the organisation to perform short-term, it is imperative on those managing it to ensure that a perception of healthy longevity is achieved. An organisation with an insecure future is hardly likely to achieve levels of human motivation or attention which will make it an effective provider of whatever goods or services form its focal tasks.

Organisations are thus continually strategically exchanging with their employees and the numerous constituencies and 'stakeholders' in their environments. They are trading goods, services, cash, experiences and meanings. They are trading in meanings and symbols as much as in material goods – building confidence in bankers, investors, the state, the press; establishing ideas of quality and reliability with customers and clients; invoking a sense of commitment and an interest in productive cooperation among employees. The 'cultural trading' aspect of organisations has long been recognised in the form of businesses' advertising products to customers. In the 1980s and 1990s we began to see non-commercial organisations engaging in something similar as governmental and educational bodies increasingly concerned themselves with building 'corporate images'. But more important than this has been the influence of the culture-excellence development in management thinking reviewed in Chapter 1 in encouraging employing organisations to trade meanings with their employees through 'culture management' in a corresponding way to that in which some of them once traded meanings with customers through advertising.

OFFICIAL AND UNOFFICIAL CULTURES

Again we are back to organisational cultures. The people working in any organisation bring with them such a multiplicity of wants and purposes that the organisation can readily fragment into disorder and chaos. The organisation is effectively a temporary and fraught coalition of coalitions which can only ever be held together by constantly negotiated and renegotiated agreements and understandings. Rules, formal authority and operating procedures can play a role in encouraging productive cooperation, but only up to a point. The essential ambiguity of situations and the associated bounded rationality of human beings, together with the tendency of each individual (let alone each human group, department or division) to go their own way, means some other binding force is needed. Managers cannot readily construct a culture to which all individuals and groups will subscribe and which will achieve this binding. To varying extents, however, managements make efforts to establish a shared culture; a set of key values and ideas about how one should behave in the organisation. We can define an organisational culture as *a set of meanings to be shared by all members of the organisation which will define what is good and bad, right and wrong and what are the appropriate ways for members of the organisation to think and behave.*

We saw in the previous chapter the efforts made within ZTC to establish such a culture. The 'winning culture' was a set of values and guiding principles espoused by the management and, as with any such attempt at corporate culture-making, we have to treat as problematic the extent to which it would become the *actual* culture of the organisation. To help with this issue, we can distinguish here between the official culture and the unofficial culture or cultures of an organisation (cf. Fook and Watson 1992). The 'official culture' of an organisation is *the system of meanings, values and norms espoused by the managerial dominant coalition*; the 'unofficial culture' or cultures of an organisation are *the systems of meanings, values and norms actually prevailing in the organisation*.

The rationale of managing an organisation 'through culture' is one of trying to make the official culture and the unofficial cultures as consonant as possible and, ideally, to make them one and the same. Those responsible for establishing ZTC can be understood as attempting to do this through the initiatives we reviewed in the last chapter. In this chapter I shall look at the extent to which there was a consonance or a 'gap' between these two aspects of culture, the official and the unofficial.

CULTURE, LANGUAGE GAMES AND DISCOURSES

How does one look at or analyse cultures? Cultures manifest themselves in the behaviours which follow from them, of course, and they are also transmitted through artefacts ranging from the clothing people wear to the layout and decoration of the buildings in which they work. However, the major vehicle for the transmission and manifestation of the values and principles which lie at the core of a culture is language. We know a culture primarily through language. And in so far as we find more than one dimension to the culture operating within an organisation, we can expect to hear spoken more than one 'language'. In the expression of the philosopher, Ludwig Wittgenstein (1953), we would expect to come across people playing more than one 'language game'.

To some extent, there will always be a variety of 'languages' spoken in any organisation. But if it goes too far, this can be to the potential detriment of effective communication, and hence productive cooperation. For effective cooperation to take place, people need a degree of common language and some sharing of priorities but also, for people not to be endlessly calculating their cynical and sectional self-interest and keeping themselves at a distance from others, there have to be assumptions and relations based on common values. Thus we saw in the culture-building efforts in ZTC the production of what I called a *rhetoric*; a language or *discourse* designed to persuade people to 'work together', 'developing' themselves in the process of helping develop the business. As I said in the previous chapter, it is an open question whether this rhetoric was an effective rhetoric, in the sense of actually persuading people to adopt the required values and associated behaviours. We shall see, in this chapter, how far the management was successful in establishing a common 'story' that everyone could subscribe to as a means towards making ZTC Ryland a moral community. As Peter Anthony (1986) suggests, for an organisation to function as a moral order, as a community, requires a 'tradition', a 'narrative' to shape it. Managers have to function as narrators, therefore – as storytellers.

Telling and listening to stories was discussed in Chapter 1 as being fundamental to human processes of making sense of the world. But storytelling, which might take the form in the broader management context of biographies of famous managers like Lee Iococca, Michael Edwardes or John Harvey Jones, or be manifested in the corporate tales and legends retold by Peters and Waterman (1982), does not just give us moral anchors and pragmatic guidelines to help us through life. The stories we engage with also provide languages or 'discourses' which I have been referring to and which influence the very way we talk about the world and, hence, the way we interpret and act towards it. The discourse of the childhood fairy tale and nursery rhyme, incorporating such discursive expressions as 'beautiful princess' and 'handsome prince', helps boys and girls structure the gender and hierarchical aspects of the world through which they move and, hence, influences how they act with respect to such matters. Correspondingly, a corporate discourse privileging such terms as customer satisfaction, teamwork or competitive advantage shapes the way people behave, in so far as they incorporate that discourse into their working lives.

Having deployed a battery of terms like story, narrative, rhetorics, languages and language games I need to settle on one term to conceptualise the idea of there being whole ways of talking about issues which influence understandings and which function to persuade people to act in particular ways. I shall use the term 'discourse' for this purpose. A discourse, in this sense, is *a connected set of statements, concepts, terms and expressions which constitutes a way of talking or writing about a particular issue, thus framing the way people understand and act with respect to that issue.*

This concept connects power and language by suggesting a connection between the way words are used and how people act as a consequence of using them in a particular way. As Michel Foucault (1980) points out, a discourse establishes its own notion of what the 'truth' is with regard to the issue it covers. The present book, for example, is developing its own discourse and its own 'truths' as part of its author's rhetorical enterprise of influencing his readers, linking together terms and concepts such as strategic exchange, culture, dialogue, rhetoric, the nature of being human, work organisation, productive cooperation, managerial work and so on.

All of these terms, the concept of discourse among them, are tools being put to work throughout the book in an attempt to influence the way people think about management and, if such a bold statement can be risked, to influence how they go about it.

ZTC's top management had attempted to do the same for its population of managers and employees. What I am going to argue now is that it partly succeeded, in so far as it created a discourse with the potential to shape a common pattern of behaviour. But it was failing to realise this potential during the period of my study, because that discourse coexisted with other discourses, and one in particular, with which it clashed. And that clash led to doubt, confusion and frustration.

TWO COMPETING DISCOURSES

For an organisation to achieve the degree of productive cooperation necessary for it to survive healthily into the long-term, there needs to be, I have argued, not too great a gap between the official and the unofficial cultures of the organisation; between the managerially espoused and the 'actually prevailing' set of meanings, values and norms. We cannot, however, straightforwardly identify in ZTC's Ryland plant a coherent unofficial culture which can be directly contrasted to the unusually coherent official culture developed through the DOC, BIP and PDP programmes. This is why I need to utilise the notion of rival discourses. The official culture clearly has its own discourse; what I shall call an *empowerment, skills and growth discourse* represented by the sorts of rhetorics explored in the last chapter. But the unofficial or 'actual' culture involves an oddly confused mixture of this discourse with a rival *control, jobs and costs discourse.* Within ZTC Ryland we can find individuals operating almost entirely in the language and values of the empowerment discourse and we can find others confining themselves largely to the control discourse. But the bulk of managers with whom I worked and spoke could be heard confusingly and confusedly switching back and forth between the two discourses. This is not a matter of being bilingual, so to speak. The two discourses are more than just two languages: they are two ways of looking at the world, two frames of reference, two orientations towards action. They are both ways of talking about, thinking about and acting towards customers, employees, technologies, departments other than one's own, and so on.

The attempt being made in ZTC Ryland to establish a new way of talking about and acting towards work issues is not, in general terms, an unusual one. Robert Westwood (1987), for example, considers the discourse developed around the concept of 'participation' in a chemical company he studied. He stresses the way managerial attempts to establish this discourse involved trying to 'close off' other meanings. This process of closure involves presenting 'coherence, order, unitary meaning, reason-(ableness) and naturalness' in establishing new rhetorics. He speaks of 'definitional imperialism' in the rhetorical efforts of the management at Tridy. In ZTC Ryland, it is not so much a matter of 'the management' as a unified body imposing a new language and way of thinking on non-managers. It is more a matter of some managers who have embraced the newer rhetorics endeavouring to spread these among all managers and, through them, among all employees.

Part of my own work in the company, indeed, was to encourage managers to define themselves as primarily 'business managers', rather than departmental or functional managers. A simple illustration of the sort of closure process that Westwood is referring to can be seen in the way those responsible for implementing the Business Improvement Programme and the Personal Development Scheme at Ryland would correct any manager who let slip the word 'job'. Employees, in the new scheme of things, were in 'skill grades' instead of 'jobs' and could be required to carry out any task appropriate to their skill level. Hence, nobody 'owned' a job. To use the term 'job' was to be slapped down by, for example, the injunction to 'wash your mouth out'. I heard this expression used several times by members of the organisation development team and, early on in my membership of that group, when I said something about 'job design in the factory' I was told, 'For God's sake don't use that term; "job" is a dirty word here.'

There was frequent resistance among managers to 'language reform' and attempts by the reformers to achieve discursive closure. But it was a resistance which typically involved a recognition of what the 'correct' terms were meant to be. For example, one of the managers who was rather resistant to the new style kept mentioning the word 'job' to me in a conversation I was having with him about how he might most usefully allocate a trainee to tasks in his department. Towards the end of the conversation he suddenly stopped in mid-sentence:

'Whoops, I've been using illegal language; I'm not meant to talk about jobs. Never mind, the bugger has asked me to find him a job. So it's a job I'll find him.'

The notion of a job was not one that this man was willing to have closed off to him, any more than he would deny himself the use of the word 'job'.

To help use this idea of rival discourses to look at some particular aspects of culture and strategy at Ryland, the two discourses can be set out in a way which shows what they would sound like were they each to be articulated in a pure form. We can then look at how the two vocabularies then tended to be drawn on in different ways by managers in practice.

The *empowerment, skills and growth discourse*, were it to be used by managers in a pure form, would speak of a company in which the efforts of everyone in the company are applied to help 'grow the business' through providing an excellent service to customers, be they external customers for products and services, or other departments within the business. A 'culture' is developing in which people 'proactively' seek to apply their 'competences and skills' to meet opportunities which further the strategic intent of major growth. Continuous improvement is sought in all activities. Behaving in this way makes work essentially rewarding, especially through the benefits which derive from enhancing one's 'personal skills'. To help this occur, all employees are 'empowered' by the company's provision of whatever skill training or development the employee feels would help them increase their contribution. And as people increase their capacity to contribute through developing themselves and their skills, so they gain advancement in grading and hence higher material rewards. Higher rewards can also be gained whilst operating in a given grade through receiving performance-related pay for behaviours which fit with the values of the company's 'winning culture'. These include working with others in 'problem-solving teams', being flexible in the tasks one is willing to undertake, seeking new ways of doing things and contributing ideas towards the growth of the business. To support the principle of empowering employees as contributors to the business, the terms and conditions of all groups are being 'harmonised' to produce a 'classless society'. People are also empowered by being regularly briefed on both broad business matters and operational issues. Employees are welcome to join trade unions but should recognise that they are expected to work closely with their own managers in tackling employment problems. They should not feel the need to turn to union representatives to approach management on their part.

The *control, jobs and costs discourse*, were it to be used by managers in a pure form, would describe a company whose employees are primarily there to do the 'job' for which they are recruited and trained. Senior management decide the direction of the company under guidance from the two big companies which own and control it. Managers direct their department or function to follow this direction, carefully monitoring and controlling costs so that the accounting ratios of the main controlling company are adhered to. Should costs rise too much for the return being obtained, savings are rapidly made, including through 'losing heads': reducing the headcount. Production managers give primary emphasis to meeting month-end targets and train people to whatever level they need to do their jobs as efficiently as possible. The ex-hourly-paid, and a lot of the staff grades, basically want to get their day's work done as quickly as possible for the best money the unions can negotiate for them. They worry about the state of the business because they are concerned about security. But they do not worry too much, because they have got used to regular redundancies over the past twenty years as the nature and size of the business have changed. They used to feel that this was done fairly, with decent compensation, but, like employees at all levels, they are increasingly resentful of the reduced terms insisted on by the main owning company. Such resentment is also added to by the changes to the pension scheme. It is not surprising or unreasonable for employees to look to the unions to defend them. The unions' powers ought to be reduced, but managers cannot be expected to turn their efforts from the regular pressures on output and costs to look after staff when the company itself appears to care less and less about any of its people, managers included. The personnel department keeps launching new schemes on grading, teamworking, appraisals and performance-related pay. There are some good ideas in these, like there were in TQM and the DOC (culture change) scheme. It is OK to keep up to date with new management ideas, but often these schemes are pushed through by managers trying to make a reputation and a career, who do not stay on to see them through. So new people come along with new ideas, new organisation structures. This keeps us on our toes and we go along with it – up to a point. But you can't risk being too taken in. Take your eye off the ball, off the output, off the costs for too long, and you get abused.

In a sense, these are two scripts which are available to players on the managerial stage in ZTC Ryland. I have constructed them from words heard in hundreds of conversations and dialogues. They mix descriptions of perceived realities, how things are, with notions of how things *ought* to be. Some managers who in principle might like to speak the language of the first script feel themselves forced by circumstances to adopt much of the second script. Equally there are managers determined to make the empowerment discourse the natural language of the organisation and there are managers, especially at the more junior levels, who are most at ease speaking in the second tongue, albeit using various dialects. The empowerment, skills and growth discourse clearly incorporates elements from the various attempts to develop a new official culture for the newly merged ZTC, looked at in the last chapter. Elements of the language of Total Quality Management (TQM) and 'team-briefing' which had originated in the pre-ZTC days at Ryland are also there. The control, jobs and costs discourse has a mixture of elements of rather traditional ideas about people and about management (each person gets on with their designated job) with elements arising from the controlling style of ZEC (the accounting ratios, the alleged worsening of employee benefits). It is also a language which recognises the domineering personal style of the most senior manager at Ryland ('you get abused').

These discourses, like all human language, are tools which the managers use not just to communicate with each other and pursue personal projects, but also to make sense of the world around them. They are reminiscent of the two theories about people – theory X and theory Y – that Douglas McGregor said could be found in the understandings of human nature of different managers (see p. 19) and might also be seen to have elements, in the control discourse, of what are often called 'Taylorist' or 'Scientific Management' principles of work organisation and, in the empowerment discourse, of 'democratic humanist' theories of work motivation, job enrichment and the like (Watson 1986: Chapter 4). The two discourses do indeed display these influences, but they are not directly derived from any of them. They are particular combinations of ideas and discursive resources used by sets of actors in a particular organisational setting to make sense of and act towards their circumstances.

WHAT ABOUT MY EMPOWERMENT?

To develop my point about managers using mixtures of elements from the two discourses, I shall now report a conversation I had with Jim Aspley, a senior manager in the Ryland ZTC plant. The conversation also takes us back to my key underlying theme; that of the importance of recognising the way in which managers go about shaping their own lives at the same time as they are contributing to the shaping of the organisation which employs them. Jim Aspley starts off by talking about the nature of his relationship with the company:

'If you look at it you can see that I've given a lot to this company. It is a lot. I'm not saying the company hasn't looked after me. But it needed to, didn't it, to get the sort of commitment it has got from people like me, from Bill from Jerry or Phil. We were talking about this the other day when we were having a belly-ache, the four of us, over this rotten deal they're doing on the pensions. We slaved to set up the original abc facility you know. It was part of our lives for years. Do you think they recognise that now, Tony – do they?'
   'Who are "they"?'
   'The people who are running things now. I'm not sure whether they really believe in all this team-working stuff and empowering talk that we've gone for in the last few years. I would like to know. I'm serious.'
   'Go on.'
   'Well, you know I can bullshit. I mean you've heard me. But I do believe all that stuff. I have taken it seriously. I didn't realise it until you asked me all that earlier about what I believe management is, but I didn't really have much of an idea about "management", other than that I was responsible for sorting out the shop and the people so that we got the stuff out at month end. I just thought it was a basic, you know, an ordinary decent way to treat people; to be straight with them, not to treat them like mugs and to respect the fact that they have feelings. But this idea that you can build people up so that they feel they own the job and they want to do, not just a good job, but a better job – you know continuous improvement and all that – well it's given me a sort of idea of what I ought to be doing as a manager.'

In developing this point, Jim Aspley said: 'I get paid to get certain results. I'm not sure if they are the right results.' I interrupted his flow to ask what he meant by this reference to 'not the right results'. He explained:

'For the business. I'm here, it seems, to produce the bits to meet the month-end target. You know all the arguments on this. What I would like would be to get closer to the discussions about why we are doing it this way; get a look more at the customer's end of things, if I can go back to the quality jargon.'

On the issue of achieving his output targets within his department, Aspley observed:

'To get my people to perform, and continuously improve – like I think they really have – I have a relationship with them. I think they do a lot of what they do because they owe it. It's partly because they see me, I honestly believe this – and you can ask around to see if I'm right – as a decent bloke who always sees them right. Yes, and having swallowed a lot of this personal development stuff, I've helped them get a lot more out of working here than they might have.'

And after some further explanation of his personal management style (to which I shall return in a later chapter) he turned to ZTC's employment practices:

'Going back to this pension thing and all these other things we were talking about the other day – taking out another 10 per cent heads, and all that. Goodness knows, I don't shirk having to make people redundant, I've been doing it for God knows how long. But do we have to keep just doing what someone else decides? I really wonder whether we are valued at all. The pension problem is only a symptom. Do the people running this company recognise what we put into all this? What about my empowerment? What about my personal development?'

It is important to remember that this is a senior manager speaking. He speaks as a manager, but he also speaks as an employee. His unhappiness about the way he is treated as an employee is interpreted in the light of the concepts he has acquired from the company itself. He articulates his concerns using discursive resources acquired during the period of development of the new culture: 'What about my empowerment? What about my personal development?' He recognises that the company 'speaks', as another manager once put it to me, 'with forked tongue'. He asks the question about whether the people currently in charge 'really believe in all this team-working stuff and empowering talk'. He is getting close here to my own notion of a discourse, as he does at other points such as when he alludes to 'this personal development stuff', or when he refers to going 'back to the quality jargon' (looking at the 'customer's end of things'). At other points he simply drops in terms from the empowerment discourse, such as the reference to 'continuous improvement' (a term very much associated with the Total Quality Management initiative at Ryland).

Jim Aspley does not just draw on terms from the empowerment discourse, however. He refers to meeting the 'month-end target', a concept dominating the life of many of the Ryland managers and to be found on their lips to an increasing degree as each month moved towards its close. He is speaking critically of these practices. However, he appears to use without hesitation the control discourse language typical of the bulk of managers in the plant when he refers to redundancies as 'taking out . . . heads'. Making people redundant had indeed become, as more than one person put it to me, 'part of the way of life' of Ryland's managers (the business had been becoming a less and less labour-intensive one for many years – leaving aside issues of contraction or cost-cutting). It was not having to 'get rid' as such (to use a term sometimes deployed, and which I personally found even more distasteful) that Jim was questioning, it was a matter of being required to carry out strategies decided elsewhere. The question was not simply the one of how this fitted with the broad notion of all employees being 'empowered', but can be seen as recognising a tension between this kind of imposed decision and the principles so heavily stressed during the Developing Organisational Capability (DOC) project of a form of strategy-making which involved, as the Change Champions' and Change Agents' scripts had it, moving 'information and ideas from the bottom to the top and back again in continuous dialogue'. Jim Aspley had spoken these words to scores if not hundreds of employees during that culture-change programme, as, similarly, he had uttered the words 'we must question the conventional wisdom which can be expressed as "the bosses do the thinking and the rest of the organisation the executing"'.

CULTURE TALK: GUNS AND ROSES

All of the managers that I worked with, spoke to and interviewed at ZTC Ryland had been involved in this culture-change programme and many of them had acted as change champions and change agents. Their involvement had rarely been a passive one. One of the discursive resources used in that programme was that of 'culture': to help people make sense of and talk about the changes which were being sought, this concept was made considerable use of. It was on the piece of plastic which many employees, not just managers, carried in their wallets and handbags in the form of the 'winning culture' statements. But how was this linguistic tool, this concept of culture, being used in practice by managers making sense of and talking about the situation in ZTC Ryland in the period of change following the main thrusts of the attempts to establish a new official culture?

In my core interviews with managers I asked them directly what the notion of culture meant to them. I heard it used every day and was interested to know the extent to which a concept brought into managerial discourse from sociology and anthropology would be formally defined by such lay users. Would the managers in ZTC, for example, follow the common pattern that I had noted among management students of telling me that it was 'the way we do things around here' (a term first reported in the literature by Deal and Kennedy 1982)? Or would they follow the more sophisticated social science usage and recognise that it involved a lot more than its surface manifestations: that culture, as Edgar Schein (1985) stresses, involves values, assumptions, ways of thinking and feeling as well as ways of behaving.

A small number of managers told me that it was not a concept they understood. But their saying this, I felt, was often as much a form of resistance to the newer discourse, or to the people associated with it, as a real lack of understanding. Henry Dunkirk responded to my question about what the term meant to him with 'Nothing. Not a thing to me.' He wondered why 'they' do not refer to 'changing the equipment or changing the practices':

> 'Why does it have to be the word "culture"? It always amazes me when you get team briefs and they come in with these big words and half the people don't understand what they mean. Why don't they put it in layman's terms that everybody can understand? I don't understand half the words myself. I am sure they come across these fancy words and say, "Oh I must use that".'

Dick Eastwood, a more senior manager than Dunkirk, but, like him, a man who liked to be known as a 'plain speaker', explained that he had actually removed the term from a team-briefing document which had been passed to him to pass on to the managers who reported to him (who would then use it to brief shop floor employees). He said he was removing it partly because he did not 'fully understand it, quite frankly'. He was 'searching around for some words which are more meaningful; it would be perhaps "type of company"' or he could 'go out into the shop and say the style of the company is changing, and they would know more of what I meant', but:

> '. . . go out there and say "the culture is changing" and I don't think it would mean a thing. I may be cynical, but we are too good at producing these overhead foils, projectors and things like, where the world revolves around ZTC. But getting the message over is something different.'

Another manager said he thought it was just a fancy word and another, winking as he spoke, asked in a tone of mock naivety: 'it's something to do with a race or a nation, isn't it?'

The majority of managers were, however, quite willing to attempt to define the term. There were a few definitions which restricted the concept to the level of behaviour, such as 'it describes acceptable behaviour; it's the way we normally behave' and 'It's just a way of going about doing things'. But more typical were 'getting people thinking on the same lines and going in the same direction'; 'it is your attitudes to the job and how you see the company'. Values were mentioned by a few managers, as in 'it's the underlying values behind what people do' and a range of statements recognised the idea of patterns existing 'below the surface', as in:

> 'It is what ties everything together within ZTC – an unseen framework within which one operates or how one can relate to somebody who also works for

> ZTC and actually realise that we are in the same company and are working together.'

> 'It is to do with the way we interact together and with the systems – the subconscious ones, if you like, that occur under the way we all act together – that makes us different from other companies.'

Various managers explained that the concept first became meaningful to them when they recognised its power in comparing one organisation with another. John Stapleford said, for example, that he did not understand it when he first came across it 'under DOC' but that 'it then made sense when I thought about comparing ZEC and Parry'. It was not just a different way of doing things, he realised, it was 'a different thought process; a different learning curve'. Phil Wollaton in fact used the notion, which he said was about the 'character of the company', to sketch the respective cultures of the three organisations which had owned the Ryland site. He started with the company which had owned it prior to Parry:

> 'Its character was very, very traditional, labour-intensive, solid, run by the foreman and all this kind of thing. Parry was laid back, more technology-led; their successes were measured in technological achievements rather than their sales output. Up until a year ago the culture of ZTC was one of taking over the world: we'll start by taking over Poland and then it will be Russia; everybody will succumb to our obvious power. But this did not become the case. It is now a matter of finding a culture which will help us survive; recognising we do not have a God-given right to stay in business; that we could all lose our jobs; that we must survive and find our way through it.'

Having asked managers to tell me what the concept of culture meant to them, I asked them about whether and how they saw the culture changing at Ryland. There was universal agreement that the culture was changing. One type of comment on this reflected on the process of change more than the content. Eddie Elton, very much a user of the control discourse, suggested that

> 'We try to bring too many things on too quick. We change directors all the time and each one has his own strategy or culture. We blitz that down: "Come on lads, get your coats off, here we go again . . . forget what we have done and how we did it". We keep going off on yet another bleeding track; another railway line or another dark alley or whatever. Half-way down there someone will change direction again.'

Garry Borrowash, a manager in the finance function, generally favoured the empowerment discourse, but also questioned some of the processes of culture change:

> 'It has got to be a culture of change, but it has got to be change because the world and the customers require it, not because some swine decides they are going to have a change for their own sake, or for them to make an impression.'

This way of seeing many changes as serving the careers of those introducing them is something I see as generally expresssed as part of the control discourse. But here we see it, in a sense, intruding into the language of an individual who was generally a user of the empowerment style of expression.

Whether or not individuals expressed a willingness to embrace the term 'culture', I nevertheless asked them whether they thought the culture (adding 'whatever that might be' where appropriate) was changing. There was a distinct pattern in responses in that those managers who had expressed unease with the concept of culture, whilst always happily attempting to answer my question, tended to relate 'culture change' to specific issues, rather than to the whole pattern of assumptions, values and behaviours. One of the engineering managers, for example, focused on relations with the trade unions, welcoming the move away from ritualistic bargaining which left the workforce with the view that they 'needed' unions to represent them in such a process. Another manager pointed to more flexible work practices. He said that 'A typical thing in the old culture was that staff could not drive vans; now we even see ladies driving stacker trucks. Staff and hourly paid was a big thing.' I asked what the new culture was and was told 'It is people working together because the job needs it.'

These two managers were speaking positively of the changes they had in mind. Other references to culture change which had a specific focus were more negative, however. And these were generally ones relating to the employment policies of the company. Garry Borrowash was well aware that it was a matter of what people believed to be the case that was crucial in this area. He said the culture was changing, and that people:

> '. . . do not know where we are and where we are going. They are not prepared to do as much as they did. You hear rumblings: "The company does not care so much for me – I am not going to care for the company". It may not be true, but in the transition period you do not know one way or the other. The pension fund illustrates this; it may well be that the ZEC one is better, but because they won't tell you whether it is worse or better (they have just said you have got to join it from this date).'

Dick Eastwood focused on similar issues;

> 'People are finding it difficult to realise who they are working for. The announcing of reduced severance terms two weeks before announcing a redundancy: Parry would not have done that to us.'

The majority of ZTC Ryland managers were not only happy to use the concept of culture, but spoke about the cultural changes they perceived to be happening as broad ones, rather than as changes in specific aspects of the life of the organisation. And the most common theme was one of inconsistency or confusion within the culture. One of the sharpest formulations of this that I heard came with a comment made by a manager to others in a meeting. He commented that:

> 'What we have got is a guns and roses culture.'
> 'What the hell's that, Barry?', he was asked.

'It's a rock group or something, isn't it?', added another.

'It is. And what a racket!', which was followed with:

'Do you reckon Barry's saying ZTC is a racket?', at which point Barry explained himself:

'We've got guns pointed at us. But they've got flowers sticking out of the barrels. "Watch it, else you'll get the bullet. But enjoy the sweet flowers – get some personal development in."'

'OK. OK,' intervened the person chairing the meeting, which was about managers encouraging their 'team leaders' to implement the personal development scheme. 'Order, order. A rose by any other ... Let's get down to business,' whereupon the episode ended with one of the managers pointing two fingers, pistol like, at the chair person:

'Bang, bang.'

In an interview, and expressing himself less colourfully than Barry Thrumpton had in the personal development meeting, Terry Carlton spoke to me of an attempt to move from a 'rule-oriented and procedure-based culture in which people are frustrated because they cannot do the things they want to get on with', to one where people are 'treated as equals and have more freedom to take risks and to take responsibility'. This change was in evidence, 'but it's wavering all over the place'. Phil Wollaton, saw real attempts to 'empower people' but this would fail if there was not a rethinking of organisational structures: 'you can't empower here and there and not do a lot to the structures to make this a normal way of going on'. Trevor Smalley also alluded to structural issues, in saying that the division of the company into various businesses meant that 'ZTC does not have a culture; it is just a mixture of subcultures.'

Tommy Bulwell thought that the culture had become 'inwards looking out . . . subdued, demoralised'. The cultures that 'we were trying get' were 'positive and outward, modern'. But people were now 'looking over their shoulders':

'We have gone through all the hypes of DOC and TQM and BIP (there were no super buzz-names before that) and I identified with the sort of culture. You saw it in the idea that you have to "sell our way out of these difficult situations lads, we are not going to cost-reduce our way out of these things". I identified with that kind of culture. In the last few years we have been through about four different games – the winning culture, DOC, BIP, TQM – and we have got to the point now where are back in the old "don't trust management" role. Since the year dot the reality is that management have always exploited the workers and unions have actually reduced that down in most companies. Personnel directors will admit it that there is exploitation . . . that is a pot pourri of cultural problems in all that.'

This type of view was expressed in a more focused way by Jack Hockley, whose 'greatest fear' was 'that they are going to destroy all the good work that we put onto this site if they keep pushing and pushing and pushing the bottom end like they are doing'. He feared that 'they will destroy everything' and answered my query as to what he meant by the 'bottom end' with:

'Pushing them by getting rid, I mean. How the hell can you preach this flexibility, this development, at the same time as you are getting rid? As someone said to me yesterday – an operator – "Why am I in here now doing the best I can, getting this product out, when tomorrow morning you can give me a brown envelope?" I had no answer.'

Repeatedly, managers spoke of being used to making people redundant and of having seen it as an unfortunate necessity over the years at Ryland as the shape of the business changed. But its current use was increasingly being questioned, especially in the light of the type of official culture aspired to for ZTC. Indeed it was not unusual for managers to connect trends in the actual or 'unofficial' culture in ZTC Ryland to problems of national British culture. Peter Manthorpe commented that:

'There is a big cultural problem in this approach to solving cost problems by getting rid of people. This seems typical in Britain now. We have to think again. I don't like inefficiency and it has been right to get rid of slack but, beyond that, of seeing the way of cutting your cost structure in terms of getting rid of people. It will kill us – as a country – not just us.'

In many conversations like this, strong emotions were expressed, with the notion of culture being used to enable managers to connect specific issues to larger patterns and broader trends, not just in ZTC, but at the national level too. There was a common fear that a vicious circle of mistrust was being created which would destroy the company. This was seen as following from many trends occurring currently, from pensions and severance terms to cost-cutting through 'losing heads' and, indeed, the overall style of strategy-making at the top of the company. Managers at all levels at Ryland spoke of this problem; the strength of feeling engendered by it was indicated by Ken Donington, who spoke of there being 'less discussion nowadays with top management'. He vigorously banged his desk as he explained that:

'Decisions are just taken. Mistrust is worse than it ever was in the oldest days. There seems to be someone carrying guns around at the high levels.'
'Why "guns" Ken? It makes a change from the talk of "knives being out" that I have heard you use before?'
'The difference between a knife and a gun is that you get the feeling that with a knife, you might survive it. But you can't a gun. It is instant. This is where the uncertainty comes in this place. Overnight, you could be without a job. The danger is that, although the really conscientious ones like me will continue to work, a lot of those will become less and less conscientious. So the uncertainty tends to breed negativity. People are just getting turned off.'

Donington was not the first one, as we have seen, to deploy metaphors using guns. But he said nothing of roses.

BUSINESS TALK: UP SHIT CREEK WITHOUT A STRATEGY?

In the conversation which opened this chapter, Chris Wilford related the concept of strategy to the question of where 'ZTC was going'. He implied that an organisation only had a strategy when its management knew what the direction was to be and what 'the job in hand' was being done 'for'. He further suggested that strategies were only really an issue when an organisation was facing problems of survival. And ZTC was in such a position. It needed a strategy, he felt, in the way the canoeist 'up shit creek' needs a paddle.

In the same way that the notion of 'winning culture' was part of the official rhetoric of ZTC, a key element of the *empowerment, skills and development discourse*, so the concept of 'strategic intent' formed a key discursive resource intended to help people frame their thoughts and behaviours. We saw in the last chapter that a concept of strategic intent was conceived to function as a 'guiding light' for all employees in making their contribution to ZTC's ambitious growth target.

The principle of a strategic intent acting as this guiding light was central to the Developing Organisational Capability (DOC) programme which means that all of the managers covered in my study had been closely identified with the process of encouraging all employees to work with the intention of relating all of their behaviours to the direction of the ZTC business as a whole. In this period of changed ownership, economic recession and a new managing director, what were managers' views on ZTC's business situation and what did the notion of 'strategic position' mean to them? To what extent did the managers speak as if they were becoming the broad 'business managers' that the personnel director, the organisation development executive and I were trying to encourage them to be? To help answer these questions I asked all of those I interviewed about how they saw the general business situation of ZTC and how they would characterise its 'broad strategic position'. I also asked about the extent to which they felt that managers generally had an influence on strategy. To contextualise all of this, I asked them what they felt were the 'key characteristics of the best businesses in the world today'.

We have already seen evidence of the frustration of some managers at their exclusion from policy or strategy issues in ZTC, something which was poignantly expressed by Jim Aspley's rhetorical question: 'What about my empowerment?' The idea that managers, indeed employees generally, across the whole of the organisation should have an input into the fulfilling of the strategic intent was central to the official culture and to the way that was articulated to the whole workforce through the Developing Organisational Capability (DOC) process. This process, and the close involvement of many of the Ryland managers in it, can be seen as an important factor likely to encourage an expectation that each manager should have influence beyond their specific departmental or functional responsibilities. But a more general factor relating to such a possible orientation could be that revealed in Chapter 3, where a clear pattern emerged in which managers revealed a basic orientation towards being 'in control', rather than being controlled or led by others. This, in itself, would not necessarily be a strong push towards a desire to influence business strategy. But when it is put together with the powerful arguments of the DOC process about the strategic need for contributions from 'below' towards achieving business growth and the growing recognition that changes had to made if the company was to survive, it is likely to encourage a desire for managers, as one put it, to 'at the very least get closer than we are to discussions about the direction we are to take as a business'.

But what sort of general direction did the managers feel a modern business should follow? I was interested to learn about the managers' conception of a 'good business', not just because this would provide some indication of the basic criteria they might have in mind when evaluating the strategic position of their own organisation, but also because it might tell us something about the take-up of discursive resources from the newer managerial rhetorics. Indeed the talk was very much characterised by references which we might associate with more 'fashionable' thinking. References to the best businesses being 'customer-focused' dominated responses. This was distinguished from more traditional approaches in which businesses would be 'technologically led' or 'product led', focusing more on what the people in the company wanted to produce, rather than 'what the customers might want to buy'. There was a common recognition that ideas about how businesses should be run were changing. And a number of managers seemed keen to emphasise that they were not, for example, simply 'mouthing fashionable nostrums' but 'saying what I really believe'. Statements were made like, 'I try to avoid the jargon, but when it comes down to it [the best businesses] are very responsive to what the customers want'. Another said that it was a matter of having a 'winning culture' (qualifying this statement with 'to put it in a phrase – a corny phrase, perhaps').

In speaking of 'customer focus' there was a tendency to stress the idea of 'focus' in its own right, as in 'it's not just a matter of focusing on the customer because customers are important; you need focus to give people something to concentrate on, something to prevent them all wandering off in their own little directions'. A manufacturing manager stressed the notion of 'proper focus' which, he said, meant 'selling what you can make and making what you can sell'. I asked whether these 'were your own words or a phrase you have picked up?'. He did not know, but explained that he did not 'like being technology-led. It means spending a lot of money and coming up with features that people don't necessarily want – like on the [product] we are producing here in fact'.

The best businesses were not only seen as 'looking outwards' when deciding what to produce, but as being 'flexible', 'responsive', 'speedy when it comes to meeting new needs'. Words like 'empowerment', central to the officially preferred empowerment, skills and growth discourse, were, interestingly, not used a great deal when individuals were talking about other businesses, at least not in a direct way. Words like values and culture were occasionally used, but more typical was the use of terms like 'high commitment', 'pulling together as if the whole company was just one person', being 'oriented to the customer and organised so that people don't waste all their time competing internally', and 'having a happy workforce which is working with you rather than against you'. A statement which I would select as typifying the views of the ZTC Ryland managers of what a business should be like suggested that:

> 'It is a customer focus; a willingness to have a goal or objective which is communicable to the people. However large the business is, you have to pull it together as an entity with a team, with a dedicated set of managers who understand the objectives. Any company who does that is going to succeed, quite frankly. If the market is there, someone is going to fill it. And the company with these attributes is the one who is going to fill it. Of course, once you become number one or number two you have got to be careful to maintain it. You can easily slip and have to pull yourself up now and again and; like some American companies have said, we had to get back to the knitting.'

Most of the conceptions of the 'best businesses' combined attention to *external* customer requirements with issues of *internal* cultural orientation, as in this statement. A key role for managers is one of looking outwards and then gaining the commitment of those inside to meeting these external requirements. The ideas expressed by managers were close to those underpinning the official culture of ZTC Ryland and my interpretation of the fact that managers tended to avoid using the specific language of the official ZTC discourse is that they did this to demonstrate that, in the phrase quoted earlier, they 'really believed' in the principles they were enunciating. They were not just stating them because they 'had fallen for fashionable jargon' or, in an even more colourful phrase used by one woman, 'liked parroting DOC-speak'.

When managers were asked to move to the specific situation of ZTC and what they believed to be its 'broad strategic position at the moment', there was a complete switch of language style. As one manager said 'now we really are going from the sublime to the ridiculous'. Individuals' responses often started with a single word or short phrase, like 'dodgy', 'struggling', 'up against it', 'in the shit', 'fighting for survival', 'retrenchment', 'defending the fortress'. The pattern was similar across the range of managers I interviewed, with the exception of one or two of the more junior ones who said they did not really know about these matters which, as one said, they were willing to 'leave to the blokes paid to sort out all of that'. To look again for a statement that typifies the rest, I would cite the words of the man who started with the word 'Dodgy'. He continued:

> 'It's very uncomfortable at the moment. We are under attack from companies at home and overseas. The international side is zilch and the whole link-up with

Siegfried has muddied the water. If I was recommending someone to buy shares I would probably say no.'

There was widespread recognition that ZTC were a 'tiny player on the global scene' and that the old strategic intent of becoming fifth in the world was a 'thing of the past, now we are in bed with Siegfried'. But no manager or director within ZTC Ryland claimed to have a clear picture of what being 40 per cent owned by the German giant was going to mean in practice. Two senior people put it to me that perhaps the Ryland managers should all work hard to make good relationships with Siegfried and do what they could to encourage Siegfried to buy out ZEC's share in the company. Others managers spoke of their fears of, as one put it, 'letting ourselves get swallowed up and spat out' by the German company. Time and again I witnessed groups of managers debating the possible benefits and the possible dangers of becoming integrated into Siegfried. In line with my own strategic exchange view of how organisations function, these discussions often focused on what it was that ZTC had to 'trade' with Siegfried. Positions varied between ones that saw ZTC as having techno-logical skills and knowledge that could contribute significantly to the Siegfried position in world markets, to ones which spoke of ZTC as being 'just a distributor for Siegfried products' and of Ryland as becoming 'just a warehouse for German hardware'. A senior manager put it graphically:

'It's survival now and how to get Siegfried interested in us. They are not interested in anything we do at the moment. Somebody said to me recently, "We've been raped". I said it's worse than that, "We've taken all our clothes off and they've said 'no thank you'". It's hurtful. I can't see what we can offer them. I can't see what product they want; why would they want our switch when they've got their own equivalent? And they've got factories in East Germany needing work. They could use us as a place to support their products. If we were really lucky we could get the spares work. We are all dressed up and nowhere to go. Nobody's coming through the door. They are not looking at our capacity.'

Generally there was considerable distrust of Siegfried beneath the puzzle-ment of what that company's interest was. But this did not seem to be a matter of fear of a foreign company as such. In fact, a not uncommon argument was that a German company might have less of a 'British short-termist' attitude. Such an attitude was associated with ZEC, the current controlling interest in ZTC, who were said, for example, to think along the lines: 'short-term profits are not too good, so let's hack something out of it'. It was particularly felt that the 'ZEC philosophy might not be best for a high-tech company'. One holder of this view observed:

'We have got two owners with different philosophies. ZEC bought us because they wanted a reasonable return over a period. But I am not sure how willing they are to invest their wonderful money mountain in us. And Siegfried's interest is unclear. In theory we should be making their business switch – we can do it cheaper than in Germany. So where is it? We are trying. But I suspect they bought us so that we would not compete with them in overseas markets.

Overall, we have a situation where managers across the levels in Ryland can only talk about the strategy of their own company in speculative terms. Yet they are employed by a company that put enormous effort and resource into establishing itself as a business which would involve people across the organisation in developing the business. When directly asked about the extent to which managers generally were contributing to the strategy-making in ZTC they, not surprisingly, gave a largely negative response. However, it was not a straightforwardly negative response in the sense that managers simply blamed 'the company' for excluding them from important decisions. Such a view was expressed by a number of people, sometimes with bitterness. But I was surprised by the number of managers who said that they could perhaps be blamed themselves for, in one phrase used, 'not insisting on being more bloody proactive'. It was commented, for example that 'I am a strong believer that you can change things if you really want to. Too many people hide behind the excuse that there is nothing I can do about that'. Another such comment was:

> 'Managers believe that they can't influence the management of the company but, if only they knew, they can. They *are* the management but are always saying that "they" will not let us do this or that. I know that I have got influence, but a lot of managers do not realise that the source of the answers to many of the knotty problems that they've got is in themselves. They actually know the answers, if only they could cogently put it together and present it.'

I was probably wrong to have been surprised by the number of people who spoke in this way. Some of the individuals who spoke in this way to me were well aware of my own arguments about the foolishness of managers not simply 'waiting to see' what more senior managers would decide. The conversation about the new managing director reported in the previous chapter (p. 103) illustrates this; the individuals in that meeting seemed genuinely anxious not to be in a position to be accused of being 'wimps and cowards'. One might also see the reluctance to accept a lack of 'empowerment' among managers themselves as a further illustration of the importance to these men and women of being 'in control' rather than 'controlled', as demonstrated in Chapter 3. But a further dimension probably lies in a deeper matter of the individual defending their concept of 'self'. A director of one of the businesses at Ryland told me 'I know I am being pushed around. I feel foolish about it at times. But then I say to myself that I could assert myself if I really felt like it. And I will – soon.' Two of his fellow directors left ZTC, however, giving, among other reasons, their frustration at not being able to influence strategic matters. One of them spoke of directors who were staying:

> 'Perhaps they are happy being told what is what in their own business by ZEC or the corporate bullies. I doubt that though. I think the ones who are staying

either haven't had an offer [from another employer], are flattered at having been recently promoted, or are fooling themselves that sooner or later somebody will listen to them. They can take it from me, they are wasting their time.'

There was a strong feeling across the managers in ZTC that strategic matters had not just been 'taken back to the top table', as one Ryland man put it, but were in the hands of Paul Syston alone. It was a reversal with a vengeance of the principles of strategic intent originally taken up by ZTC from the ideas of Hamel and Prahalad. It was reversion to what these authors and consultants call a 'strategic hierarchy' approach in which 'senior management makes strategy and lower levels execute it' (1989: 75). Hamel and Prahalad condemn this as involving an 'elitist view of management' which leads to a situation in which 'middle managers buffeted by circumstances that seem to be beyond their control desperately want to believe that top management has all the answers. And top management, in turn, hesitates to admit it does not for fear of demoralising lower level employees'. However, many of the ZTC Ryland managers were unhappy about accepting this relatively passive role in the strategic hierarchy. They had come to believe that more should be expected of managers 'who like to think they are managers with a capital M', to quote the words of Geoff Clifton.

Over the course of my year in ZTC I observed a trend whereby a significant proportion of Ryland managers became increasingly restive about this shift back to a strategic hierarchy. In part I may have perceived this as managers reflecting back to me my own increasingly well-known view that managers who did not involve themselves in strategic matters were not really managers (and remember that one of my formal tasks was to help establish this view of management among Ryland managers). However, I believe the most significant factor behind the trend was an increasing recognition of the trouble that the company, and the Ryland plant in particular, was in. As Chris Wilford was suggesting at the beginning of this chapter, strategic matters come more to the fore the more obvious it is that management is a matter of managing for survival. And survival was an issue that managers were increasingly talking about: 'nothing concentrates the mind on business strategy like knowing you're about to go out of business the next day', a commercial manager said at one meeting I attended.

ESCAPING THE GIANT BROWN ENVELOPE

I saw most clearly the trend of managers coming to terms with a need to assert themselves instead of waiting for 'decisions from above' whilst attending the weekly meetings of the Ryland manufacturing managers every Tuesday lunchtime. The original purposes of these meetings had been to help coordinate innovations on employment matters. But, as it became increasingly obvious that there was a serious question about whether there would be for much longer any manufacturing work for the factory to employ people on, the focus of discussions turned to actions to defend the continued existence of the factory.

The manufacturing managers increasingly realised that such problems as the currently poor order book, the lack of new products coming 'on stream', a nearly saturated market for the main product and the allegedly comparatively high costs of manufacturing at Ryland were bringing the plant's survival into doubt. The regular bouts of redundancy were seen as beginning to bleed the factory's lifeblood. 'We are spiralling down and down like a rocket' said one of the managers on what I felt was a significant day. It was the day when one man said, 'Look, we keep coming along here, bitching about things and mourning. It's no good keeping mourning.' This introduction of the word 'mourning' seemed to invite a possibly carthartic process, whereby individuals spoke about their feelings in terms such as 'I am depressed', 'I just can't take much more of this lying down and getting walked over', and 'Sod it, we are clearly going out of business.' A passionate speech was then made by Gerry Cropwell, who spoke of having a 'genuine passion for keeping this place going'. At the end of the speech there was a silence. Gerry then asked, 'So what are we going to do?'

I must take care not to over-dramatise this process. For weeks subsequently, these managers, as one person said, 'simply talked round and round the problem'. But week after week I was noting interpolations such as: 'So what are we going to do to influence things?'; 'We can't wait for the drive to come from the top table'; 'You can make history or you can let history happen to you'; 'Everything does seem stacked against us but don't let us roll over and let them do it to us.' It seemed that none of the managers wanted to assert themselves and take on the role of, as it was put at one point, 'leading a rearguard action and getting your bollocks bitten off by Ted Meadows'. Eventually, the problem of 'getting something to happen' was partly solved by the personnel executive who chaired the meeting organising a series of separate 'working groups' which would each tackle one facet of the problem of what was variously labelled 'filling the factory' or 'saving Ryland'. There were thus groups looking at such issues as contract manufacturing into the factory; reducing costs; improving coordination between manufacturing and other functions; persuading corporate management to bring one of the new products that was otherwise destined for another factory to Ryland, and coordinating 'good news' about Rylands that could be broadcast to 'hype up our image'.

These groups were under way at the time I left ZTC, but the last meeting of this series which I attended was a far from positive one. Rumours of further redundancies which might include managers themselves were handled with grim gallows humour such as, 'Next week we should get champagne in instead of coffee, so that we can get pissed as we hand each other our brown envelopes' ('getting a brown envelope' being the normal term for receiving a notification of redundancy). But a much more sombre note was struck when Dick Mansfield offered the thought:

'Don't you think we are all being a bit parochial about this. We are saying "fill our factory". We are saying "give us work". Have we really considered whether that is what we are here for? It's all very fancy talking about being strategic and influencing Syston. But we are just looking after ourselves aren't we? Is this really being strategic? Is the company here to provide jobs, or are the jobs here because the business needs them done?'

Harry Basford followed this with an observation which led Mansfield to look around the table and say 'That's flattened it, hasn't it?'. Basford's point was:

'Nobody's said a thing here about the mission statement which Syston produced months ago now. Do you remember what it says? It says bugger all about making anything. The company is here to provide solutions to people's telecommications problems. Those solutions might involve making things ourselves. But they are equally likely not to. You work out what people need and go abroad to get it made. Bye bye Ryland.'

The comments by Mansfield and Basford were followed with a further burst of gallows humour, starting with a quip that 'we are now into flattening the factory instead of filling the factory' and culminating in the conjuring up of the horrid and surreal image of Paul Syston 'coming along and measuring up the Ryland site so that he can get us all into one bloody great giant brown envelope'.

This almost frantic outburst of black humour was followed by a contrastingly philosophical discussion of what the job of managers should be. Harry Basford put forward the argument that their prime responsibility was to maintain 'the viability of the company as a whole and not to defend your own patch of it or the jobs of the people who work for you'. This led to heated dispute as others argued that they could not, morally, 'let this place go down the pan with all the people who have put their lives into it, us included', as one of them put it. Eventually, however, a general agreement was reached when Mansfield and Basford between them explained that they were by no means arguing for 'giving up' and 'jumping overboard so that ZTC can stay afloat with whoever is left to sail in her'. They said that a case had to be worked out which would show that manufacturing at Ryland was 'strategically more sensible' than 'buying in'. And that would mean that they would really have to change 'the way we manage' to make that a reality and not just a piece of 'Ryland special pleading'. The person chairing the meeting then spoke of 'closing on that note of challenge' but the final words spoken in the meeting took the theme back to that of how free the managers really were to manage: 'That's all very well, and I'll fight to the death to do what I can. But the real fight is going to be the fight to be allowed to manage.'

Later that afternoon, one of the managers who had been at the meeting said to me:

> 'I bet you've never seen anything like this outfit. There's so much potential here. But we have this terrific knack of throwing it all away. Every time we decide to go for something we get ourselves all psyched up. We take aim. And then we shoot ourselves in the foot. Why? Tell me why?'

This was not an easy question to answer. But in the next chapter I shall attempt to make sense of the factors which lead to the phenomenon found in organisations generally whereby people can come to feel that they are 'going round and round in circles', to borrow another phrase used by this same manager to describe his current experience of managing in ZTC. The events and the problems in ZTC Ryland present a powerful illustration of the tendency by which the *means* chosen by the managers of all organisations to achieve certain *ends* can come to subvert them, rather than serve them. To manage successfully is to be constantly aware of this danger and to work continuously to minimise it.

Chapter 6

Means, ends and going around in circles

'The new structure and mission will soon be in place. We've got the grading structure in place. The action team is moving towards MRP2 and we are getting the PDP into place. What we now want to do is to look at metrics. To make sure that we are meeting the business's new strategy we need to put in place the right metrics. Graham?'

'OK. I agree with you, Mike. We've got to make sure that we are getting it right. I don't think anybody would disagree with that, would they?'

'I was hoping not. But Tony won't agree with it. Look at his face. He hates metrics. He gets upset every time we talk about measuring anything. Why do you get so twisted up on measures, Tony?'

'I don't really. It's not measures as such that I get bothered about. It's the sort of approach that goes with it; all that "putting in place" crap.'

'Aha. We are using the wrong words again are we, groan groan?'

'It's not just words. It seems to me that management is not really about putting systems in place, putting structures in place, putting metrics in place. Of course, you need all of these things. But in themselves they achieve nothing. I think there is though, if I can borrow one of Jim's favourite phrases, a "mindset" among a lot of the managers here that believes that if you get the "right" systems, measures and all that, then the place will more or less manage itself. That's what I mean by "crap". You know that, to me, management is all about making and remaking understandings and agreements, persuading people, building trust, encouraging people to find new and better ways of doing things and –'

'But surely you've first got to put basic procedures and structures in place? – Whoops, I've used the dreaded phrase.'

'Yes, of course. "Basic ones", as you say. But let me just say something about the "dreaded phrase". It's not just my obsession with words. Haven't you noticed that whenever politicians are in a flap about the economy or the health service or whatever, they increasingly turn to that hollow phrase; they are "putting in place measures" to do this, "putting in place policies" to solve that. It's just like they say they are "making things absolutely clear" when they want to pull the wool over people's eyes.'

'Come on, get off your soap box. You –'

'No, I am talking about what happens here really. The more I hear managers talking about putting things in place, the more I get the impression that they are not confronting the fact that what they really need to be doing is getting out and about and talking to customers, talking to people in the factory and in the offices. They want to manage by remote control.'

'That's crap, Tony. We are not in trouble because we've depended on structures and systems. We are in trouble because we've depended on bad ones. Well, it's a combination of that and finding that our systems were knocked off course by unexpected changes beyond our control. What we need to do is to – and I am deliberately going to use the term – put in place more bomb-proof systems; one's which will not be blown off course. And that is where having good metrics comes in. You identify the important things your business needs to do to win in the market place and you set up indicators to tell you whether you are doing them. Dead simple.'

'I wish it was.'

MEANS AND ENDS

My contributions to this part of a meeting in ZTC Ryland called to discuss setting up managerial performance indicators were not the cool, calm and objective utterances of a social science researcher playing the role of 'fly on the wall' data collector. At this meeting I was playing hard the 'participant' part of my participant observer role within the company's management. I felt very strongly about the issues I was addressing, not least because of my conviction that the sort of 'management by remote control' that I was criticising would, if relied upon in ZTC Ryland, lead to more and more people losing their jobs at the plant. Among these would be a good number of my own friends and neighbours. However, this does not mean that I was not speaking as a social scientist in the sense that I was drawing on my sociological knowledge and theoretical understanding of how organisations work when playing my role as a committed and combative member of the 'management team'.

On various occasions when I took part in management meetings of this kind I played a role which I used to describe with mock solemnity as that of a 'creative subversive'. This was well understood by most of those I worked closely with and was recognised as an aspect of why I was there. It was understood that I would use my 'expert' knowledge and my experience of other organisations to raise questions within managerial decision-making processes that otherwise might not be asked. The quality of thinking and decision-making would thus be enhanced. My questioning and my critical interventions as 'licensed fool' were to be constructive, in intention at least. As I have explained more than once in previous chapters, part of the role which was negotiated for me when I joined ZTC involved helping develop managers' awareness of their need to act as broader 'business managers', rather than as people in charge of their specific area of responsibility. The view shared by the personnel director, the organisation development executive and myself was that managers should carry out their specific roles as a means towards the development of the business as a whole, and not as an end in itself. It was in this spirit of attacking tendencies to let means become more significant than the ends which they were devised to serve that my contributions to the above conversation were made.

If one takes the view that the essential rationale of the management of an organisation is to ensure that the organisation exchanges material and symbolic resources with all the parties or stakeholders involved with it to achieve its long-term survival, then it follows that any division of labour of that management into different levels, functions and responsibilities is only justified as long as it serves as a means towards the achieving of that broader end. A research and development manager's job, for example, is not one of devising new products as such, however much such a role might excite and inspire them. It is to devise products which the organisation can trade with its customers to maintain its long-term viability. And, going beyond the issue of managers' roles, a corresponding argument applies to all the systems, procedures, missions, values and 'metrics' that go along with these roles. It is immensely important to recognise this and to appreciate what has always seemed to me to be one of the most sociologically significant aspects of how organisations function. I refer to the fact that the means established within organisations to manage their long-term survival (the whole gamut of structures, roles, symbols, policies and practices), however 'right' they may be when they are set up, have a tendency to 'go wrong' and become ends in themselves, thus undermining the ends for which they were devised.

This was a tendency that I felt was being ignored in the position taken by Graham Ockbrook in the meeting on metrics. He had argued that certain problems in ZTC Ryland had come about because they had either operated with the 'wrong' systems or had found the 'right' systems getting 'blown off course' by unexpected circumstances. At the meeting I had gone on to agree with him that indeed some structures and systems in organisations would be more effective than others, given the prevailing circumstances. In the spirit of the classical advocates of rhetorical technique (of whom we will hear more in the next chapter), I also conceded to him the value of having arrangements which were less susceptible to being blown off course than others might be. This was the point of having 'flexible arrangements'. But then, having softened my debating opponent with these hints of agreement, I pushed forward my claim that it was 'madness to look for the Holy Grail of the perfect, all-singing all-dancing organisational structure and culture that would solve all problems for all times'. This piece of rhetorical bluster was less effective than it might have been ('What the hell's a Holy Grail?', asked one colleague) but at least I made with some impact my point that all systems had the potential to go wrong. 'Oh I see', said another colleague: 'it's Sod's law and Murphy's law that you are on about.'

The principle I had in mind was that of the *paradox of consequences*, a central concept underlying much of the work of the great sociologist Max

Weber (1968). But to move to such terminology in a management meeting, away from the principles of Sod or Murphy, whoever they might be, was less than appealing. I cannot avoid such a task here, however. Weber identified a trend underlying the development of modern societies whereby more and more aspects of social and working life were subjected to the application of *formal rationality*, something which did not, however, lead to a generally more rational control over the world, in the sense of achieving the broader purposes and values of human beings. By formal rationality Weber meant the careful and calculated choice of appropriate means to achieving specific ends. This rationalisation process involved the growth of scientific and technological ways of thinking and acting and to the development of money-based exchange systems, accountancy techniques of cost management and benefit analysis and, accompanying all of this, bureaucratic ways of organising administration and industry.

What all of these diverse matters have in common is the careful and rational devising of the most efficient way to solve any particular problem. One calculates the most 'efficient' way (lowest inputs for highest outputs) to get from A to B, as opposed to travelling the route which is prescribed by tradition, priest, parent, friend, or dictator. Technical calculation is of the essence. All being well, one gets to A at the lowest cost to oneself. But, in the world of human institutions, things rarely work out in this simple way. Human arrangements do not have the predictability of the machine. A modern gun (or should I say weapon system) is a formally rational device. It will reliably move a piece of metal at a carefully calculated speed through a precisely worked out trajectory to have a deliberately chosen effect on whatever target its sights are set on. Formal rationality is thus demonstrated. But put the gun or weapon system into the context of human relationships, and unintended and less 'rational' broader outcomes may result. The guns issued for defensive purposes may turn into weapons of aggression as some of the defenders fall out with others, for example. And to turn to a different area of life, pills scientifically devised to improve lives through bringing sleep or reducing pain may be used to take life. Public bureaucracies set up to provide fair and just government can become the means whereby officials give themselves security and career advantage. And the private bureaucracies of the business world can correspondingly come to grief as departmental empires are constructed and people do their jobs for the sake of doing their jobs, as opposed to focusing on the level and quality of goods and service delivery which will continue to justify that organisation's long-term existence in the eyes of its 'stakeholders'.

In each of these cases, the means devised to achieve ends come to undermine, rather than serve, those ends. This is the paradox of consequences. It suggests that whatever system or structure managers establish in their organisation, and however 'rationally' they might have worked it out, it will be subject to decay. George Ritzer (1993) calls this tendency the 'irrationality of rationality' and sees it coming about in the ways the advantages of increased efficiency, predictability, calculability and control – through the substitution of non-human for human technology associated with the spread of the 'fast-food principles' ('McDonaldisation') to the whole of social life – may have considerable negative unintended consequences. Robert Burns, in looking at the damage done by his plough to the nest of a mouse, observed that the 'best laid plans of mice and men gang aft agley'. The mouse had no expectation that a ploughshare might crash through its nest when it set about constructing it. But managers setting up the systems and procedures that compose a work organisation need to be aware that, whatever they construct, their plans can 'gang agley' – go wrong, not just because an unexpected catastrophe occurs, as it did in the life of Burns' mouse, but because the human beings who 'people' those arrangements bring their personal or sectional interests, self-defence strategies and priorities to bear on them and interpret their instructions in the light of all the inadequacies of understanding that characterise human efforts at communication.

I had to put all of this much more simply in the management meeting, where I was questioning the value of putting too much reliance on what I labelled 'bureaucratic performance indicators'. I explained that any structure, system or procedure contained within it the seeds of its own destruction because people would find ways of operating it to meet their own purposes, whether that be to advance their own personal interests, justify their existence or give them a quiet life. Too much target-setting and too much emphasis on numerical performance measures can lead to people working up to that formally stated level and no further (cf. Gouldner 1954). Charles Bunny argued that the way to avoid this problem was to have the 'right' measures. He said that the key aim of the business should be 'sustained growth' and that, therefore, he would 'not measure people against standard produced hours'. He would not measure business performance on profit alone and 'because empowerment is so important' he would 'measure things like the number of appraisals done and the number of days spent training'. My argument was just the same about these, I said. It was valuable to have measures of these things. But they should not become anything more than indicators. If they were emphasised too much, they would be 'ends in themselves'. Such indicators could function like the speedometer in a car. This gives valuable information to the driver of a car. But any driver who decided always to ensure that the dial gave a pre-specified reading would hardly be an effective driver.

The metaphor of management performance indicators and metrics as a car speedometer proved to be very helpful in the discussion. It was taken up by Mark Cossall, who had a background in quality management. He started by saying that 'the great quality guru, Deming' was against the use of management targets and measures. He said that what was desirable was for measures to be applied by the people doing a particular type of work to guide themselves. They 'owned' the measures and applied them to themselves to check that they were achieving what they 'wanted to achieve'. This was like the car driver looking at the speedometer to help them travel to their chosen destination. But if the measures and targets were ones imposed by managers on others, then they became 'constraining and not empowering'.

At this point the conversation moved on to other aspects of the broad phenomenon of means getting in the way of the ends for which they had been devised. Was it not because of the way that this sort of thing had happened, I asked, that the company was changing the payment system to get rid of the variety of bonuses, which no longer related to the sorts of return which they were originally designed to encourage. A colleague from the employee relations area commented that it seemed to him that all incentive schemes had this potential to 'decay'. And could 'the overtime syndrome' be another case of this phenomenon, he asked? Overtime payments were often a perfect example of this tendency towards the irrationality of rationality manifesting itself and means coming to act as ends in themselves, I agreed. Overtime existed as a clearly rational device to cope with 'extra' work, over and above the normally expected schedules. Martin Hillside commented:

'And I have no doubt that a significant number of our managers are *making* overtime. We have got to look at this policy of paying our junior managers for overtime. There are managers coming in here at weekends because they have got a team of people in to do work which they could have got done during the week. This not only creates the cost for us of their extra pay, but we have to pay the operatives as well. And on top of all that we are encouraging all the inefficiency that goes on during the main shift. You can be bloody sure that if there was not overtime going, they would get a lot of that work out by working more smartly in the normal hours.'

Graham Ockbrook agreed that this happened, but said that it was simply the outcome of 'bloody slack management'. Nobody disagreed with him, but I pointed out that to avoid such problems arising there needed to be some understanding of why such patterns tended to arise. Before jumping in with tighter controls we needed to recognise that employees tend to seek a predictable and regular level of income and will 'bend' incentive or overtime systems to achieve this. 'Aha', said a voice, making itself heard for the first time, 'Hawthorne experiments'. 'Three cheers for management courses', came back another.

Partly because I knew that one of the managers present was seen as a main culprit of such a habit, I went on from this to raise the case of the use of the 'all-in-one' electronic mail system as a way of avoiding directly communicating with people. I pointed out that such a device was justified as a means of improving communications, but that it was alleged by a number of managers that 'certain individuals' were using their new ability quickly and easily to send out messages as an excuse not to 'walk around the factory and chat things over'. This example of 'unintended consequences' caused much amusement with some of the managers present, because they were familiar with the allegation and knew to whom it applied. The individual involved, however, showed no recognition of this but moved the conversation on with:

> 'What about car phones then? They again were issued to help us be efficient. But look what happens. When you get one of these calls from someone in their car you know it will go on and on and bloody on. People are using their car phone to help pass the time when they are on a boring drive. If I know a call coming in for me is on a car phone, I think twice about accepting it. Too many of them lead to unnecessary long time-wasting conversations. Yeah, and there's the call charge cost as well, of course.'

One of the consequences of this meeting, in addition to my achieving a purpose of fending off the establishment of a new set of 'metrics', was that I was invited to speak at a subsequent meeting about this general problem of means and ends. This came about because I suggested that it seemed to me that the whole business was at risk because it was 'characterised from top to bottom by the extent to which means were getting in the way of realising ends'. I said that I had the impression that the company was full of people busying themselves with activities whose contribution to the health of the business was apparent neither to themselves nor to me. However, I never formally presented my overall analysis in these terms to a formal meeting. Instead I used it in informal discussions with individuals within senior management who were interested in making sense of what was happening in the company in broad terms. I judged that the analysis might have greater impact if I 'delivered' it this way, rather than putting it forward in a management meeting, where it would tend to arouse interpersonal arguments and tensions between managers which could be counter-productive.

LIFE IN THE IRON CAGE?

In the early years of the twentieth century, Max Weber worried that the growth of formal rationality and the spreading dominance of bureaucratic organisations would lead to a situation in which the citizens of modern societies would come to be trapped in an 'iron cage'. They would become caught up as cogs in a great machine, where they would neither be able to achieve any significant purposes of their own nor contribute to realising the purposes for which such organisations were originally conceived. ZTC Ryland did not wholly fit this gloomy image, but there were times when I felt that it was becoming, if not an iron cage, then a great labour camp, in which there would be a group of people labouring away in one corner doing the equivalent of breaking stones, whilst over in another corner there would be a group engaged in something akin to sewing mailbags. Yet other groups would be sitting in endless meetings discussing what had happened in previous meetings and what might happen in subsequent meetings whilst, all over the place, there were groups of people sitting at desks and computer terminals writing documents, gathering figures and otherwise adding to the great glacier flow of paper. In the middle of all this there were people making circuit-boards and assembling telephone systems. And elsewhere there were people designing boards and systems. But how all these activities fitted together and made sense as an overall system of productive cooperation was not easy to see.

My feelings about this were similar to those I heard expressed by the Canadian management academic and writer, Henry Mintzberg, who was researching within the British National Health Service at the time I was at ZTC. He commented that he would sit in management meetings and look out of the window of the conference room to see ambulances going back and forth. He found it difficult to relate what he saw going on in those meetings to what was going on at 'ground level' in the hospital. I felt much the same in moving about between management offices and management meetings. One often saw people very happily and efficiently working away at what they were doing in their 'segment' of the organisation, whether or not that effort could be seen as contributing to the organisation as a whole.

There were also people working within constraints which they disliked and sometimes resented. The most significant case of this seemed to be the phenomenon within the manufacturing function which was widely referred to as the 'month-end syndrome'. It was described to me by Ron Hucknall as:

> 'a fundamentally destructive force. It focuses everything on getting output through the door. This is to a specified level at the end of each fixed calendar period. The month-end syndrome, I reckon, gives the key focus to the whole organisation. It's the way we measure output and everything is geared to that. Manufacturing are oriented to getting things into the warehouse. That's their target. My target, if I could change things, would be getting it to the customer and paid for. The culture at the moment is defined as 'you get output'. And output is defined as stuff in the warehouse. Success is stuff shipped at the warehouse, whether we need it now or not. It may be rubbish inventory, because we don't know whether it works.'

Jim Somercotes said of the month-end emphasis: 'It is, to be honest, stupid. I know it. All the manufacturing people know it. But we insist on operating in this way.' This was said to me in private but a similar comment was made in a meeting by a senior manufacturing manager: 'The business is run totally back to front. Nobody says what the business wants. I am simply locked into fixed lead times and the month-end targets.' 'And this means', added one of his colleagues, 'you spend all your time fixing figures rather than getting the job done.' I asked Jim Somercotes why this situation was tolerated:

'In some ways it is good for the business. It sets targets and focuses people's attention on what they need to achieve. That is fine when you are in an expanding business, so I used to agree with it. But when the business is contracting like ours now is – well. What you are doing is forcing more work in progress into the system than you necessarily need and you are running at such a pitch that ultimately you will fall off the cliff.'

Somercotes believed that there was a fear of moving to systems which better fitted the newer circumstances. In fact, he said, there were 'political reasons' for showing 'just how much we can get out of this factory. This means that we actually overproduce.' He went on from this to tell me 'what it is like to be a production manager in this outfit' and described a situation in which the monthly cycle would typically start as it was doing that week:

'I am virtually on waiting time now because the parts and the boards I need haven't come through. I am ducking and weaving around, putting operators on jobs that we would not choose to do. This is because if I lose the hours I can't recover them.'

As each week went by there would be a 'harder and harder scrabble' to catch up on this lost time and 'by the last week and the last few days of the month everybody is going absolutely bloody mad to get the stuff into the warehouse'. I was told by various managers that to meet the month-end target it was not unknown for incomplete or faulty products to be taken into the warehouse at the last minute of the final week, only to be secretly retrieved the following Monday for completion or rectification. I heard stories, which may well have been apocryphal, of products being driven out of the gate in front of senior managers, as if they were going for delivery when, in fact, they were to be driven back into the factory once the feared director had gone home for the night.

Another broad and general example of managerial techniques and procedures showing a tendency to become self-serving was the approach often allegedly taken to reducing costs. As we will see in Chapter 8, stories about ludicrous attempts to reduce costs were central to the humour of ZTC Ryland. At this stage, however, I shall give just one illustration of the type of frustration managers across the business told me of when talking about cost-cutting attempts:

'A lot of people have a very blinkered view. Take, for instance, finance. They have got a very strict set of rules which they apply and these don't always reflect the reality of (a) being in business and (b) customer requirements. And so you get all sorts of constraints put on you. Let me give you an example. In my budget two years ago I was going to spend half a million pounds on postage to send parcels out to customers, and this was based on the volume we knew we had to do multiplied by the cost of each package; good junior school sort of stuff. The accountants said "You've got to cut your budget and Ted Meadows says that figure is too high." My response was "I don't care what Ted Meadows says, that is the figure and I stand by it." They come back, "But he still says it's too high." "OK then," I said, "cut it in half. It will make no difference." And when it came back it was a quarter of a million pounds; it had been cut in half. Now he's got his objectives, he had to cut the budget and he saw this big chunk of money. And because he doesn't understand what happens, he just arbitrarily cuts it.'

'So what did you do?', I asked.

'Nothing, I remained dignified, saying that this sort of thing is so stupid I am not prepared to discuss it. I went over budget by a quarter of a million pounds. This illustrates that somebody who is a financial whiz, no doubt, is so focused on getting a bottom line right that he is not prepared to find out what he is doing. You know, "Cut this out, cut that, three less heads"; it's quite arbitrary.'

In contrast to this broad example of means becoming detached from their ends, I would give, as an example of the myriad ways in which smaller activities could be similarly characterised, the induction procedure for people joining ZTC Ryland. I was part of a group reviewing this process and judging the success of the new practices and documents which had been designed by a 'Business Action Team'. The new induction process had thus been created by the application of this modern and 'progressive' principle of teamworking in which people from various levels in the personnel organisation had worked together to solve the problem of what had been seen as an inadequate procedure. The resulting event for the new employee lasted for a day with a group of new starters receiving a welcome and a talk about the nature and state of the business from a director in the main conference room. A high-quality folder full of information about the business and its organisational structure and about the site, its welfare provisions, the bank, the canteen and so on was provided. There was then a tour of the site. This took new employees to such locations as the personnel office, the bank, the social club, the library and the medical centre. What it did not do, however, was to take anyone into a single location in which the company's products were being designed, developed, manufactured, tested, stored or marketed. In the second half of the day the individual would go to their own department to receive an induction into the working of that department. Although each individual had been provided by the morning's activities with an effective mental map of the amenities available on the site, they had no mental map of what occurred in the various productive activities into which their own departmental efforts might be expected to link.

It is important to stress that the group which had devised this induction procedure were highly dedicated and enthusiastic and could justifiably claim that their efforts represented what one of them called a 'very professional piece of personnel practice'. And it is equally important to point out that the group received my observations about the exclusion from the tour of the 'working bits' of the factory as valuable comment and as a helpful suggestion in the spirit of 'continuous improvement'. One of the group's members said:

> 'This is culturally worrying. However well we do what we do, it is no good doing it within the walls of our own little boxes. Yeah, we've done a really professional piece of personnel work. But, in a way, we have not worked as much in the spirit of the culture we are trying to build as we should have done. We should be working to keep people out of their little boxes, not inducting them into them.'

WORKING IN LITTLE BOXES?

The notion of people in organisations confining themselves to the 'boxes' of their formal bureaucratic location is something very effectively conceptualised by the American social scientist and management researcher Rosabeth Moss Kanter (1983) as *segmentalism*, a condition which could be contrasted to that associated with successful and innovative organisations. In her study of the factors which were present in successfully innovative American companies, Kanter found what she called an 'entrepreneurial spirit' combined with a participative way of approaching problems. This leads to a structure and culture which she characterises as 'integrative'. It involves a willingness to combine ideas from unconnected sources, to 'embrace change and to seek opportunities to test limits'. Problems are seen as 'wholes related to larger wholes' (1983: 27) and such organisations 'reduce rancorous conflict and isolation between organisational units'; they 'create mechanisms for exchange of information and new ideas across organisational boundaries'; they 'ensure that multiple perspectives will be taken into account in decisions'. And, above all, they 'provide coherence and direction to the whole organisation' (1983: 28).

Segmentalism, on the other hand, involves 'compartmentalising actions, events and problems' and keeping each piece isolated from the others. Problems are seen narrowly and not as connected to other problems. Companies with segmented cultures, says Kanter, are likely to have segmented structures. And what this means is:

> a large number of compartments walled off from one another – department from department, level from level, field office from HQ, labour force from management and men from women. Even innovation tends to be given to a specialist department.

This concept of segmentalism seems to me to be a powerful one. It suggests a strong connection between behaviours, structures and culture. It recognises a culture in which 'them and us' distinctions exist not just between senior and junior people, but between members of different functions, departments, and genders. It suggests a particular way of looking at the world. It is a world of people operating, as my colleague put it, within the walls of their 'own little boxes'. This was precisely what the founders of

ZTC had wanted to avoid. But it was a condition prevalent within the company. The enormous investment in the 'Developing Organisational Capability' programme was intended to encourage people to think holistically; to consider how they could contribute to achieving the 'strategic intent'; to look for ways of bringing their 'core competencies' to bear on solving problems faced by the business; to subscribe to a 'winning culture' in which responsiveness to customers came before sectional loyalty or functional interests. The winning culture, at least in its original form, had prioritised 'bringing people together'. These words were written on the plastic cards which everybody was meant to carry around. They were, in effect, an invitation to leap the walls of the departmental and functional boxes.

The logic originally adopted by ZTC of following the principle of 'realised strategy' (actively working towards the strategic intent, as opposed to following a strategic plan), of developing a simple but flexible set of structures (the integrated grading structure, for example) and of managing through values and culture rather than command and constraint was consistent with Kanter's pattern of the integrative organisation. It was a logic which would have helped ZTC cope with the unexpected changes in circumstance which were always likely to arise and could have made it less prone to the worst excesses of the paradox of consequences; the problems of means becoming ends in themselves. But, as we have seen, things did not work out in this way. Many of the managers in ZTC Ryland had, however, been influenced by the culture change programmes in which they had been involved. As we saw in the last chapter, they had two contrasting discourses available to them, two languages in which they could talk about and address the day-to-day problems they met. Their familiarity with the language of the newer management ideas meant that they were well equipped to analyse problems in the way the company was being run. They did not have the concept of segmentalism to draw on when doing such analyses, as far as I was aware, but much of what they talked about when reflecting on the key issues needing attention in the company resonated with Kanter's concept and the insights it encapsulates.

In my core interviews with managers I asked them all, towards the end of the interview, what they would treat as their priorities if they found themselves in the position of 'taking over the company tomorrow'. Tommy Bulwell spoke in terms which suggest a considerable sensitivity to the dangers of means becoming ends in themselves. He said that there was a danger that on taking over the company he would instigate 'yet another investigation' into what happens, implying that many of the various 'reports we write, the business managers' reports, the soft reports', together with the 'levels of authorisation and delegation', achieved little. What was needed, instead, was simply to 'free up managers to manage'. He pointed to an inconsistency in Paul Syston's behaviour. On the one hand he was 'tightening up on authorisation' while on the other, he was saying 'God help the one that takes three months to get to me'. What this meant was that people were 'fiddling the dates on all sorts of things'. Therefore:

> 'I would try to remove every single constraint which is making people compete with each other instead of fighting the outside world. There is a hell of a lot of defending your patch and diverting attention away from the outside world.'

A constant theme was the need to focus attention much more on customers and to combine this with more 'talking to people' rather than working through systems and documents. Geoff Clifton spoke of the 'communication process' being vital and how 'DOC started the process of opening this up, but nothing has happened'. He went on:

> 'I would then start hacking away at some of these weighty procedures and processes and documentation which just slow the whole process down. I am just having to review a twenty-two page document which tells you how to put a change in a requirement specification; twenty-two bloody pages! I thought, "how can I condense it?" and then I thought, "why should I condense it, why is it there in the first place?" The reason is very apparent. We have organised ourselves into functional cells and communications between those functional cells is by bits of paper. So a guy wants a change doing. We know it is going to affect the product, the market, the way we make it, the way we design it. What we could do is ask who is the focal point for deciding whether or not this change goes in (by and large, it is the business planning and marketing guy who takes the rap for it). We would then put it in, make a proposal. He can then say "justify it" – across the table. OK, so we see an impact on manufacturing. So I pick up the telephone and I say let's talk about it. After two days we could decide if this is a goer or not. But instead of this, we have a process where this piece of paper goes from here to there for this person's comments and that person's signature. Three months later we still don't know whether we can do it. Lots of paper has been generated and a lot of time has been wasted, and you might have lost the market opportunity. You are too late.'

His recipe was therefore:

> 'Processes, procedures: let's try and reduce them. You do need structure but you do not need it to be so rigid that you can't breath without writing it in some form, 1 2 3, a b c.'

Geoff Clifton was anxious to encourage people to recognise the broader business implications of specific practices like the maintaining of certain levels of work in progress:

> 'The next thing I would address would be recognising that we are a manufacturing company and that what goes through that door pays for all of us. I would want to pull up the floor-boards and ask why we have got such high levels of work in progress. I don't understand it. They tell me they can't change it. I cannot see that it is more than that is the way we have always done it.'

This was clearly a matter of seeing certain practices existing as ends in themselves. The level of work in progress did not serve any end beyond doing things according to tradition, it is suggested. Alan Bridgford took the view that much of the very organisation of ZTC existed for reasons other than ones contributing to business effectiveness. His priority would be:

> '. . . to bang my head on organisation and say that I do not believe that we are thoroughly organised in a sensible way. I think we are organised partly on "How can we find this guy a job?". Following the merger of ZEC and Parry and there was a lot of "This little bit can stay in place, that little bit can go over there". I was amazed that when ZTC was first formed that they did not bite the bullet there and then. The Stock Market was expecting it, the industry was expecting it. We should have cut something like 5,000 to 10,000 jobs. We should have closed a number of sites and both rationalised and slimmed ourselves down.'

Many of the managers, especially those at a more senior level, spoke of, as one put it, 'needing to lift our eyes up from the detail' to look at questions about what the business was producing, and why. Ken Donnington, for example, gave his priority:

> 'It would be asking which way are we going: what are the new products and what are we going to do? Are we doing new things or developing existing ones or fattening the cow or what? We have got to go one way or another; we can't hedge our bets. That's what's happening, though. It is criminal really.'

Mary Southwell suggested that it was widely felt among employees that 'so much money is spent on unnecessary things'. She included here the various company newspapers, the 'posh cars and all these dos' and also my own involvement in the company! The ritualism of life in the company bothered Mary and she tried to discourage her staff from working in such a style:

> 'There are a lot of people doing things because that was the way things were done historically. I am always telling my staff, "Stop and think why. Don't just photocopy because it always was". I say when they inherit a job, "Ask 'why is it done this way?'"'.'

Dick Eastwood was especially radical about reviewing activities:

> 'I would take a wall as big as this one and draw on it the complete structure of the business, everything from top to bottom. I'd then order a box of red pens and I would put a circle around all the bloody things that aren't necessary. I would streamline the operation. I have already threatened to do this. I don't think anybody anywhere has that picture. So you would ask, "Why is that then? Why is that there? Why are there two of those, one there and one there? What do they do?" That would be really something, wouldn't it? You'd say "Your box has just gone off the chart".'

Eastwood then referred to a report prepared by a consultancy company, before moving on to some fundamental strategic issues, ones which we saw being confronted by a group of managers towards the end of the last chapter (some months later than the following words were spoken, however):

'There is a suggestion that a customer's order goes through fourteen sets of hands before it comes to manufacturing. My great big chart would help me sort that out.

'I think, and this is absolute heresy this is, I might sit back for a time and work out what the company was about: whether we are manufacturers or just providers of solutions and not necessarily hardware. This would fit the history of this site. When I came here we used to make paint, we used to make metalwork bits, we used to make screws, we used to make cables, we used to make wooden cabinets. As technologies changed we have moved, so that our major skill is in electronics. We stopped all windings. We are not into windings, we are into electronics. Now, you may reach a stage where you say, "We do not want to make coils. We do not want to make cabinets. Do we really want to make equipment at all? Should we just buy it in and just make systems and do system tests?".'

Throughout the general statements about what each individual would do to change the company, there were specific illustrations of the sorts of problem which needed to be overcome. Harry Basford, for example, having spoken of his priorities as 'changing how we deal with customers and emphasising the importance of developing people' gave a specific instance of what worried him:

'There are some very worrying things about how we deal with customers. I had a business contact who does a lot of business with us who said that they would give us first go at a contract – a networked PABX. I got on to the relevant person who said, "I'll see to it." A week later I got another call from my contact, saying they had heard nothing. I pushed it again but another week later I had a call saying they could not wait any longer. So we lost it. The reaction here when I raised it at board level was that they didn't like me criticising another senior manager.'

Jim Somercotes also connected means–ends issues to managerial politics. He would prioritise problems over materials which, he believed, were largely out of control. But, he felt:

'You can't point the finger to a particular group of people and say, "They have cocked it up".'

However, when I pressed Somercotes on why it was that, by his account, there was £33 million worth of inventory on the site, 20 per cent of which was 'dead and redundant', he asked me to switch off my tape recorder. He then explained that the forecasting system which had in large part led to this state of affairs had been established by an individual who was now one of the senior directors and who was unwilling to accept criticism of 'his effing system'.

Examples of problems like this grounded the generalisations offered by managers about how they would change the company and, taken together, they confirmed in a multitude of ways the impression that managers were conscious of jobs, structures, systems, procedures and behaviours in ZTC existing for ends other than the overall quality of performance of 'the business'. And, it was often stressed, the poor performance of the business was in the interest of nobody.

THE POWER OF SYMBOLS: SECURITY LOCKS AND MOTOR CARS

About half-way through the time I was at ZTC Ryland, security locks appeared on the doors of many of the office buildings across the site. To gain entry to a building one had to know its code. Every two weeks the occupants of a particular building, or a section of a building, would be given a new code. There was considerable speculation about the reasons for this development. The official story was simply that the corporate headquarters had instructed the site engineer to fit these locks to improve commercial security. In effect, however, many people saw the innovation as one which 'locked them into' their various little boxes. The first day they were in operation I stood with a group of manufacturing supervisors ('team leaders') waiting to be told over the newly installed door-phone the code required to get into an engineering building. Among a variety of scornful comments was:

> 'The buggers have never wanted to talk to us. And just as we are getting them to think about design for manufacture, they go and ruddy lock us out.'

My own office at that time was in a building which mainly housed engineering and business planning offices, and the most popular explanation among the people I heard talking about the new locks was that they had been installed in response to complaints from staff that 'hourly paids' had been coming into the building in their dirty overalls to use the staff lavatories. This, we might say, was an expression of the unofficial culture of an organisation which had at the centre of its new official culture the principles of 'harmonisation' and a 'classless society' (see p. 116). When I pointed out the irony of this, in a conversation with several of the directors who worked on the site, one of them said 'It was nothing to do with us', to which another replied, 'You've got to admit, though, in cultural terms it is a real own-goal.' In response to my argument that you could hardly argue for the necessity to the 'winning culture' of 'bringing people together' and then introduce devices which seemed to epitomise the idea that people on the site could not and should not trust each other, it was suggested, 'Oh, they never thought of that. The idea is to keep outsiders who get onto the site from getting into the buildings.'

Symbols are key elements in the expression of any culture. In their impact as bearers of a cultural message undermining the principles of the espoused new culture of equality, the door-locks seemed to me to be rivalled only by the allocation to managers of company cars. Being someone almost as ignorant about motor cars as I am uninterested in them,

I was never able to fully understand the way many of my colleagues could work out the place in the managerial pecking order of any given individual by reference to the make, size, engine capacity and so on of their car. It was pointed out to me more than once that the individuals who were most identified with the policy of harmonisation were, as one woman manager put it, no less 'infected with the "what car does he drive" syndrome' than any others.

It was this same manager, Jane Lowdham, whom I was speaking to one day in the corridor of one of the office buildings when the topic of difficulties she was having with an accountant in the finance function arose. Midway through speculating about the extent to which the problem was caused by the normal tensions between her function and that of finance, and the extent to which it was because 'he finds it difficult to relate to women', the 'man himself' as Jane put it, appeared further down the corridor. 'Let's go and catch him, so you can see what you think.' Racing down the corridor in pursuit of the man, we failed to catch up with him before he went through one of the doors into the finance offices. The door clicked shut precisely as we arrived at it. We could not get through it –we did not know the code of the lock. 'Oh, we'll forget it,' said Jane: 'He's safely locked in his fortress.'

What had been referred on another occasion as 'little boxes' had, on this occasion, become a matter of 'fortresses'. The existence of the locks was symbolically reinforcing tensions between finance and the marketing function in this case, just as it was the tension between design and manufacturing in the earlier case where the design engineers were referred to as 'locking out' manufacturing people.

TICK-LISTS, BELLS AND WHISTLES AND 'NO IN SPADES'

Criticisms of the design engineers were made not only by manufacturing managers, however. A common criticism was that the engineers were too prone to designing products which enabled them to demonstrate their engineering talent for its own sake, rather than showing how it could be a means towards better satisfying customers. A marketing manager said, for example:

> 'They think we can sell on tick-lists. They have this idea that if we say to customers, "the system can do this, and this and this", then they will want it, regardless of cost. How do we get them to realise that you've got to start from what the customers want, and to realise that customers can actually be put off by too many features.'

A common theme of concern among managers was the lack in the business systems part of the organisation of new products. They often pointed out that a great deal of time, money and effort had gone into the 'Hornet project', a telephone system which one man described as having 'all the bells and whistles that you can imagine. But it was far too expensive and it was far too late.' A parallel was drawn by various people with other major British engineering developments, such as the early warning apparatus developed for the British Nimrod aircraft, where projects had been cancelled after enormous investment because they 'tried to do too much'. 'It's the British engineering culture' said one senior manager, himself a former engineer:

'We've got to move from an engineering-led culture to a market-led one. If railway engineers think they can run the trains because they like running trains, rather than running them for passengers, then they will end up out of a job. And it's the same with our people. They have got to learn the lesson that telephone systems are used by people, and not by engineers who like playing with the bloody things. Look at this telephone on my desk. It's got a calculator on it. Who would possibly want a calculator on their telephone? We sold plenty of these. But the cost was higher because of all the tick-list goodies that people probably hardly ever used. We wouldn't get away with that in today's market-place.'

And if anyone ever wanted evidence about the need for telephones to be simple, then I would be well-placed to provide it, by reporting how common I found it to be for managers in ZTC Ryland to be unable to use their own office telephones fully! Because I often interviewed managers in their own offices it became necessary to divert calls to another office, or to the individual's secretary. I was astonished how often it was the case, in the very company that had made the telephones, that managers did not know how to use the most basic 'extra' functions on them. This was ironic in itself, at the level of managers not knowing about their own products, but it was also ironic in that such difficulties could have provided such a powerful marketing lesson to the management as a whole. But perhaps this is precisely the point; there was no such thing as a 'management as a whole'. The non-engineering managers, who had problems with their telephones, rarely discussed such matters as 'the product' with the engineering managers – who presumably did know how their telephones worked.

Alan Bridgford, who seemed to be to one of the most strategically aware of the managers I met in ZTC Ryland, was very worried that the structure of the company was inappropriate for the sort of business that telecommunications was becoming. The whole drift of technology, he argued, was towards the integration of the various 'elements' of a telecommunication system. Yet ZTC was developing these elements as if they were 'owned' by the part of the organisational structure which produced them, instead of their being conceived and developed to provide 'integrated solutions' to customers. He illustrated this:

'If a customer turns up tomorrow, and this actually happened. . . . Well, we had a tender in from an underground railway company. He said, "What I want is to buy some CMUXs from you and I want to buy some 140 megabit line systems and I want a network management system.'' The answer is no, because those elements have never been designed to be managed. My job is to manage elements that have not been conceived as going with others in the overall system. I have got one interface out of CMUX and a completely different style of interface out of the 140 megabits – because 140 megabits is point-to-point. This customer wants a turnkey solution. Now if this was a product called Hercules – a pan-European railway telecoms system where the customer is saying, "I think what I want is some system Xs, I want some ISSXs, I want some transmission kit, I want it all brought together and I want it managed as an overall system" – the answer is no in spades now. This is because the businesses do not have a way forward in terms of how we manage all of our products in ZTC. We don't even do it within the business, let alone between them. It is a question of a strategy of how our products relate to each other and how we can sell all these products together in a world-wide turnkey style market.'

DIFFERENTIATION AND INTEGRATION: THE PERSONNEL FUNCTION

Organisational structures follow the logic of a division of labour, as ZTC have done by dividing themselves into several main 'businesses' and then by further sub-dividing the efforts in these businesses into various specialisms, departments and functions. But, as I said earlier, these divisions are only means towards the end of the effective performance of the whole organisation. The *differentiation* of an organisation into various compartments has always to be accompanied by efforts at *integration*, to ensure that the efficiencies gained by the compartmentalising are not lost and strategic effectiveness threatened in the way that Alan Bridgford was concerned about (cf. Lawrence and Lorsch 1967).

The personnel function of an organisation is a facet of the division of labour of the modern organisation, in that it specialises in various employment aspects of the broad management task, so relieving general managers of some of the employee-related tasks they would otherwise have to carry out. But the personnel function, if it is one with more than an old-fashioned welfare role in the organisation, also has a particular role in bringing about the integration of the organisation. This tends to bring it into tension with non-personnel managers.

The tensions and conflicts which frequently arise between personnel and other managers have been closely analysed in previous studies by Karen Legge (1978) and by myself (Watson 1977). These tensions were as strong in ZTC Ryland as in any organisation I have ever investigated. Such tensions have in large part to be understood, I have argued previously (Watson 1977, 1986), as resulting from the way that the personnel function has a particularly integrative and strategic role to play which brings it into conflict with managers who have both more specific (departmental, say) goals to fulfil and more short-term (output, say) tasks to carry out. Thus, for example, the personnel department has to develop the workforce as a whole through training. But when they go to departmental managers to release a particular individual to go on a course, those managers may resist losing that individual's services at that time. The tension between the long-term and the short-term thus becomes manifest through a tension between line managers and personnel managers. To take another example, a departmental manager may wish to pay a bonus to staff which that department's budget can afford. But the personnel manager has to veto it because it would lead to wage claims in other departments, which would not be able to afford them. In this case the tension between departmental priorities and the wage costs of the organisation as a whole become manifest in a similar departmental–personnel conflict. As I have said:

> The ultimate rationale of the personnel department is one of keeping the organisation as a whole going on a long-term basis through maintaining the staffing resource and coping with the conflicts and contradictions which arise wherever and whenever people are employed. But this long-term or more *strategic* emphasis and the necessity of constantly keeping in mind the state of the organisation as a whole can clash with the more specific short-term and sectional priorities of managers who are less concerned with what is ultimately the organisation's most problematic aspect: its human element.
>
> (Watson 1986: 195).

What this recognises, in sociological terms, is a structural conflict in the sense that the division of responsibilities creates a potential for people to clash with each other. It is a conflict which can be managed more or less well, and how well it is managed will be influenced by the broad cultural context of the organisation as well as by both the personal characteristics and the interpersonal skills of the people involved. At ZTC Ryland the tensions were considerable, with frequent and sometimes bitter clashes occurring between personnel and other managers. Many managers commented that there were positive and helpful members of the personnel department, but that there were a number of people who were arrogant and 'reluctant ever to come out of their ivory towers'; others who were 'well-meaning but because they came straight from college do not understand the realities of shopfloor life' and yet others who 'see personnel as a good area to make their mark and prove how bloody wonderful their theories are'.

The personnel function contained the organisation development function and was responsible for many of the important innovations occurring on human resourcing issues. But it was far from uncommon for managers to say that whilst they agreed with the spirit of many of these innovations, they were suspicious of them because they found the motives of some of the key personnel innovators suspect:

'They are far more interested in steam-rollering in these new things so that they can move on in their careers than they are in trying to understand people and show them how these new ideas will advantage everybody.'

A big problem facing the personnel function was that it was simultaneously trying to introduce 'progressive' policies – changing the culture to meet the principles of the *empowerment, skills and growth* discourse which we examined in Chapter 5 – and policing the organisation as the agents of those who operated terms of the alternative *control, costs and jobs* discourse. This meant, as one personnel manager put it:

'I hear plenty slagging off of Personnel. Because we are seen as having this traditional role which involves blocking people on things like recruitment and forcing them on things like redundancy, we are not appreciated when we attempt to take barriers away so that they can manage better. The Personal Development Programme and the Business Improvement Plan are seen as things done to them, rather than as things enabling them to manage better.'

A common complaint among managers was that the personnel department was far too big and that it did not take its fair share of cuts, especially redundancies, when these were applied elsewhere. The department was described by one as 'a great black hole sucking in and spewing out paperwork'; another commented that 'too much time is spent on record-keeping, paper-pushing and information-gathering and not enough on dealing with people and getting new ideas under way'. The theme of means coming to be ends in themselves can readily be inferred from many of these kinds of statement about the personnel function. Such a notion was colourfully expressed to me:

'I have this theory that if you connect enough computers up they don't compute anything because they spend so long talking to each other. If you connect enough personnel people up they don't personnel anything because they spend too long talking to each other. This is cynical, I suppose, but I don't understand why they don't relate.'

This individual, like a lot of others, spoke of the need which they had of a *service* from personnel. But they often felt that they were getting too little of this and that what they were getting was far too expensive. A popular view among manufacturing managers was that each main manu-facturing area might have its own personnel officer. This would save on overheads, but it was also seen, I suspect, as a way of removing one of the major sources of constraint on how the managers went about their daily tasks.

One development in the sphere of personnel management which was strongly welcomed by many managers was the changing approach to industrial relations. This was, again, in part welcomed because it involved a limiting on the constraints imposed on the freedom of managers 'to manage their own patch' – this time by the trade unions, rather than by the personnel function. However, there was also a welcome for the move away from time-wasting and what one engineering manager called the 'empty ritual' of the way wage negotiations had previously been carried out. The management would have 'a mandate for 8 per cent', he explained, 'so they come along to the union and offer 6 per cent and the union argue it up to six and three-quarters and they don't accept this but go along and argue it somewhere else and it could become 7 per cent and a bit and they know when they get towards the end of procedure there is half a per cent'. The effect of this was that it 'proved to everybody on the shop floor or anywhere in this business that "the union get me my dues"':

> ' "The union cracked them in the end, you know," people would say; "the union sorted them – the company would have got away with 5 per cent but for the unions. I owe my allegiance to the unions." Today there is a difference, and people are beginning to realise that the company when it says something means it; it is going to do it. It might have several attempts at it [laughs] . . . but sooner or later it is going to do it. If you walk round here now and talk to people, they have that impression that, say, the management is going to declare a CR [compulsory redundancy]; the management is going to name people. And they really expect the management to name them, whereas two years ago they would not.'

As one personnel manager put it, 'We used to put all this effort into employee relations problems which, in the end, simply had the effect of creating more industrial relations problems.' This was surely, if ever there was one, a case of the paradox of consequences – of means coming to subvert the ends for which they were designed – with an aspect of personnel work coming to exacerbate the very problems it was meant to reduce. 'We have', he said, 'broken out of that vicious circle at least.' However, he did not believe that there was necessarily any 'real shift of power' towards the management in any of this:

> 'Sure, we are on top in some ways at the moment. They can't block us on everything we want to do. But they are still trying to trip us up wherever they think they can get away with it. Just think what will happen if we are not careful when, sorry if, business starts to boom again.'

Here, we see a suggestion that the most basic manifestation of segmentalism, a 'them and us' relationship between the management and its workforce, was endemic in the company, in spite of all the efforts to 'develop people', 'empower people' and create a 'winning culture'.

FADS, FANCIES AND GOING THROUGH THE MOTIONS

I am conscious of there being an element of the tragic in the story I am telling. If we were to see ZTC as a Shakespearean character rather than as a business organisation, we would see our hero starting out from a difficult birth to take on the world with a sense of what Macbeth called a 'vaulting ambition, which o'erleaps itself'. From being a minor player on the world stage, our character sets out to become one of the five dominant world figures. But not only do circumstances on that world stage turn out to be less auspicious than was hoped for, but some flaw deep within our hero's character holds him back from meeting his dreamed of destiny. I say 'he' and not 'she' here because I simply cannot see ZTC as a she. Yet might it not be that we have a character confused about whether they want to be a hard *he*, who ruthlessly cuts costs and axes 'heads', or a soft *she*, who nurtures skills and 'empowers' her children?

Rather than getting caught up in gender metaphors, perhaps we would do better to go back to a notion of a clash of languages or discourses? To switch back and forth between two languages is not a problem in itself. To be bilingual is possibly to be better placed to survive in the world than to be monolingual. But what if it is a matter of 'speaking with a forked tongue'? Now that is dangerous. People come not to trust you and will not cooperate with you. A good degree of that has certainly happened to our hero. But perhaps the problem is even worse; what if our hero is 'hearing voices'? One minute a voice says, 'Build people up, look after them' and the next minute another voice says 'Off with their heads'. To borrow the words of King Lear, 'that way madness lies'.

This is perhaps going too far; portraying ZTC as a mad and tragic character. But I did hear people talking about ZTC as a 'sick company' and I did hear it said 'they must be mad', as the company continued to act in seemingly self-contradictory ways, claiming to be 'developing' people and encouraging 'personal growth' at the same time as people were kept well aware that an axe was continually hovering over their heads. To talk in this way is perhaps going too far, in that it is treating an organisation as a being which is in some way 'mad' because it is inconsistent when, in reality, no organisation is a being or an entity. To personify the organisation is to forget that organisations are always coalitions of interests which fight out their different positions. Indeed, that is the theoretical position on which this study is based. But another part of the theoretical position taken here is one that implies that nobody can ever really know what they are doing in managing an organisation, given the boundedness of their own rationality and the terrifyingly ambiguous nature of the world. And, to revert undeterred to my metaphor of ZTC as a tragic dramatic hero, we can see the company as getting into severe difficulties in trying to cope with a difficult and challenging world because it is too unsure of itself and of what language it needs to speak to make clear sense of its situation.

The outcome of this incipient madness is a descent into 'going through the motions' in the range of ways we have reviewed in this chapter. So many of the activities undertaken were potentially appropriate means of achieving long-term business survival, but so many of them ended up being ritualistically acted out as ends in themselves. The term 'going through the motions' was one which I heard used by managers of a variety of different managerial activities which they knew could have much greater effect than they were in fact having. Consider the words, for example, of a senior manager who argued strongly for the value of managers carrying out regular appraisal interviews with their employees, something which all ZTC Ryland managers were formally required to do:

> 'I get the impression that a lot of people are just going through the routine. Appraisal does not have the commitment of the directors. I have not been appraised in years. And nothing happens as a result of it and so employees regard it as a bit of a fag and the manager regards it as a bit of a fag. So the two of them go through the sometimes embarrassing routine of something they know at the end of the day is bloody meaningless.'

I found managers frequently saying that they believed in such things as teamworking or Total Quality Management but worried about how these tended to become 'flavours of the month', 'hypy things', 'more fads with fancy names' rather than, as Don Littleover put it, 'the sort of thing you do naturally as part of being a good manager'. Littleover went on to suggest:

> 'There is a sort of disease here. And it could be the death of us. We set out to do some really good things. DOC was brilliant. It really worked at building the sort of culture a business like this needs. BIP was completely necessary. It is common sense. TQM seems to me the only reasonable way to manage a high-tech operation. Team briefing's a good idea, problem-solving teams are a good idea. But look at what we do with all these things. We give them a fancy name, we hype them up. We over-egg the pudding with launches and posters and pamphlets and glossy brochures and pocket-cards. People expect the world. It is as if the company grabs at every good idea that comes along and treats it as if it were a magic fad, a new cure-all. If only we would take these management good ideas to heart and incorporate into some basic hard work. Then we would get there. Instead of that we keep chasing rainbows; going through the motions without thinking out properly what we are doing things for.'

In these words, one of ZTC's own managers is offering a powerful critique of his own company. He sets the criticisms within the notion of what 'good managers' naturally do. This implies that he has a concept, a theory even, of what being a 'good manager' entails. In the next chapter we will look at the theories that managers hold about their work, in the sense of ideas which underpin their practice, or which might underpin their practice were they free to manage in the way they suggest they would prefer.

Chapter 7

Managing Management
Theory, practice and emotion

'I wouldn't regard myself as someone who has ever been trained to be a manager. I was thrown in at the deep end when I began. I didn't know how I was going to survive – sink or swim, like. I suppose I knew I could hack it at the end of the day though, using my native wits and all that. I think I soon learned to manage.'

'To manage?'

'To keep my head above water. Oh I didn't mean to "be a manager" in the sense you are talking about. I mean just surviving to the end of the week, or the month more like, without getting into too much trouble or upsetting too many folk.'

'But is that really different from "being a manager"?'

'Perhaps it isn't. I don't know. I must admit that in spite of all the courses I've been on and all that management book stuff that I've swallowed, I still rely on my wits, my devastating charm, to do the job. Sometimes I think I haven't learned anything and other times I think that I am learning all the time. I don't think I am as likely to sink beneath the tide as I might have been early on.'

'You're a better swimmer than you were?'

'I like that: learning to manage is like learning to swim. It's sort of instinctive but you still need to learn; perhaps not learn, but become more confident. Yes, you get confidence as you try out different things and as you find that you can get on with people. I don't think I've learned that much on the management courses except that there aren't book answers. I've got confidence from the courses; largely from being with other managers who are in the same boat as yourself. You get on with these people and you get to think "Yeah I can hack this as well as the best of them".'

'What did you mean by "finding that you can get on with people"?'

'OK. Let me think a minute. I like the swimming idea but it's also like learning to speak. You need speaking, speech I mean, to relate to people and to get your way don't you? But you are always developing that skill aren't you? You go from mumbling to speaking in sentences. I'm quite good at joined-up talking. Don't get me wrong. I'm not saying that I manage by bullshitting. I am not that kind of person. I talk to people all the time. I am building relationships, yeah? I'm not just surface charm you know [laughing]; you've got to be sincere or they'll soon rumble you, whether it's a big customer or an ordinary board-stuffer – especially the ordinary board-stuffer, come to that.'

LEARNING TO MANAGE AND MANAGING TO LEARN

Gordon Radcliffe, in answering a question I put to him about the management training he received, talks in terms close to one of my own main themes; that of managerial work being about managing not only in the formal sense of doing the work of a 'manager' but also in the sense of coping, or 'managing to survive'. His words suggest that learning to be a manager involves a great deal more than receiving a formal training in management. One is learning and adapting all the time. Like many of the other managers with whom I discussed training, there is a recognition of the value of formal management training, but a greater stress on its function as, for example, a booster of confidence rather than as a direct source of skills or knowledge. This can be related to the argument presented earlier that managers have a sense that being a manager is not just a matter of what you know or even of what you can do, but is tied into a concept of what 'sort of person you are', a key part of the individual's process of strategic exchange with the world around them. This appeared to be an important concept to managers when we looked at their orientation to work in Chapter 3 and focused on their concern with personal control and the apparent need of the individual to relate their approach to managerial work to their personal concept of self.

Gordon Radcliffe takes up a further theme which plays an important part in this study; that of the role of language in the carrying out of managerial work. He introduced the intriguing concept – which is new to me at least – of 'joined up talking' to imply the manager's need for a sophisticated level of linguistic skill. But he seemed anxious not to imply that he used his own skill in this area in a superficial or manipulative way ('bullshitting', 'surface charm'). There is indeed a moral tone in his reference to sincerity and building relationships. But this moral concern is one related to a simple pragmatism. To be insincere is to risk being 'rumbled', whether by a customer or a woman shopfloor worker (the 'ordinary board-stuffer').

The theme of a marriage of the moral and the pragmatic suggested by Radcliffe's words and the further tying-in of this with the individual's concept of self is something which we can see running through managers' accounts of how they learned to *manage management*. Later we will see this theme playing a part in the way that managers 'theorise' about their work, before going on to relate these issues to the importance of trust in organisational relationships.

The provision of management training, development and education in ZTC seemed to me to be at as a high a level as, if not at a higher level than, in any other large British company. The managers with whom I discussed training referred to a considerable range of different activities in which they engaged, ranging from Diploma in Management Studies and

Master of Business Administration courses studied by part-time and block release, to a series of one-week custom-designed courses, 'Management One, Two and Three', provided by a major University Business School, to more focused courses on planning techniques, total quality management, team-building and developing self awareness. Use was also made of adventure training, where managers were sent to Scotland to climb mountains and swim in the ice-cold sea. Universities, consultants, as well as their own management development specialists and experienced managers were used as resources to deliver this range of provision. However, as might be expected from the picture painted in the last chapter of an unsystematic approach in the company to the appraisal process (one function of which is meant to be highlighting the appropriate development activity for each person), there seemed to be little pattern in the allocation of managers to courses. This was something Terry Carlton hoped would change as the company began to take appraisal and career development more seriously. He explained that the company had tended to have 'the sheep-dip kind of culture'. There was:

> '. . . a menu of courses where they had to nominate people. I always got nominated. "He's a bright lad; let's put him on this course." Whether this had any relation to my capability or my needs did not come into it. I didn't really take it seriously.'

Carlton said that early on in his managerial career the training received was 'absolutely zero'. After ten years he got 'bucketfuls of the stuff', which he thought was 'all back to front'. Other individuals spoke of identifying needs for themselves and having to fight to get onto courses. Phil Wollaton spoke of being sent on 'Management One, you know the basic Lego course'. The course

> '. . . wasn't readily offered. I had to push. It was sort of there and you could insist you went on it and people would then say "there's been a cancellation – you can go on it now."'

Generally, managers were rather ambivalent about the courses they had attended. There was a suspicion that a course was really something of, as one man put it, 'a jolly'. Courses were, in the words of another, 'definitely seen as a good thing, but nobody is quite sure of what it is they are good for'. Geoff Clifton had concluded that courses tended to 'overlap with each other; you get fed up with building things out of Lego'. In attempting to identify what it was that courses were 'good for', managers often spoke of them helping build personal confidence and, through enabling them to mix with people from other companies or other parts of their own company, preventing the individual from 'becoming insular'. Confidence could be boosted by finding out that 'other people are facing the same problems as you', by learning that 'nobody has the right answers so your stab at them is as good as the next bloke's'. Dick Eastwood was especially appreciative of the opportunity to develop his confidence in giving formal presentations ('never underestimate how nerve-wracking many people find that, however senior or experienced they are'). He passed on what he saw as an invaluable rule: 'I'll always remember what the trainer on this said: "it doesn't matter whatever happens, even if your trousers fall down: you do not apologise when giving a presentation".'

Courses involving managers from other parts of ZTC were seen as helpful in establishing contacts, and even something more:

'These courses have been very useful. Some of it has been a bit Janet and John. But, overall, it is valuable – if nothing else, because you are with a group of your peers. It's a strange thing that you can work with people every day of your life, but when you have been on a course with them, well two years later you see them in the yard and it's, "Hale fellow, well met". There's a strange bond when you've been on a course together, especially off-site. I don't understand this but it's true.'

A common theme among managers was that the significant management learning came from a process of trial and error after you had been 'thrown in at the deep end' (a popular phrase in this context). One not only learned from one's own successes and failures but by looking at others, especially at senior managers one worked with:

'Of course you have got other managers around you and above you. You ask yourself, "Do I look like him? I wouldn't like to look like him for all the tea in China."'

Some managers spoke of particular experienced individuals with whom they had set up informal mentoring relationships, and this seemed to be especially important with the women managers. Sometimes managers could identify people on whom they had partly modelled their own behaviour:

'I have watched a lot of people, a lot of managers. I have worked with some absolutely brilliant, absolutely super managers. The biggest influence on my career was a guy called Dan Stanton. He was very much a people's manager; he always had the time of day to spend just a few moments talking to him or her, saying "How's your wife?", "Is your mother any better?", "How are your kids today?". He did that every day. He walked round his patch with me in tow. I learned more during that six to nine-month period about people management than ever before. The only thing that he had that I hadn't was a memory for people's names. He used to say, "Is your 'arry all right?", or "Is your Joan all right?", or "How's your young Simon?" I have to say, "Is your husband all right?", or "Is your littl'un OK?" I felt that that gave the individuals a little bit of closeness to him. I thought that was super.'

Sometimes 'lessons remembered' were more specific, and not necessarily easily received at first;

'I was influenced by various people. One case is old Joe, a superintendent I worked for who was fiery and loudmouthed – but anybody would do anything for him, the total opposite to Ted. I'll never forget him and I remember coming back after a two-week course and within the first five minutes I got an almighty bollocking: "Production is down." "But I wasn't here." "That's got nothing to do with it: you are in charge of the department and the production is your responsibility." I saw eventually what this means: it is irrelevant whether you are there or not. You should have it all tied up so that it will carry on without you when you are away.'

A number of managers related the length or the complexity of the learning process to the need to build up through experience an ability to adapt responses to varying circumstances, and especially to the circumstance of human individual differences. One senior man said:

'I am still learning. I think it is mainly by experience and no other way. I burnt my fingers a few times and thought perhaps that is not the route to do it. Gradually over a period of time you build up this experience. You have got to recognise that each unit within the human resource is different and you have to learn quickly to learn the differences. I learned a lot here being a purchase expeditor, because each supplier you dealt with had a representative on the other end of the phone and they all reacted to different approaches. Some of them wanted a big stick, some of them wanted coaxing, some of them wanted jollying along, some of them wanted avoiding and so on. I am now doing all this with the team I am pulling together: where they are weak and where I can leave them to get on with it.'

The other unique circumstance at the heart of the learning process is managers themselves. Nick Attenborough spoke of picking up principles from the courses he attended. The course would 'apply a principle to us all' but 'we each modify that principle or that procedure or that learning to suit ourselves and we discard a lot of it, accepting just a bit of it'. He said something similar with regard to learning from 'your own manager'. You observe how they do things, but how you operate relates to 'the sort of person you are'. Attenborough illustrated this by referring to 'other managers who will wait for things to come through to them from back in the chain'. Attenborough would not do this: 'I go and chase up to see what the problem is and what can be done about it.' And this was because 'I am the sort of person who sees my patch as part of something bigger. Others don't.' Henry Dunkirk, a very different style of manager, and one who prided himself on his outspokenness and truthfulness, also spoke in terms of drawing on observations of others within the process of shaping his unique self; 'I think you pick up pieces from everybody you work for, the good and the bad, but you mould yourself into the way you think'.

Many of the other statements made to me about what was learned from management courses can also be fitted into the idea of the individual 'moulding' or shaping themselves as they confront different experiences in their managerial lives. There were references to 'picking up things' which 'bubble under' and then 'come to the surface when you need them' and there was more than one reference to a subconscious process of learning occurring on courses. Andy Tollerton gave a useful account of the sort of process alluded to by various managers. When 'you get back from the course', he explained, 'you ask what you have learned and realise that, specifically, it is nothing – apart from understanding':

> 'You don't come back and say on the Monday morning, "I've got to do this" or "I've got to change that". But you obviously do learn and these things come back to you. They come into play later on. Courses don't help you turn the world over. They give you things to think about, even if you don't agree with what is being said.'

I asked Tollerton if he could illustrate this. He cited a course run by a large consulting company called 'Results through People'. It had, he said, been 'originally designed for salesmen, but had been modified for managers on the grounds that a manager's job is to sell themselves'. He said:

> 'There were two things stuck with me. First, there was psycho-cybernetics: if you believe you can do it then you will do it. If you believe you can't do it, then you probably won't succeed. Second, there was a definition of a successful negotiation. We spent a whole day trying to decide what this was and we concluded that it was a situation where both parties are satisfied and would come back again.'

These were things which Andy Tollerton said influenced him in his managerial practice. Managers often cited fairly simple guiding principles or 'rules of thumb' like these, or like Dick Eastwood's rule of never apologising when giving a presentation. Such rules or principles may appear rather trite, but it is better, I suggest, to see them simply as surface manifestations of a series of understandings developed through the manager's life and career. Such understandings are not easy to articulate and therefore we see a tendency to quote a few simple formulas which are readily put into words. Difficult as it may be to get managers to articulate these deeper understandings, it is nevertheless worth while attempting to locate the principles or theories which underpin them.

MANAGERS AS PRACTICAL THEORISTS

In his studies of managerial behaviour, Iain Mangham has adopted a theoretical position corresponding in a number of ways to my own. His perspective, like my own, suggests that 'individuals may be seen as uniquely self-aware beings who define, designate, evaluate, plan and organise their actions through a process of internal conversation' (Mangham 1986: 31). Earlier I discussed the way that human thinking can be understood as involving 'debates with oneself' through engaging with the series of arguments about the world which one encounters as one moves through life (see pp. 23–5). In the process of learning about managerial work, managers engage in continuous and regular 'internal conversations' as they make sense of what they are doing and exert control over their situations. But, as they face each new situation, they cannot possibly find the time to engage in a detailed thinking-out of what is to be done. Mangham draws on the classic writing of Chester Barnard (1938) to deal with this point. He cites Barnard's view of management as an art and his view that in 'the common-sense, everyday, practical knowledge necessary to the practice of the arts, there is much that is not susceptible to verbal statement'. The 'know-how' of the executive arts is 'acquired by persistent, habitual experience and is often called intuitive'. As Mangham says, most executives, much of the time, 'act intuitively, that is to say without reflection, because what they do is to realise performances with which they are familiar' (1988: 71). I was intrigued to know whether it was possible to persuade managers to attempt some reflection on the principles which underlay their personal managerial practice. I asked them whether there were any theories which they had picked up or developed for themselves about how they might do their jobs.

I was well aware that the word 'theory' was not one likely to receive too favourable a reaction from the typical British manager. And given that there was a degree of impatience among many managers in ZTC Ryland with the regular introduction of new managerial 'fads and fancies', as we saw in the last chapter, there might be a particular resistance to notions of managerial theory in this company. Garry Borrowash, for example, spoke especially forcefully about 'flavours of the month':

'I would much rather have a practical pragmatic approach to management rather than spouting theories. People can spout theories until the cows come home. Reading more theoretical books about this that and the other can be interesting. If you are going to bring that in you don't just say, "Let's bring that in". You say "How could we apply that to this or that real problem?" I can illustrate this: on the accounting side there are quite a lot of wonderful philosophies and methodologies around. They are flavours of the month, things like activity-based costing and throughput accounting. The more you learn about it the more you realise it will be a disaster if you say "Ah, activity-based costing, that is the thing for our company". Instead, you say, "That is interesting, what can I learn from this that I can apply to doing a revision to our systems to improve the situation the company is in?" Otherwise, it is a bit like politicians who follow dogmas, like monetarism. I think these people are dangerous. They make decisions based on those theories without actually sitting down and using common sense; actually thinking about it, rather than simply following a principle. People will follow philosophies which are not proven and read patterns into things, patterns which aren't there. Economists are terrible at this.'

We can see here a preference for a combination of principle and pragmatism, not a complete rejection of theoretical principles. I was happy to force the issue in my interviews by using the word 'theory' and I was ready to make the point, as indeed I needed to, that I neither saw theories as the preserve of academics nor as something to be separated from practice. I had long believed that social science theories were not of an essentially different order from those of non-social scientists. I had written before:

> Most human actions – including many of those which have become almost habitual – are informed by ideas of how one thing connects with another or how one event or action leads to another. These, in effect, are theories and, in this sense, poor practice is likely to follow from poor theory.
>
> (Watson 1986:14).

An activity as complex as the management of work organisations inevitably involves drawing on complicated theoretical ideas, however consciously or unconsciously this may be done and however wise or foolish the theoretical propositions may be. Management practice involves dealing with people, dealing with resources and coming to terms with the economic and social environment of the organisation being managed. The practice is therefore informed by assumptions about all these matters and about how they relate to each other.

I found that many of the managers I interviewed and talked to about theory could be persuaded to move beyond their initial dislike of the notion of theory. Eric Lenton stated his dislike very clearly:

> 'I honestly have no time for management theories, or any kind of theory really. You won't take that personally will you? I mean, that's what you do in your normal job, isn't it; teach all that theory stuff?'
>
> 'Believe me, Eric, I am as impatient as anyone with a lot of the stuff that is taught to management classes. But I–'
>
> 'There you go. That's typical academic to me; all going on about this theory and that theory and how this theory is better than that one. I suppose that's all most academics can do anyway. I would have more time for them if they talked about practical things.'
>
> 'So you are a practical man who works without theories?'
>
> 'Yes, I think that's right. But I've got a feeling that you're going to say I'm wrong about that, aren't you?'
>
> 'No, no, not at all. I accept what you say. You go around doing practical things all day. You do it all by instinct. There's absolutely no thought behind anything you do.'
>
> 'Yeah, I knew it. I see what you are getting at. Of course there is thought behind what I do. But don't, for God's sake, ask me to tell you what it is. I've got no fancy theories but I do have a pretty good idea of how things work in factories, in business, in, well, you know.'
>
> 'OK. Let's forget about "fancy theories" and talk about "how things work", as you put it.'

Where Lenton used this notion of ideas about 'how things work', other managers used a variety of their own terms to describe whatever patterning in their thinking they felt able to articulate in response to my question about theories. Garry Borrowash, for example, had agreed that people do have 'theories'. 'Yes', he said, 'Everybody must do. The hardest thing is coming down and saying what the heck they are. That is when you sit down and write your own book.' This enabled me to ask what would go 'in your book'. Jane Trowell referred to a 'matter of philosophy', this being 'you must follow an open-door policy', whilst Dick Mansfield spoke his 'basic beliefs' to characterise his view that 'everybody has a point of view and managers don't own all the good ideas; this means you have to listen to people'. Carol Rowsley, who had both a first degree in management studies and had completed an MBA course, spoke of 'a way of life'. In response to my question about theories she said:

'This is difficult. I've absorbed them, I suppose. I use them subconsciously. I probably expound on them to people at work when they need to understand why this happened this way or that. But I've not consciously sat down and thought I'll take on Maslow's hierarchy of needs. It's all really a matter of the way you think about things; the way you approach things.'
'Can you put this in words?', I asked.
'The thing that pops into mind is listening and paying attention to people. But to me that is a way of life.'

The great majority of statements of personal theories made no reference to formal management theories and, with only one or two exceptions, they were about relating to people. The statements were typically prescriptions about how one should behave, with frequent reference to listening to people, treating people fairly and building trust. I often challenged individuals to tell me *why* they thought such principles should be successful. Mark Cossall told me that he had once attended a course on 'leadership and motivation' and that

'The theory that came out of this was that your role as manager is with making sure that people understand what they need to do and help them by removing barriers.'
'But isn't that more an operating principle rather than a theory? Could you say what the theory is behind it, in the sense, say, of the assumptions about people which it depends on?'
'Yes, it is that people want to be treated as people, as individuals. You don't change from being a person because you are working for somebody. Because somebody cleans a toilet it does not stop them from being a person. They have hopes fears, aspirations and all the rest of it. They may not have the same level of understanding or the education I have, but it does not make them any less than me. The second assumption is that if you don't explain to people what you want from people, you won't get anywhere. It's no good speaking louder, "I want this". It's like the theory of learning a foreign language, speaking to foreigners abroad. It's no good speaking to them loudly in English if they don't understand English in the first place. The other assumption is – trying not to use buzz-words – communication. I must help the individual understand. The third assumption is that if you are not consistent you have a difficulty. I don't have kids but I understand that if you don't have consistency you have big problems. But I do have animals; I know with them I have to be consistent. It's a basic belief of mine. So to move all this into my theory of management: respect for the individual really, communicating, consistency. OK?'

'Yes, it's an unusually coherent statement.'

'It's bloody difficult. Um, gut feel again: another thing is being able to say that you are wrong, being able to admit fallibility. It doesn't sound like any theory I have heard before, but . . .'

A number of managers used the notion of empowerment to label their personal 'theoretical' position and, as with Mark Cossall, I attempted to elicit what I would see as the theory behind the concept, by asking questions like 'So why does this work?'. The typical response here was to argue that people would actually enjoy their work more if they experienced 'challenge', 'stretch' or 'owning the job' or 'making a contribution'. If they enjoyed doing the work they would do it better. As one manager put it, giving full voice to the *empowerment, skills and growth discourse* discussed in Chapter 5, 'It's only through giving responsibility and ownership that you will really get continuous improvement.'

Throughout all of this we see a mixing of principle and pragmatism, a blending of the normative and the analytical. On occasions, the value basis of an individual's position was made explicit, if sometimes qualified by a warning that being moral should not be equated with being 'soft'. Andy Tollerton suggested that one of his 'rules' was that:

'You have got to get your people working for you, not going through the motions. But that is all you will get if you go around kicking hell out of people. That's not right anyway. But don't get the idea that I am a softy. I am not, ask anyone. If people act out of line, they have to be brought back.'

Terry Carlton argued that successful management depended on an explicit recognition of the values which would 'make sense of the practices you encourage'. He spoke of an experience earlier in his management career to help answer my question about the values he would hold to in practice:

'I had something simple to deal with. It was about the wearing of overalls in hot weather. I said to my boss, "Look, I am going to have a problem because most of my people think that it is not right to work in uncomfortable conditions". His response was, "They are not entitled to an opinion. Go and tell them what they are going to do and get on with it". I thought from then on, "That's wrong." I'll never forget that. I said I am never going to work long for a bloke like that. That's a value probably: it doesn't matter how insignificant people appear to be on the outside, their opinion is valuable.'

Again in these accounts I encountered the concept of the 'sort of person' the manager was, this being consistent with the idea that the manager, in developing their managerial competence, is also developing their personal 'self', shaping their individual identity both through developing a repertoire of personal practices and moulding a notion of personal integrity through a set of values. The exchange element of the phenomenon of personal strategic exchange, as I have conceptualised this process, becomes explicit on some of the managers' accounts of their 'theories'. Andy Tollerton, in revealing another of his 'rules', said:

'This is very near and dear to me: I insist on loyalty. I would prefer an average worker who was loyal to me to a high flier who didn't give a damn.'

I asked why this was.

'It is my nature. I see myself as a very loyal person; loyal to the people who work for me as well as to the company. So I expect it back. Going back to the trick cyclist on the Looking Glass course, the first thing she said to me in feeding back after my interview with her was, "I wish I had someone as loyal as you working for me."'

Similarly, Charles Bunny had been talking to managers in a company he had visited and found himself criticising their way of handling a problem:

'They are having a blitz on absenteeism. They are sending threatening letters, scaring the daylights out of people. I have been asking, "How would you respond to this kind of treatment?" and "Why do you work all the hours?". "Because we get a buzz", they say. "So why can't you create a buzz for other people?", I ask them.'

Eddie Elton who spoke of the importance of treating people 'fairly, kindly, but firmly' summed up his position:

'Yes, it is my theory of motivation, if you like, that people will do what you require of them if you treat them as you would want to be treated yourself. I always think it is nice to come to work to want to work and to want to work for somebody.'

What all of these statements and claims of managers suggest is that these 'practical men and women', who are initially reluctant to speak of theories and principles, are far from theoretically naive or unthinking in their practice. As Iain Mangham and Annie Pye say of the senior executives they studied, 'pragmatists our respondents may be, but they do not appear to act without theme and direction' (1991: 20). These authors were referring to the decision-making activities of business leaders, but the same principle applies to the day-to-day actions of the mainstream managers in ZTC Ryland, a principle which Karl Weick (1983) labels 'acting thinkingly'. The thought is in the background as one carries out one's daily managerial work. As I got Eric Lenton to admit earlier, 'Of course there is thought behind what I do'. But that thought is sufficiently in the background to *feel* as if one is acting instinctively. And it is based on a combination of what the individual, within their personal concept of self, feels is 'right' in a moral sense and has learned to be 'right' in the pragmatic terms of 'what works'. Clive Oxton illustrates these points in speaking of his use of 'team working':

'It becomes instinctive. I like the concept of team working. We tend to do most of what we do here as a team, although of course you steer the team the way you want it to go anyway. We get everybody involved. It is basic communications and team-work. It simply makes life easier.'

'Why does this work?', I asked. Oxton believed that it was the only way he could manage his department:

> 'People respond to having their ideas and views listened to, even if they are not used. I could not dictate policy in here and have an effective organisation. People would resent it. Maybe you can do this at senior levels; I simply could not at this level.'

This statement is reminiscent of the earlier claim made by Gordon Radcliffe that he would be 'rumbled' if he acted insincerely in his use of 'charm' and 'wit' to 'relate to people and get [his] way'. Acting as a dictator or operating as a 'bullshitter' is not to be avoided simply because these behaviours are morally wrong. They are also the wrong thing to do because they do not work.

CULTURE, TRUST AND MESSING EACH OTHER ABOUT

In speaking about how he could not act as a dictator in managing at his 'level', Clive Oxton says that 'maybe you can do this at senior levels'. I do not think that he was in fact suggesting that senior managers can or should act dictatorially; his words were more a matter of dissociating himself from behaviours he saw senior people in ZTC engaging in. This is suggested by something he said to me on another occasion:

> 'I've got a good culture going in my department. I'd like to think it went beyond these walls. But it doesn't. We work together in an open way here. I might be naive but I think I am trusted. I – No, I don't think I am naive. I genuinely trust the people in here. I wouldn't have the sense that I could trust them, would I, if I wasn't putting trust in them? Well, that's the problem outside these walls. The way the culture of this firm has gone is one where nobody trusts the company. I don't think that's any good at all. I've got to work against that grain to run the sort of department that I want. It's the sort of department the company should want. But they don't make it easy for me. They just say, "We're going to do this", or "The consultants say we've got to do that". How do I know it's for the best? How do I persuade my staff it's for the best?'

Oxton's words suggest a 'theory' relating effective work organisation to 'openness' and a high level of trust. The concept of trust used is one suggesting a strong level of reciprocity; a two-way exchange of understanding which leads Oxton to relate his 'sense' of being able to trust his staff to their trusting him. The stress on consistency in the account of Mark Cossall and others can also be understood as relating to the importance of reciprocity in managers' human relationships, as can Eddie Elton's espoused theory that 'people will do what you require of them if you treat them as you would want to be treated yourself'. Here is a moral principle of biblical status; a key principle in the teaching of Jesus Christ which can have meaning for Christian and non-Christian alike, I suggest. But this kind of understanding is not one which, according to Clive Oxton, exists between the managers at the level of 'the company' and departmental managers like himself. And this creates difficulty in gaining compliance in effecting changes.

I would argue that there are some important theoretical principles behind Oxton's words. Relationships based on trust and reciprocity can indeed be highly relevant to the achieving of what I have called productive cooperation. People who do not trust each other and have a strictly calculative concept of exchange are unlikely to achieve together work tasks of any complexity, or to solve organisational problems of any difficulty. One aspect of this was neatly expressed to me by a manufacturing manager:

> 'You can't keep your eye on the job, you know, on how to do it better, when you've got to keep your eye on your back all the time.'

The importance of trust relations in work contexts has been stressed by Alan Fox (1974, 1985) in work which, although from the British industrial relations writing tradition rather than the management mainstream, has considerable relevance to the notion of achieving high levels of productive cooperation (or 'excellence') in work organisations through cultural rather than structural means. Fox draws on Peter Blau's (1964) distinction between *economic* and *social* exchange. Economic exchange occurs between people when there is an expectation of carefully calculated, immediate and tightly specified return for an equivalent thing given. There is no discretion between the parties; neither side trusts the other. In social exchange, on the other hand, favours are given without expectation of immediate, specific or matching return. This creates 'diffuse future obligations' and, hence, establishes relationships of trust between the parties. Feelings of obligation and trust are established in social exchange, unlike in economic exchange, and 'social exchange therefore tends to generate a spiral of rising trust' (1964: 71).

What we might call 'traditional' work arrangements, with people employed to do highly specified tasks for a finely calculated return tied to their completion and within a hierarchically structured control regime which carefully monitors performance, fits the concept of economic exchange. This, Fox says, brings about a 'spiral of falling trust', primarily through the denial of discretion to people. For a management to dictate every detail of what people are to do and continually to check up on their performance as a condition of giving rewards is unlikely to result in those people trusting that management and hence giving to it any more than a minimal level and quality of performance.

Fox advocates the building of discretion into work arrangements to bring about 'institutionalized high trust relations' where trust is 'embodied in the rules, roles and other policies and arrangements' which some people make for others. His key argument is that the greater the degree of discretion extended to people in their work, the greater will be the sense of trust between people and the greater the sense of personal involvement. This makes possible 'problem-solving work relationships' – 'high-trust', relationships in which people:

> work to an assumption of common goals, communicate freely and without calculation, refrain from the gamesmanship of the win–lose approach, and work through their disagreements by rational discussion instead of taking up a stance of conflict and bargaining.
>
> (1985: 83).

In many ways the 'winning culture' which the founders of ZTC had set out to establish, as well as the Total Quality Management which preceded it in the time of Parry control at Ryland, accorded with these principles. Ken Donnington, who had earlier been complaining about the lack of cooperation between various departments on the Ryland site, drew on elements of the *empowerment, skills and growth* discourse during a meeting looking at 'improving communications':

> 'If you, me and all of our people were empowered and allowed to get on with the job; well, we're all bright enough to work out what needs to be done. Then we could stop all this pissing each other about. But the powers-that-be don't trust any of us at Ryland to know what's best for the company. And there's bugger-all evidence that we can trust them to know what's best for sod all.'

The terms 'messing people about' or 'pissing each other about' had been used several times during the discussion to cover a variety of different ways in which departments, sections, functions and individuals were seen, in another phrase from the empowerment discourse used by one of the participants, to be failing to 'treat each other as customers'. I would say that the participants in this meeting were working towards a fairly sophisticated sociological analysis of the situation. It was explicitly recognised that there would inevitably be career rivalry between managers, given the imminent retirement of a senior manager, and it was also noted that 'obviously each of us has our own departmental objectives which do not necessarily coincide with everybody else's'. With the exception of one individual who crossed his arms, pulled his chair back from the table and stayed conspicuously silent from the beginning of this part of the meeting, what the group was attempting to understand was the extent to which individual managers were 'keeping their heads down', 'getting involved in petty bickers', 'keeping the left hand from working with the right hand' to a greater extent than might be expected within the normal 'politicking' of a large organisation. These things were seen as happening to a greater extent than could be explained by normal career and interdepartmental politics. A deeper level of explanation was being sought.

Probably to avoid any of the specific conflicts which people had in mind from flaring up in this meeting, the terms used were kept in the kind of abstract form represented by phrases like 'pissing each other about'. This was probably analytically helpful as well, because it helped keep the analysis at an abstract and relatively general level, so enabling it to move towards the conceptual understanding implied in Ken Donnington's words; one identifying what we might call a low-trust unofficial culture encouraged by the corporate management's reluctance to 'empower' or trust the managers at Ryland (we may remember the words of Jim Aspley reported in Chapter 5; 'What about my empowerment?'). Such a culture sets the context for the 'segmentalist' tendencies analysed in Chapter 6 and the tendencies for means to get in the ways of ends and for people to be seen more 'going through the motions' rather than effectively managing. Here I can be accused of putting words into the mouths of the managers whom I was observing and listening to, and must not go too far with this. But I do wish to claim that some valuable and powerful lay social science analysis was being carried out by these managers and that there is a significant degree of correspondence between this lay theorising and some key ideas of formal social science thinking.

The background to this meeting was the growing recognition among this group of managers, discussed in Chapter 5, that the future of the whole Ryland plant was in some doubt and that strategic decisions made elsewhere could put all their jobs at risk. There was thus a pressure to understand behaviours which could undermine joint action to defend shared interests. Concepts like culture and empowerment, taken in large part from the learning process instigated by the company itself, were resources deployed to make sense of events. But these were mixed with many of the more common-sense notions, like trust, listening, showing respect to others, which we saw permeating the managers' own 'theories' reviewed above. Similar concepts appear in their notions of 'good' and 'bad' managers.

GOOD MANAGERS, BAD MANAGERS

Issues of how effective or competent managers can be judged to be by any relatively objective criteria are ones to be considered later when the implications of the arguments and information gathered across this study are brought together. The thoughts that managers themselves have about the relative merits of the managers they have known are, however, worth considering in themselves, as well for the possible light they might throw on the wider issues of managerial competence. We know from our consideration of how managers learn to manage that their experience of other managers, together with the judgements they make about those people, influences their conception of how they should themselves behave. And, since all the managers we are looking at have both been 'managed' and continue to be managed by people senior to themselves, we can regard their judgements of the qualities of other managers as useful evidence of what is and is not seen 'to work'.

To leave open issues of how effectiveness and competence might be defined, I simply asked managers to tell me about the 'best manager they had ever known' and then about the 'worst'. As we might expect from the pattern seen in Chapter 2 in which managers tended to prioritise 'people management' in their concept of what management is, being good or bad as a manager tended to be seen predominantly, but certainly not exclusively, in terms of how they related to people. This would also be expected from the fact that the managers they have the most salient experience of are those to whom they personally have related as subordinates. The emphasis on relational qualities would also accord with what we have already seen as the importance of maintaining social relationships of trust and reciprocity in 'managing to manage'.

The value of a balanced 'give and take' relationship is suggested by Don Littleover's report of a character who was once his 'boss's boss' and is someone he continues to keep in touch with:

> 'He made you feel involved. He kept me informed, made me feel that my opinion was being taken into account, is interested in me as a person. He involves me in his thought processes, confides in me. He makes clear what he wants from me and if I have problems with this helps me achieve what he requires. He was not afraid to let me do things on my own and let me have visibility.'

The willingness of the 'good' manager to delegate responsiblity and to recognise success was often mentioned, and its opposite was often highlighted in mention of 'bad' managers, as we see in Harry Basford's generalised portrait of bad managers:

> 'They let everybody else do the work but they take the credit – until there is flak going. They pass that back to their department.'

or Clive Oxton's:

> 'The worst sort – the ones that have always turned me off – give you a project to do. You do that project, he accepts it and then the report is out in his name as if he has done it. That is probably the biggest turn off you can get. The other one is the guy who delegates but doesn't really delegate. He gives the impression that he is delegating a task to you but he doesn't actually let you get on and do it. He is watching you every five minutes.'

Phil Wollaton described this the 'total opposite of empowerment'. Empowerment was something which he believed all good managers did.

Good managers were frequently said to be good listeners, but the good listeners described were seen as people who put that listening to some effect. A man who was something of a managerial hero to several managers was described, for example as:

'very focused on the success criteria – what was required by the job. To get there he was very supportive, he was a good listener.'

In this there is a suggestion that managing is not just about relating to people, but about doing this in a way which furthers business ends. Being a good manager is taken beyond the interpersonal level and the maintaining of happy relationships. Dan Smalley emphasised the need for a balance between giving attention to people and attention to the business:

'Some managers spend most of their time looking after their staff, so hence they may be "great guys". But I don't see them as good managers. On the other hand, there are the authoritarians who dictate yet are very knowledgable about the business. I don't see either of these as making the best managers. They may get the best results in the short-term but it tends to lead to labour turnover, to bitterness. So it is the balance between being knowledgable about the business – being involved with the business – but also being involved with the people.'

Dick Mansfield explained why he thought this was important in talking of his hero:

'He was a brilliant manager. He would listen to people; seek the opinion of anybody. But he was a very strong character: once he had made his mind up he would drive the thing through. He was a strong manager but he was a very warm manager and everybody felt that he was doing the best for the company and for them. It is important for you to feel that your manager is doing the best not just for you but for the business too, because the business is your livelihood. I always felt that is what he was doing.'

Terry Carlton's experience taught him that 'being nice' in itself achieved little. The worst manager he had known 'was also the nicest of them all; he was so weak in dealing with the people who worked for him that he would allow people to delegate up to him'.

In speaking of the worst managers they had known, managers regularly brought up the name of Ted Meadows, a living reality for them. He was said, for example, to be 'unthinking and absolutely uncaring about the people aspects of management; numbers of people have resigned because of him'. Reference was frequently made, for example, to how 'abusive, insulting and nasty' he frequently was and that 'the foulness of his language – aimed right at you as the total effing prat he made you out to be – was his nearest idea to motivating people'.

The reference to bad language here is interesting, because it was quite common for managers to speak of several 'old-timer manager heroes', as one man called them, who were 'rough as diamonds' or, in another case, 'a real dirty-mouthed sod'. Typically, these were figures who would give people 'a real bollocking' but who would do this in such a way that they only increased the respect in which they were held. This was a pattern I had heard of before in other industries. Quite typical here was the case of a manager who, it was said, 'was the kind of leader you would follow over the top'. And 'he would give the most almighty bollocking if you got it wrong, yet you came out of his office feeling that you were the most important person in the whole factory'. There seems here to be a mythic managerial figure who is unpretentious, down-to-earth ('He'd sit there with his shoes off and in his braces'), kind-hearted but tough-minded. These characteristics were attributed to several named individuals who had walked the shop and office floors of Parry Ryland in the 'good old days' before ZTC took shape and about whom managers would recount particular tales.

When I pressed managers to tell me just what it was that made these figures outstanding, they would use terms like 'just a mysterious quality that made you respect them, love them even'; 'a sort of indefinable charisma'; 'something that made you want to please them at whatever cost to yourself'. The readiness of these semi-mythic figures to exert authority in a direct way whilst retaining a personal respect for the individual was something managers tended to admire. The emphasis on the roughness and the plainness of their speech suggest admiration for qualities of boldness and directness. To 'call a spade a spade' and not to 'flannel people' was clearly esteemed.

It would seem that these characters whose reputations had taken on a mythic function represented an ideal in which there was a high level of reciprocal exchange between manager and managed, based on a high level of personal and emotionally charged commitment. A common feature of these individuals was the close interest shown not just in individual employees, but in their families. This was especially the case with Dan Stanton, who, we heard earlier (p. 162), remembered the circumstances of employees' wives and children and could ask after them by name. Stanton would, it was said, 'eff and blind like hell' but 'you could take it from Dan, because that was the way he was'.

The phrase 'the way he was' is reminiscent of a notion that we have come across with regard to the way managers see themselves: 'the sort of person I am'. Every manager is unique and has their own way of relating to others. 'You will always be respected for being yourself', said one person: 'You've got to think carefully about how to behave, but it's no good acting false.' We are back here to trust and a recognition that 'good managers' can take a variety of forms, as long as certain key principles are followed. John Stapleford spoke in such terms. He spoke of two of his 'own bosses'. The first was 'a nice guy' and

'his strength was, you just wanted to please the guy. If he asked you to do something you would lean over backwards to do it. He never came out and told you to do things. There was none of the big-whip syndrome. What can I say? He relied on your integrity; he gave you plenty of rope (one or two took advantage of that, but they got hauled in and people got to know what the norm was). He was not a disciplinarian.'

However, Stapleford's current boss is 'as different as chalk and cheese from that guy':

'but he is a good guy. He is honest – he will tell you if you are wrong and he will tell you if he is wrong. And he can be strict. I can't think of the words to use. The other chap was easy-going, like drinking a glass of milk; the present chap is like a nice sharp drink. It is that sort of difference, very difficult to explain. They are two different personalities but they get the same out of us.'

I asked him if he could explain this:

'I don't know why. Let me think about this. What is common to both of these blokes is that they are honest, you know. That is the overwhelming thing that comes out. This then is the overriding factor: if you can believe the guy, trust the guy, then you are half-way there. Even the job knowledge is not of great importance. It is this interaction thing: the parent syndrome, up to a point – without us really knowing what it means. You have got trust in people and, come the crunch, you can lean on the guy and know you will get some support.'

The accounts of good and bad managers are not straightforward reports of what they have experienced, of course. They give us an indication of certain benchmarks against which individuals can match their own behaviours. The rogues and heroes of the management drama are personifications of some of the principles of everyday managerial survival. Reference to constructs of good and bad managers – some based on current colleagues, some based on semi-mythical figures of the past – are resources used in the process of managing to manage.

Certain common themes run through managers' accounts of their own 'theories' and their notions of what makes a 'good' and a 'bad' manager. A reading of these themes with their frequent reference to treating people as people, to listening, to empowering and to developing relationships of reciprocity and trust might suggest that the managers at Ryland who spoke to me in these terms actually adopted a benign, participative, high-trust management style in carrying out their responsibilities. Had my research method been solely one of interviewing these managers, I could indeed have come away with a view of them as a group of highly enlightened and progressive managers, although this view would perhaps have been qualified a little by hearing so many individuals rehearse the argument that middle managers were often undermined by the dictatorial and impetuous decision-making imposed on them by the top managers.

However, my close involvement as a 'participant observer' in ZTC Ryland and my experience of working alongside many of the managers I interviewed showed that the picture was nothing like as simple as this. I did indeed see some of the most impressive managerial skill that I had ever witnessed. There were managers who would talk to me of their belief in 'empowering' their staff and who would then invite me to go and speak to any member of their department at any time and test for myself whether such principles were being applied. I did exactly this when invited and often found in those managers' departments individuals who were proud to talk of the extent of control they had over their own work tasks and the pleasure they took in being encouraged to develop themselves and their skills. But, in contrast to this, I found on frequent occasions evidence from what I heard of managers' behaviour and from what I observed at first hand of people 'pissing each other about' that a good proportion of managers fell somewhat short of the ideals they espoused when talking about managing. But I rarely found that I could put this down to simple hypocrisy.

ANGST, INSECURITY AND HUMAN FRAILTY

The more I saw of the managers at Ryland, the more I became aware of the extent of human angst, insecurity, doubt and frailty among them. I observed managers being rude to their staff, refusing to listen to advice given to them within their departments, curtly announcing unexplained decisions, losing their tempers with people from other departments, creating rows with fellow managers. I came across numerous examples of managers offending others by failing to reply to telephone calls or by writing curt memoranda or electronic mail messages, rather than explaining decisions face-to-face to people, of managers spreading malicious gossip about others, of managers failing to turn up to meetings where their presence was important. On a number of occasions I found myself mediating between managers who had fallen out with each other and who were unwilling to meet to sort out difficulties. And on three occasions, I actually found myself having to persuade a manager that it would not be advisable to go and exert physical violence against another.

Much of this behaviour was destructive and harmful, both to the quality of the working experience of people in the factory and the effectiveness of the work done. Some of it could be described as 'functional', in that it allowed people to handle normal everyday work stress by 'letting off steam' with a ritualised battle over resources or missed deadlines. But much of it contributed little to the achievement of 'productive coopera-tion'. My own view of work organisations is that they are composed of a multiplicity of different interest groups and competing individuals and that, therefore, productive cooperation is something that has to be striven for, in a context where conflicts and rivalries are inevitable. But my time in ZTC Ryland suggested that a great deal of what could be regarded as 'negative' managerial behaviour was neither an inevitable reflection of the normal conflicts of managerial politics, nor a matter of managers failing to understand the principles of successfully working with and managing other people.

To listen to a manager carefully and sincerely explaining to you in the morning the importance of treating every individual as a unique being with their own wants and worries and then, in the afternoon, to witness them storming out of a meeting with a group of supervisors who tell you that the man is an arrogant, insensitive and pig-headed dictator, makes one stop and think. To explain this event, and others like it, as simply a matter of individuals claiming to be something they are not when being interviewed by a management researcher seemed to be highly inadequate when I tried to make sense for myself of such experiences. One area of explanation could be the particular stresses and insecurities arising from ZTC's difficult business situation and from the overall cultural style currently being adopted by the corporate management. But this did not seem to me to be a good enough explanation on its own. It had also to be related to some of the major challenges at the core of being a manager, challenges which many managers, having only the feet of clay of the ordinary mortal being, found at times to be beyond them, regardless of their 'theoretical' understanding or intellectual grasp of what is required of them.

Managers not only have to 'manage people' (customers, bankers, suppliers, and so on, as well as employees), they have to manage themselves, too. Managers are human beings and they have all the human frailties and anxieties of the other people whom they seek to influence. It may be that they often have these to a greater extent than many others, given the higher expectations which may be held with regard to them.

My experience in ZTC Ryland has convinced me that we have tended to underestimate the extent of human frailty and insecurity in the lives of managers. There has long been a strand in management thinking which recognised the non-rational aspect of the 'workers', those, that is, who are 'managed'. This is the so-called 'human relations' thinking associated with Roethlisberger and Dickson (1939), Elton Mayo (1933) and the Hawthorne experiments. It suggests that workers are motivated in large part by 'sentiment' rather than by reason. But managers, it is assumed, are rational. Employees need to be shown that they belong and that they are important. Managers are given the responsibility for bringing this about. There is little question of their own insecurities and need for meaning being attended to, because they have to be seen as 'in control', as 'providing leadership', as knowing more about the work being done than those doing it know. The humanity and fragility of managers themselves is no more recognised in this human relations perspective than in the 'scientific management' tradition associated with Frederick Taylor (1911) which the human relations writers wanted to supplant.

The view of managers encouraged by the classical traditions of management thinking as the rational planners and unemotional builders of organisational systems tends artificially to set them above and apart from the action of which they need to be a part. By setting themselves above and apart from the core work of the organisation, managers put themselves in danger of knowing less and less about what is going on whilst, to justify their being above and apart, they have to put forward an impression of knowing it all. This impossible position not only leads them to outbursts of bad temper and screaming frustration, but leads to a descent into attempts to manage through systems, structures, rules, 'new initiatives', fads and techniques. And this is at the expense of working closely with others in the basic human task of getting people together, sharing ideas and developing solutions to shared problems and agreed tasks. Structures, rules and systems, instead of being means to achieving these things, become ends in themselves, as we saw in the last chapter.

In looking closely at managers as human beings, each with their own values, beliefs and strategies for shaping their lives and identities, it has become apparent that there is a significant emotional dimension to managerial work. But, as Stephen Fineman (1994) argues, this is something which normal organisational and administrative discourse suppresses or marginalises. Fineman notes Max Weber's famous analysis of the bureaucratic mode of organisation as one which 'eliminates from official business . . . love, hatred, and all personal irrational elements' (Weber 1968: 973) and he suggests that this element of the principle of bureacratic organisation has led to 'the perpetuation of a conception of organising' which has little resemblance to what people experience in organisations where;

> arguably, much of organisational life is quintessentially a sense of being 'worried about . . .', 'envious of . . .', 'comfortable with . . .', 'resentful about . . .', 'hurt by . . .', 'sad for . . .', 'bored with . . .', 'excited by . . .', 'happy with . . .', 'mad at . . .' and so on. Even the dull indifference which pervades some peoples' work experience is ususally conveyed as a 'feeling'.

These phrases are not a common part of typical analyses and texts on management. But they were part of the everyday informal discourse in Rylands. In an earlier chapter we saw how often managers spoke of their 'love' for their jobs. Yet the same people could talk, as they did, of 'what gets me down', 'what I can't stand about this place'. What the managers loved and what they hated were matters relating to their deepest personal values, and considerable emotion could be brought into play when they saw these values challenged. One manager in an interview said:

'You saw me the other day leave that meeting in a hurry. Do you want to know why I left? If I had stayed I would have ruddy thumped that know-it-all bastard. Just you wait, though, when I get the chance I'll really piss in his chips. I'm no delicate flower and I can shout my mouth off with the best of them at times. But I don't think I could ever do that: sit there and talk to blokes who are flogging their guts out as if they were dozy school kids. You've got to respect people who are doing their best. He was just showing contempt for us and all we are doing. But he thinks he knows best. Just let him come near me and look down his nose at my operation. I'll flatten the bastard.'

Reference is being made here to a value; that of respecting others. Another interpretation of the offence being taken here could be that this man's ego was being threatened. In fact I would not want to separate the values and the sense of 'self' that a person draws on in orienting their behaviour in any given situation. The way in which these two aspects of an emotional reaction to a problem can come together can be seen in the following conversation (as I remembered it when making notes shortly afterwards):

> 'I'm going to have a go at him. If you don't watch it I'll pop him one. If I can get hold of the sod, that is.'
>
> 'He's hiding from you again, is he?'
>
> 'He bloody is. He knows we've got to sort out how we allocate responsibilities in the new set-up. He's got no right to piss me about like this. I tell you I am getting really uptight.'
>
> 'But is it so urgent?'
>
> 'Yes. Well, perhaps not. But it's the principle of the thing; failing to turn up twice after we'd agreed to meet. And the always being "out" when I phone. It's sickening – using your secretary to lie for you like that.'
>
> 'Can't you let it go and just get on with what you want to handle?'
>
> 'I'm buggered if I will. I feel insulted, you know, made a prat of. I'm not usually seen as the Mr Ego in this department. But there are limits. I'm not letting anyone ignore me like this.'

morality & *ego* (handwritten margin note)

This individual is clearly making reference to moral considerations with 'it's the principle of the thing' and in stating his disapproval of the practice of 'using your secretary to lie'. Yet this is not a simple dispassionate moral judgement, unconnected to the man's personal feelings and the offence he has taken at being 'made a prat of'. He is explicit about the threat in this to his 'ego'. As we saw in Chapter 3, a person's concept of self, their values and their orientations to their work, are tightly interwoven.

How often managers at Ryland did in fact resort to violence in working out tensions between each other I would not know. To depart from the normal managerial conventions of negotiation and reasonableness to talk of the possibility of violence was probably enough in itself. As in so many other respects in the work organisation, talk is the key to action. This is not to say that because managers who speak about hitting other managers stop at talking about acts of violence rather than committing them, there is no action other than talk. But it is to say that without talk there can be no action. People talking to each other is vital to getting things done. But it also helps create the more general conditions, or the climate within which things can get done. Through talk, people persuade others to do things. But they also use language to make sense of the world and to cope with its pressures and its threats to their sanity. The role of language in thinking, persuading, joking and story-telling is a key theme of the next chapter. Managing to manage involves sophisticated linguistic skills, to a greater degree than might at first be apparent.

Chapter 8

Managing to manage
Language, humour, gender and home

'Sometimes I go home at night and ask myself what I have achieved. This happened driving home the other night: "What the hell have I done today?". I had been to the inevitable meetings of course. But the rest of it was just people coming in to see me, asking me this, telling me that. I didn't even get a glance at the mountain of paperwork until after six o' clock. You've spent the day gassing with people. It's all talk and very little action. I'm really beginning to wonder about this open-door thing.'

'What would action be?'

'Well, I do shut my door sometimes. And then it's phone, phone, phone. Sometimes I think that if it wasn't for the meetings, I'd be trapped in this office.'

'Don't you get around your department?'

'Aha, that's just it. I believe in managing by walking about. That's what worries me about all this talk, talk, talk. It keeps me from getting out there among my people. That should be key to my job. I am not doing it as much as I should.'

'So what does "managing by walking about" entail?'

'Oh, you know as well as I do. It's just walking around the department, having a word with various people; seeing how they are getting on; letting them ask me things; finding out what problems they are having. You have a bit of gossip, a bit of a laugh with certain people. It can make all the difference. Yeah, it makes a good department. It's managing, you know, by walking the job.'

'So that's what you mean by action instead of talk?'

'Precisely.'

'But it just sounds like more talk to me.'

'You sod. Yes, I see what you mean. Um, um . . . well you . . . no. There's talk and talk, you see. And there's talking and listening. Yeah, talking and listening to my people is where I have my biggest impact here. Ninety . . . no, let's say 75 or 60 per cent of the rest is a waste of time.'

MANAGING AND TALKING, TALKING AND MANAGING

Roger Sawley seems to be developing a distinction here between useful and time-wasting talk. This replaces his earlier attempt to draw a distinction between talk and action. He recognises the centrality to managerial work of talk, even if he has to be prompted to recognise this. As Rosemary Stewart noted, in reviewing the range of existing studies on managerial behaviour, 'managers talk and listen most of the time' (1983: 87). Such observations lead Dan Gowler and Karen Legge to argue that management can be seen as an oral tradition; not just in the 'literal sense' that managers spend most of their time talking, but also in an 'anthropological sense . . . as a means by which culture is generated, maintained, and transmitted from one generation to another' (1983: 199). To quote Iain Mangham again:

> Organisations are created, sustained and changed through talk. There is nothing good or bad in this world or any other but talking makes it so. Organisations, enterprises of great pitch and moment, are constituted by active, wilful individuals talking to each other . . . It is through words that [managers] appeal, persuade, request, coax, cozen, assign, declare, debate, agree, insult, confer, teach, advise, complain, irritate, anger, correct, socialize, recruit, threaten, promise, praise, ridicule, condemn and dismiss.
>
> (1986: 82)

Mangham develops the point made by Louis Pondy (1978) about language being a key skill required to make a manager an effective leader. He goes beyond Pondy's claim that language renders 'activity meaningful' and hence helps the managers explain, justify and rationalise, to argue that 'language can . . . fundamentally affect the decisions that are made' (1986: 83). And this brings me back to my arguments about rhetoric being more than a matter of persuading. Rhetorical skills are ones which deploy language to deal with *arguments*. This means that the way skills are used will influence not just the negotiations about decisions which occur between people, but will play a part in an individual's own thinking and personal decision-making process – since thinking itself can be understood as rhetorical (see pp. 23–5).

Walter Nash has argued that rhetoric is an 'ordinary human competence . . . an ordinary thing with some extraordinary manifestations, some graceful, some less so' (1989: ix). Traditionally, rhetoric has been associated with grand speeches and flights of oratory and, in recent times, the term has become almost wholly used in a pejorative way, to label talk which is contrived, fanciful and devoid of substance. Writers like Nash are keen to restore rhetoric to its proper place as a widely used human skill. To show the strength of this argument and to bring out the sophistication which can lie behind seemingly modest pieces of managerial language use, I shall analyse a small piece of managerial conversation to locate examples of the techniques and devices of rhetoric which were written about and taught by classical rhetorician's, following the lead of Aristotle, Cicero and Quintillian.

The following conversation occurred between Dick Bilborough, a personnel manager involved with developing 'skill modules' for the Personal Development Scheme, and Alan Daybrooke, a junior production manager.

I was in the process of interviewing Daybrooke when Bilborough called
into his office to seek a decision from him about preparing a skill module.
I indicated to Bilborough that my tape recorder was running. He gestured
to suggest that I could leave it on whilst he had his brief conversation with
Alan Daybrooke:

> 'Hello Alan. Sorry to interrupt. Just a quickie. You've decided?'
> 'Aha. Am I going to take on the skill module? Uhm. I think I.. Uhm. Well I . . .
> Go on, persuade me.'
> 'I wouldn't do that. It's up to you. You know the way the business needs to
> go. You know what's in it for you. You know that in the end you've got to
> persuade yourself. I'm not going to twist your arm. You're ahead of the game
> on all this. You know the score. You know what's best.'
> 'I know, I know. If I take it on I've got to own it. I know the language. I didn't
> go through the whole teamworking thing for nothing.'
> 'You got a lot out of that, didn't you?'
> 'Oh yes. Oh yes, I did. Look, I have bought into the whole personal
> development scenario. And if I can show others what empowerment can mean
> to them . . . But . . . No, I'm still not sure. You know the arguments. You tell
> them it's like making an investment. OK, they say. So the pay packet will follow.
> Well, the pay packet might follow. But people aren't sure are they? "Winning
> culture", ugh. That's all very well. But people can still go down the road. What
> do I say to people when they ask "Will another skill module under my belt stop
> me getting a brown envelope, the next time Bill's told to take out heads?" Can't
> you see their point? I mean I really do. They talk about it being a con. I don't
> agree. But I know what they mean. OK it's an honest con. But – '
> 'OK, Alan, forget it. I don't know about all that stuff. It's beyond me. It's ER,
> not my scene. Perhaps you're right. It's best that you say no.'
> 'Oh, sod it. All right. I'll do it.'

To take a key element of Nash's concept of rhetoric, there is a process of
'witting' persuasion going on here. Dick Bilborough was very anxious that
Alan Daybrooke should undertake this task. But rhetoric involves more
than just persuasion, as Nash (1989: 1) argues:

> In rhetoric there is always an element of complicity; it can be magnilo-
> quent, or charming, or forceful, or devious, but whatever its manner it
> seeks assiduously to involve an accomplice in its designs.

Bilborough was working assiduously to fulfil his designs on Daybrooke,
although we do not know the contents of the script he might have followed
in earlier conversations with him. These are echoed here, however, in
references to 'business needs' and to 'what's in it' for Alan. What is perhaps
most significant in this conversation, however, is that Alan Daybrooke is not
so much here being persuaded, at least in a direct way, as arguing with
himself. This is explicitly recognised by Bilborough and we see Daybrooke
utilising a whole series of rhetorical devices and discursive resources in
working out his own position. Daybrooke's skill in achieving complicity is
a skill of letting Bilborough himself deploy the arguments and set them
out to work against whatever contrary arguments may be in his mind.

Dick Bilborough's opening words were judiciously chosen. Even though the term 'Just a quickie' is very much a cliché of organisational life, Bilborough can be seen as using it to imply that there is not a lot needing to be said. Note, too, that his question is not worded 'Have you decided?', which might invite the answer 'no'. It is worded 'You've decided?', and was spoken with a hinted reading: 'Of course you've decided, there's no need for debate.' As soon as Daybrooke responds he can be seen as drawing on his own supply of techniques of rhetoric. He starts with perhaps the best known of all of them, the rhetorical question: 'Am I going to take on this skill module?' In fact, we see here a hint of *anthypophora*. In saying 'I think I . . .' he is on the point of producing an answer to his own question, so demonstrating his skill with this particular variant of the rhetorical question. But Bilborough comes back with an even more subtle burst of classical rhetorical figures. In the sentences, 'You know the way the business needs to go. You know what's in it for you. You know that in the end you've got to persuade yourself' we see *anaphora* (the repetition of the first words of a sequence of constructions; 'you know', 'you know', 'you know'), *parison* (the use of the matched constructions across the three 'legs' of this construction) and *personification* (treating the business as if it were a living entity with 'needs'). And in the same small speech this master factory rhetorician indulges in a spot of *comprobatio* (flattering Daybrooke with 'You're ahead of the game on all this') followed with a taste of *epitropis* in the form of a recognition of his listener's discerning judgement: 'You know what's best'. Later we see the silver-tongued Bilborough turning to wield the stick of irony when he says the opposite to what we all know he 'really means': 'It's best that you don't . . .'.

Alan Daybrooke's armoury of rhetorical devices is no less impressive, however, even though, at first sight, he is the person being persuaded rather the one doing the addressing. He is, in effect, engaged in argument with himself and if we apply the concepts of the classical rhetorician to his utterances we not only come across the standard tropes of *simile* ('it's like making an investment') and *metaphor* ('I've got to own it'; 'buying into') but a range of others. *Synecdoche* is used as part of one figurative reference to redundancy ('take out heads', where the part stands for the whole – the redundant peoples' heads for their whole person). And *metonymy*, a trope where an element of a principle stands for that broader principle, is utilised in two other references: redundancy is referred to through mention of going 'down the road' and receiving a 'brown envelope'.

In Daybrooke's words we can also find the tropes of *epizouxis* ('I know, I know' and 'Oh yes. Oh yes'), *antithesis* (the '*whole* teamworking thing for *nothing*') and even *epanorthesis* ('So the pay packet will follow. Well, the pay packet might follow') where a phrase is repeated and modified to develop a point. And in trying to resolve a potential conflict between the view of some of his colleagues that the personal development scheme is a 'con' and his own view that such a position exaggerates elements of manipulation or insincerity behind the policy, he resorts to an *oxymoron*, with the phrase 'honest con'. Almost as if to match that rhetorical flourish, Bilborough counters with a bluff of *aporia*, pretending that he cannot puzzle out these matters: 'I don't know about all that stuff. It's beyond me. It's ER, not my scene'. As an employee development specialist, Bilborough could play this hand; saying that these were ER (employee relations) matters, and not something he could expect to understand. However, both Daybrooke and I knew that he understood all these issues very well. And he knew that we knew. His flourish amounted to a more stylish way of saying that he did not want to engage with such issues. His hope, we might guess, was that Daybrooke should work out for himself the counter arguments to such an 'anti-change' position. Bilborough seems aware of the fact that Daybrooke's process of thinking about the decision he needed to make about working on a skill module was a matter of 'arguing with himself'.

In carrying out the above analysis I astonished myself at the number of rhetorical tropes I was able to find in such a small piece of seemingly mundane discourse. In reporting my analysis I am making a serious point. But I have to concede that I was knowingly using the rhetorician's technique of lightening a rather 'heavy' argument with a touch of humour through mixing the ponderous Latin and Greek terms of classical rhetoric with a hint of a rather 'knockabout' medieval joust in which our two knights take turns to display the magnificent weapons in their respective armouries. As I said in the opening pages of this book, humour is a very serious matter.

THE SERIOUSNESS OF HUMOUR: MUSICAL CHAIRS, BANANA GANNETS, THE PRINCESS AND THE GOOSECRAP

Humour is a much broader phenomenon than the telling of jokes and funny stories. It involves all forms of communication which create within people feelings of amusement and a predisposition to express that emotion through laughter. Humour is woven closely into the fabric of everyday life and is only at its most obvious when it takes the shape of formal jokes, explicitly signalled quips or deliberate piss-takes. It sometimes simply gives a nuance to a piece of communication through the use of a particular tone of voice, a carefully chosen word or phrase or a piece of body language; Steve Loscoe banging his head on his desk when talking about whether management is a 'real job', for example (see p. 29).

Gordon Radcliffe's term 'joined-up talking' or his ambiguously self-mocking references to his 'devastating charm' (see p. 159) lightened an otherwise serious reflection on learning to be a manager, so enhancing his communicative effectiveness and demonstrating his possession of everyday rhetorical skills. To insert a touch of humour into one's conversation with another is to assist the process of exchange; the person listening is rewarded for their willingness to listen. They get something back for giving the speaker their attention. We can see another facet of this in the adding of a spark of humour to what was essentially an angry and aggressive piece of talk with the phrase 'pissing in his chips' by the manager who was, at the same time, talking of 'thumping' another manager or 'flattening the bastard' (p. 180). I was quite disturbed by that conversation with an individual whom I liked and respected. But I was greatly tickled by the notion of him urinating in someone's fish supper. I found myself relishing the phrase, repeating it over and over in my mind as I walked home that night (and even looking it up in one of my dictionaries of slang – true academic that I am!). In this way, perhaps, the humorous phrase functioned to help me retain my affection for an individual who somewhat frightened me with his unexpected talk of violence. My listening to his diatribe was rewarded with an amusing and colourful linguistic titbit. Was this consciously intended? Partially, I suspect. It can be understood as another facet of an intuitively developed mundane rhetorical skill. It also demonstrated a skill in managing the finer points of strategic exchange.

Humour is far from a trivial or an incidental matter in the conduct of management, or any other human activity, for that matter. To investigate humour is to go into some of the very basic questions about what it is to be human and to use culture to make sense of the world and to survive in it. At the funeral of the comedian Benny Hill, the novelist Anthony Burgess spoke of Hill's comedy as not just diverting people from 'headaches, indigestion and paying taxes' but as holding

> a vision of the truth of what we really are. And what we really are is a strange mixture of animals and angels, endowed with a gift of seeing how absurd the human situation is.
>
> (Burgess 1992)

This view puts our capacity for humour at the centre of our humanness. Burgess is engaging in an intellectual level of analysis unlikely to have been heard from Hill. But it might well have been heard from another comedian, Ken Dodd, who takes from his extensive reading on humour an ancient view associated originally with Aristotle, that 'most comedy is the perception of incongruity':

> It is seeing things from a different angle, juggling with concepts, having a mind not rooted in logic. A comic is always saying 'What if . . .' What if, instead of laughing, your nose turned blue or your ears lit up.
>
> (Dodd quoted by Montgomery 1991: 34)

The effect of humour raising the question 'what if?' ties in with Burgess's notion of our capacity to see the absurdity of the human situation. Humour functions in the same way as I argued fiction and story-telling generally does (see pp. 21–3). It allows us to confront and come to terms with the threats and dangers of the world around us. Laughter allows us to cope emotionally with that which could frighten us into madness: the fragility of our identities and the contingency of our social location. We laugh at what frightens us. We have to contemplate the horrors around us. Maintaining our sanity is like the tight-rope walker maintaining their balance whilst crossing a high gorge over a roaring torrent. The tight-rope walker has to glance down from time to time to remember they are so precariously placed. If they too readily take for granted their balance, they might relax too much and tumble into the torrent. Correspondingly, we have to recognise the absurdity of our human condition. To be able, most of the time, to take for granted the normality of what we do we have occasionally to suspend that taken-for-grantedness, whether by watching a play or taking part in a 'laugh' at work.

Why is this? It is because the taken-for-grantedness of a sense of order and control is not a 'given' which is set up for us: it is a human accomplishment. We forget this at our peril. And the incongruities of humorous episodes function as reminders; whether it be the absurdity of one man urinating in another's packet of chips or the surreal notion of 'joined-up speaking'. We are peeping over the precipice every time we use a funny phrase or engage with a joke. Marriage is a serious matter for most adults, for example, and adultery is a threat to it. So we joke about adultery, just as we watch plays and read books about it. As Carol Clewlow says, in her ironically titled novel, *A Woman's Guide to Adultery*:

> Adultery's a good subject for jokes because it's a sad business and the saddest things in life are also, often, the funniest. Life, after all, is a tragi-comedy, a confusion of laughter and tears, of humour and hurt, without so much as a chalk mark to separate the two.
> 'I never know when you're joking.'
> 'I'm always joking. Only all my jokes are serious.'
> I said that once to Paul.

Being made redundant is no less serious an issue in people's lives than adultery. It was a potential reality for every single employee, managers included, in ZTC Ryland. And it was joked about endlessly, as we saw for example, in the surreal gallows humour of the managers in Chapter 5 who contemplated the whole workforce being packed into a 'giant brown envelope'. The regular joking about the threat of redundancy can be seen as an attempt to handle sources of insecurity external to the individual. The tension that people felt as a result of the lack of control over their lives created by employment insecurity was lessened by the act of laughing together with others who were similarly stressed. But the need in every human being to maintain control of their inner lives means that they also have to handle all those internal insecurities identified in Chapter 1 as threatening the integrity of the concept of self and producing the constant need in people to create and re-create their identities. When English people joke about the alleged stupidity of the Irish or meanness of the Scots, they are contemplating the range of different possibilities which could apply to themselves. By implying through the joke that they are not stupid or mean, they are dabbling with the notion that they might indeed be so. They are confronting that which they want to reject, just like the managers joking about redundancy. The emotional experience of laughing along with others at what they do not wish to apply to themselves is a reassertion of personal control.

Two of the key thinkers who are regularly referred to by writers trying to theorise about humour, Bergson and Freud, both recognised, says Mary Douglas (1975), the connection between joking and the maintenance (or loss) of control. Taking the classic joke of someone slipping on a banana skin, she observes:

> For both, the essence of the joke is that something formal is attacked by something informal, something organised and controlled, by something vital, energetic, an upsurge of life for Bergson, of libido for Freud. The common denominator underlying both approaches is the joke is seen as an attack on control.
>
> (1975: 95)

That which we laugh at – the experience of being hurt and humiliated by falling on the floor, or the experience of receiving a redundancy notice – is contemplated and our fear of it tamed by the social experience of 'the laugh'.

In their analysis of humour and practical joking in a factory workshop, Boland and Hoffman, observe that 'while humour serves to celebrate an individual's existing identity it also asserts its fragility and ultimate equivocality' (1983: 193). How the practical joke plays with people's workplace identities in this way can be illustrated by an episode which took place in the ZTC Ryland boardroom. The event was one of the regular senior manager meetings known as 'control meetings' (jokingly referred to sometimes as 'out-of-control meetings'). The meeting was chaired by the director of the function whose activities were receiving their monthly review. The normal procedure was for the director to sit in the chair at the head of the table. But at one meeting when the director was late arriving, one of the attending executives decided to take this seat; 'Let's see what he does'. The rest of the group all moved towards the same end of the table, so leaving just one vacant chair, out on a limb.

When Jonathan arrived he reacted by quickly covering his initial fluster and taking the seat left for him. His different physical position appeared to make it difficult for him to maintain his usual domination of the meeting and a fairly heated argument about some issue developed between two individuals, which Jonathan found difficult to manage. However, he was then called out of the meeting by his secretary to take a telephone call. While he was out there was a further shuffling of chairs and the vacant chair which greeted Jonathan on his return was that between the two men who had been arguing. One could almost read on his face when he returned his debating whether or not to show recognition of the game that was being played. He took the seat, however, with a rather tensely spoken quip, 'Ah, I might as well be the rose between two thorns'. 'Between two pricks, more like', added someone else. At this there was laughter all round and the tension dissipated. The senior man in a meeting, a director of the business trying to chair a meeting of his executive team in the company boardroom, had been recognised as the senior man at the same time as his status was temporarily subverted. The next time he was called out by his secretary, the group discussed their experiment and came to the conclusion that it had 'done him good'. 'We got much less of the Jonathan monologue after that little prank' said the originator of the joke. In this demonstration of what Radcliffe-Brown, in his classical anthropological discussion of joking, called joking's 'peculiar combination of friendliness and antagonism' (1940: 196) control and authority has been both challenged and reaffirmed. But a change had occurred – the relationship between the manager and his subordinates had been subtly modified. It had been rendered more manageable.

Humour plays a part in the negotiating of relationships between people in the workplace, this case suggests. It became a major resource for me, and indeed the managers I worked with, in my own negotiating of a role in the factory as a hybrid insider/outsider. Humour was sometimes used as a sort of social litmus paper, as it often is with a newcomer, to check whether they will 'fit in' and will constitute a threat neither to the daily pattern of interaction and banter, nor to people's particular organisational interests. I needed to establish with managers that I was a pleasant companion to work with but, more important, that I was not yet another consultant looking at their work, or a pretentious and remote academic on a patronising visit to the 'real world'. Being located in the personnel department, which was resented for its powerful influence by many non-personnel managers, I also had partially to distance myself from that function. One opportunity to do this arose early on at a meeting where the shortage of bananas provided with the working lunch was apparently a regular issue.

As I left the conference block with a group of managers, following this meeting, the conversation turned from issues about performance-related pay to the sandwiches, fruit and fizzy drinks with which we had been provided. I was told:

'You've certainly wised up pretty quickly to how things work around here.'

'Oh, thank you. How do you mean?'

'You got here early enough to make sure you got a banana', to which another manager, whose name I had not yet picked up, added:

'There were three bananas last week; lots the week before, but only two today.'

'I don't know what's wrong with Harry', commented Bill (Harry being the personnel manager who organised the lunch), 'he knows everybody wants bananas but he doesn't arrange it when he books the lunch.'

'Don't complain, though, I'm sure you're pleased to see that the power of Personnel has it limits', I offered.

'Yeah, and you made sure you got in ahead of the usual personnel banana gannets. Well done.'

At this point the banana topic was suddenly dropped and the rather feeble humour quickly interrupted by a surprisingly aggressive question, shot at me by Phil Wollaton, as we crossed the road outside the conference block:

'What do you think of all these management gurus then?'

This was a serious challenge, and I had to distance myself from both consultants and popular management writers who 'think they know it all'. The humorous and the serious were working hand in hand in a social testing process. No joke, it would seem is 'just a joke'.

Humour functions at a variety of levels at the same time. A complex agenda of issues were addressed at Jonathan Bestwood's control meeting, looked at earlier. But this is not to say that people were not simply having fun, at the same time as playing about with issues of control. There is a surface level which has a significance in its own right, independently of the deeper level processes which may be occurring. Humour within management meetings can quite simply 'lubricate' proceedings and relieve the tedium of much of the business which has to be conducted. But this does not mean that there are not deeper currents beneath the surface ripples which are thrown up. At one long management meeting the conversation switched very quickly from a serious and detailed examination of factory loading into an almost bizarre comedy session. The change occurred when one member of the group arrived late and apologised, explaining that he had been helping Ted Meadows prepare a speech for an imminent royal visit to the site to open a new engineering block. Contributions from various participants followed:

'I hope Ted's not going to eff and blind at the Princess.'

'Eff off, Your Majesty.'

'Did you know that it's very common for people to dream that the Queen is coming to visit them for a cup of tea. They get all anxious that the house is nice and clean.'

'Have you got the engineering block all neat for the opening then, Jim?'

'And you've got the fancy fish for the fish pond?'

'I did. They cost a packet. But they've gone. The herons off the gravel pits keep coming and getting them.'

'What are you going to do about the geese? They make the grass beside the lake dead slippery. "Oh what a lovely lake Mr Meadows" [in mock royal female voice]. Splash. "Sorry Ma'am".'

'Sorry Ma'am. You haven't found any missing inventory down there have you?'

'Ted's going to get us all over there, cleaning up the goose crap before she arrives.'

'It's not the goose crap that's the problem. It's the mud they keep bringing right up to the nice shiny front of the building.'

'Get away. Are you telling me the geese are trying to jump the queue for a word with Her Majesty?'

'No. They keep coming up and having a go at the windows.'

'They what?'

'They try to mate with their reflections.'

'They'd better not do that when she comes. Ted'll have to say, "Excuse me Ma'am while I tell the geese to fuck off".'

At one level this was simply a hilarious episode punctuating a tedious meeting. At the deeper levels there were all sorts of possible meanings, some of which would no doubt be meat and drink to the Freudian analyst, with references to dreams, sex, excrement, deep water, missing hardware and a wet princess. Particular anxieties about the visit itself were clearly being addressed, as well as normal tensions of life in the Ryland site (which is set alongside a lake which was once a gravel pit and is now a bird sanctuary). There is the issue of missing inventory (a serious issue for some present) and there is the omnipresent shadow of Ted Meadows himself – a daily source of worry for every manager in that room and a standing threat to each man's self respect, given Meadows' habit of viciously and verbally abusing his managers. They knew very well that there was no chance of his slipping into his foul-mouthed mode of address in front of the Princess. But there is joy to be found in fantasising about his losing control in this way. As was the case with Jonathan Bestwood's executives, Ted Field's team have ritualistically challenged the leader's authority and at the same time adjusted to it. As Steve Linstead says, in looking at the role of humour in maintaining an organisational culture, humour has the 'capacity to both resist a dominant formulation and also to accommodate it' (1985: 762). Stories of all kinds also play a key role in the cultures of organisations.

HIGH STORIES, LOW STORIES AND TALKING DIRTY

If we look at the managerial literature on corporate cultures, which I argued has been so important in shifting management thinking in recent years, we will note the stress put by writers like Tom Peters on the stories which are told within organisations (See p. 23). Peters and Austin borrow Alan Wilkins distinction between 'high story' and 'low story' companies with the former using stories 'to motivate, teach and spread enthusiasm, loyalty and commitment' and the latter allowing stories to circulate which 'perpetuate cynicism, distrust and disbelief' (1985: 279). I collected as many stories as I could within ZTC Ryland, and the pattern was one in which there was an enormous dominance of 'low stories'. Among the exceptions to this were stories about the Parry past, when there were tales of heroic efforts to complete projects in very short periods of time. Dick Mansfield explained that he liked to tell people positive stories:

> 'Not long ago, someone wanted a telephone exchange and in twenty-four hours we delivered. That is the sort of place it is; if you give people the right message and tell them what you want they can perform bloody miracles here – it has. It has happened time and time again. I remember in the 1970s we produced as much in three days as we did in five. We have always been good in this way. And we are known for it.'

But these were not the sort of stories which were generally being recounted now:

> 'The stories are about how people have been allowed to go without us saying goodbye to them. They have just gone without anyone giving them any recognition. Forty years service have just drifted away. That is a sad thing which never would have happened in the past. We lost thousands of people in the past but we always recognised in some way the people that were going.'

The other type of positive stories were ones about certain widely respected and semi-mythical managers of the past, as we heard when looking at conceptions of good and bad managers in Chapter 7. But the bulk of the Ryland tales were negative ones. Almost totally dominating the stories told to me, when I asked the managers I interviewed to pass on stories they thought were typical of the ones told on the site, were anecdotes, myths and jokes with Ted Meadows as the villain or butt. I asked Mark Cossall, who had a personal collection of such stories, why this should be:

> 'He is the visible power figure. He represents the culture. He signals it. He is the "Simon says". If the stories about him didn't exist, people would create them.'

He recounted some of the tales, tying them into observations about other facets of the culture:

> 'It's part of the culture here that the place is kept reasonably tidy because he goes around on a Saturday morning. He bollocks people if things are untidy. He expects managers to shift things, to jump to it. It's told that when he first joined he went to one of our factories in Northern Ireland where they had laid out some automated test equipment as per workflow. He said, "I don't care what the effing workflow is, I want them in a straight line." Then there's the output thing. Output is so important at the end of the month that it is rumoured that bricks in boxes have been put into the warehouse to signify output. Then there are the cutting-in-half stories. Ted would look at invoices and say, "You can't possibly want that much, so cut that order in half." So people used to double up quantities. And there were minimum amount orders so you paid more

than you needed. Then there was encouraging people to go second class to London while, so the tales went, he drove down in his Jag. You'll also hear stories about doors on offices. In the finance department, certain people were told they should walk the job and therefore didn't need doors on their offices. But, at the same time, the story goes, he asked, "Where is the chesterfield for my office?" The unwritten rule is that there is one law for the rich and one for the poor. Then there is the terrorist joke: "What's the difference between Ted Meadows and a terrorist?" "You can negotiate with a terrorist."'

I heard time and again about the 'cutting-in-half' stories. Some of them were clearly apocryphal, such as the one in which joiners 'put in for twelve-foot lengths and got six-foot ones' and the one about safety boots, where the recipient of the halved order is said to have telephoned Meadows to ask 'What am I to do with all these left boots?' A story that I was assured by more than one individual was completely true was about an order for signmaker's letters of the alphabet:

'Gerry wanted to put up some signs – exit, no entry, etc. He decided the smart thing to do was to get some cardboard and stick his own letters on. He worked it all out and counted up the letters needed: two or three X's, twelve E's etc. He translated this onto a requisition – twelve I's etc. It then went to Ted, who crossed out the twelve and put six. All the high numbers were crossed out, halved. When Gerry got this, he said, "What shall we do?" I said, "Put them up '-X-T'". I am determined that this guy is going to understand. So Gerry put up "D-G-R". Ted walks round the warehouse: "What the bloody hell does this say?" Then, quick as a flash he said, "I bet this is because I cut the numbers down. Why didn't you tell me?"'

Andy Tollerton told me his variant of the popular office door story;

'Here's a really silly thing. I am having two of my managers moving into a new office on the shopfloor, nearer to their people. Ted came in the other day saying, "Let's go and see how it's coming along". He was collaring me for it not being done yet. Anyway, he said, "It is not having a door on it". He instructed that it won't have a door. My people are pinging off the wall about this. One of them has been here thirty years and now he's being told you can no longer have a door, even though the quality group next to the area have a door. Ted's leaving of course. So the door has been delivered and it is going up on the first of April, the day after he leaves.'

Another manager told me that 'there are office doors that Ted insisted be taken off hidden all over this site. The day he goes people will be digging them up all over the place'.

Here was a symbol of rebellion. In a use of stories not just to feed cynicism but to defend people's sense of self against a tyrannical senior manager, Ken Donnington had a fund of stories which generally mocked managerial pretensions:

'You know Maurice, well he had this handkerchief in his top pocket (he is a bit of a, snob anyway). He was walking around with a visitor and there were these two lads lifting some heavy stuff and sweating a lot. One of them just takes Maurice's handkerchief, wipes his face with it and puts it right back. Maurice was livid. Another good one: there was this bloke Fred Berkeley – as rough as arseholes – a pre-former. A senior guy was going around and asked 'Could you tell me what you are doing please?" Fred says, 'You take this fucker and you put it in this bugger here and then you do this to the bastard." My favourite story, though, is when this bloke – we think it might have been Fred again – phones up the General Manager and this voice says, "Are you the bloke in charge, are you the bloke who gets things done?" This went on and he then said, "Will you get that effing coffee machine working?" Donald was furious.'

Stories do not all circulate by word of mouth alone, as these scurrilous tales undoubtedly did. There were various unofficial documents which were circulated around the Ryland offices and workshops and which appeared on notice-boards. The following story may or may not have originated in ZTC. I think that it may have been circulated like the broadside ballads of earlier centuries; getting passed from hand to hand around the country and being adapted to fit local circumstances, its general relevance being given a local touch by the changing of key names. I came across this same story only days after being given it by a manager in ZTC Ryland, but this time in a large local hospital. Instead of ZTC it told of the NHS. The ZTC version, however, was:

Once upon a time, ZTC and the Japanese decided to have a boat race. Both teams practised long and hard to reach their peak performance. On the big day, they were as ready as they could be. The Japanese won by a mile.

Afterwards, the ZTC team became very discouraged by the loss and morale sagged. Senior management decided that the reason for the crushing defeat had to be found, and a project team was set up to investigate the problem and recommend appropriate action. Their conclusion: the problem was that the Japanese team had eight people rowing and one person steering. The ZTC team had one person rowing and eight people steering.

Senior management immediately hired a consultancy company to do a study on the team's structure. Millions of pounds and several months later they concluded that: too many people were steering and not enough rowing. To prevent losing to the Japanese the next year, the team structure was changed to four 'steering managers', three 'senior steering managers' and one 'executive steering manager'. A performance and appraisal system was set up to give the person rowing the boat more incentive to work harder and become a key performer. 'We must give him empowerment and enrichment. This ought to do it.'

The next year, the Japanese won by two miles. ZTC laid off the rower for poor performance, sold off all the paddles, cancelled all capital investment for new equipment and halted development of a new canoe, awarded high performance awards to the consultants and distributed the money saved to senior management.

In this story we see a powerful satire of the ZTC Ryland tendency to allow means to subvert ends, in the variety of ways examined in Chapter 6. There is also a scepticism about newer management discourses and control techniques. Top management are portrayed as incompetent, lacking confidence in their own managerial judgements and, above all, financially self-seeking. The manager who gave me the story took bitter satisfaction in reading it and in passing it on. It resonated loudly with attitudes common among Ryland managers.

KEEPING YOUR FEET ON THE GROUND

As Yannis Gabriel says, 'Stories, gossip, myths and jokes may represent attempts to humanize the impersonal spaces of bureaucratic organisations, to mark them as human territory' but they also 'strengthen the individual in his/her daily engagement with them' (1991: 873). Ken Donnington's fondness for stories which undermined managerial pomposity by setting linguistic crudity against pomp and authority reflected his personal attitude to status issues in the factory. But the use of such language was also a cultural device used by various of the factory managers to express their resentment of, or at least their ambivalence towards, the higher levels of the company hierarchy. Donnington's challenge to propriety and authority echoes the massive incongruity of his colleagues' insertion of rough 'factory language' into the arch respectability of royal protocol in the fantasised version of the Princess's visit and its imagined subversion by muddy-footed amorous geese.

In a sense, all of this was a matter of managers 'keeping their feet on the ground'. 'God help us, if we begin to take ourselves too seriously', said a colleague to me one day, following a piece of foolery in which we had jointly engaged. He had written on the white board above his desk some piece of folk wisdom – in Spanish. In partial mockery of this, I wrote above my desk a piece of mock Latin, *Fac Meam Diem* (make my day). 'If you can understand Spanish I am sure you can understand that', I said, tongue in cheek. His response was fast and, I thought, brilliant: 'Oh yes, no problem: "fuck me daily" – the Ryland motto.'

The telling of stories and the retailing of work-related jokes at ZTC Ryland tied in very little with the official culture of the company. They did very little to support and spread the 'winning culture'. They were predominantly 'low' stories which either subverted authority or aided adjustment to deprivations, worries and insecurities. Managers widely disapproved of the short-termist, cost-cutting approach which had arisen with the ZEC regime as much as they resented the behaviour of the senior managers effecting these policies and practices. Yet the stories and jokes about foolish and self-cancelling cost-cutting practices and about the bullying behaviour of Ted Meadows were as current in those areas of the plant where he rarely directly intervened as in the manufacturing area where he held particular functional responsibilities. As Mark Cossall suggested, he epitomised the culture of the plant as a whole. It might be more accurate, though, to say that he provided a focus for the development of a cynical and defensive unofficial culture.

Cynicism was an attitude adopted with immense reluctance by managers at an individual level. It was expressed in stories and jokes, and in what a secretary taking minutes at a management meeting one day called 'ritual belly-aching sessions'. One might say the culture handled the hurt and kept it from cutting too deeply into the souls of men and women deeply committed to a company many had worked for and identified with for many years. I had the following conversation with a manager, crossing the yard, on my last day in the plant:

> 'I've just come from empowering six of my staff.'
> 'Oh good, you are keeping up the battle, then?'
> 'Oh yes. I've just empowered them by telling them they are redundant, out, finished.'
> 'That's a bit cynical isn't it? I thought you believed in empowerment and all that?'
> 'Of course I do. I am dead serious. They have been empowered by being set free from this place. They will have to use all their skills and resources to cope in the big wide world.'

Joking was never more serious. And management could go on being managed.

WOMEN IN A MAN'S WORLD?

The workforce at ZTC Ryland was not a completely male-dominated one. The office-based departments, as in most organisations, employed large proportions of women secretarial and administrative workers. And the factory departments were not the traditionally male preserves seen in traditional engineering works. Much of the production work was done by women, especially in the 'board shops' where components were added to circuit-boards ('board-stuffing'). Generally, then, being a woman employee at Ryland was less likely to feel like being a stranger in a male-dominated world than it might in more traditional manufacturing enterprises. But, ironically, it made being a woman manager feel all the more a 'woman in a man's world', as Caroline Wymswold observed:

> 'It's not that the men [managers] aren't used to having women around them. I still have to remind some of them that I'm not a secretary or a tea-maker. They're generally very decent to me, I must say. But that's part of the problem. It's the language thing that keeps reminding you that you are a woman in a man's world. Every time they swear, they apologise. I really hate that. Sometimes I say something like 'Shit!'. There's no noticeable reaction, but I can tell it makes them uneasy.'

As we have seen, much of the normal managerial repartee involved the use of rough or bad language, which we would normally associate with a masculine rather than a gender-mixed environment. Whether or not women managers at Ryland minded the use of bad language, the men generally assumed they did and, whether consciously or not, they sometimes created a degree of tension by acting more 'respectably' than they were comfortable with. One man said:

> 'I know I've got to get used to it. But you can't clear the air in the way you normally do, when there's a woman there, by going "sodding bastard thing" and that sort of, you know, letting off steam.'

Overt forms of discrimination against women managers at Ryland rarely went beyond the 'whoops, ladies present' apology for bad language or the common chairman's 'Good morning, gentlemen and, sorry, lady'. I observed both of these patterns frequently and sometimes had to avoid visibly wincing. 'The truth of it', a woman personnel manager told me:

> 'is that there are so few women managers here that the men have nothing to feel threatened by. We are not chasing their jobs to any real extent. Yet a lot of them are clearly threatened on some other level, something psychological I suppose. You sense it with some of them. They are being very "nice". There's something patronising in their tone – "Thank you, my dear" – and you think, "This bloke could turn nasty if he thought a woman might be a real rival to him." It's the way they keep at it, always reminding you of your place with this "dearie" stuff.'

Carol Rowsley spoke of the unrelenting pressure of male comments and terms:

> 'You get tired of albeit jovial comments about home life interrupting work and there are all the "my dear" phrases ("hell or damn, sorry my dear, ladies in the room"). But the sort of thing you get is, like one I always remember, a chap in a meeting said his wife was collecting the car from the garage and another one turned round and said, "you mean you let your wife drive it home?" There is one manager who calls me "little girl". It's his style: "you do this, little one".'

Mary Southwell suggested that these tensions arose from the 'the age old thing of men and women' which she felt had partly been brought on themselves by women because 'they pass it on to their sons that they should get themselves a wife and "you will expect her to iron your shirts and wash your socks and cook your meals". He then expects this all the time.' She thought that it had 'been proved so much now that women will do [top management] jobs better than men' and that men are aware of this. She believed that a male manager in her department covered up his concerns about this with jokes. But she felt the seriousness beneath the joking:

> 'One of my peers, he is always saying it as a joke but I feel that he means it, "Oh you are a woman." Like, one day I was sitting at the boss's desk and he says, "What are you doing there?" I thought he was just joking but he went

on, "It doesn't suit you anyway." I said "Why?" He said "Because you are a woman". He makes these jokes, but I always sense there is more underneath them. His wife is always at home, caring for him. And he has got two sons. So I wonder?'

In my core interviews I asked men and women managers exactly the same initial question on the gender issue: 'Do you think the pressures on women managers are the same as on men?' I did not ask directly about discrimination, and the above responses emerged as facets of the 'pressures' which women faced. The male respondents said little that was inconsistent with women's accounts of the attitudes of men towards women managers at Ryland. Men typically observed how few women managers there were, and it was by no means unusual for them to comment that, for example, 'it is male-dominated and it has always been very chauvinist and still is to a large extent' or 'we are sexist and we do discriminate, to be honest. We don't mean to be, mind you, but we do subconsciously.'

What the men and women pointed to, time and again, as the main pressure on women was that of the women 'continually having to prove themselves'. Other studies have found women reporting things very similar to the Ryland women. Scase and Goffee, for example, report that 'many of the women in our survey are acutely aware' of what, following Rosabeth Moss Kanter (1977), they see as the 'pressure to perform' created by the visibility of women in organisations where women managers tend to be 'tokens' (1989: 112). One man, quite typically, commented that 'a lot of the pressure is in women themselves because they believe that they have to prove themselves as much better than male managers doing similar jobs'. He said that 'the impression comes across that they are striving to be super managers just to stand still'. The men tended to comment that not all women managers were like this, and some were concerned about the limitations of such a belief, for example:

'Those who feel that they've got twice the journey to cover set off with a disability. It's a self-limiting perception. I tend to think that as long as you go on thinking that you have got to work twice as hard to be successful, that will go on happening to you.'

What is interesting about the frequency with which men pointed to this pressure to outperform men is that few of them, in practice, had had dealings with more than two or three women managers at most, as they often pointed out. It seemed that there was a conventional wisdom within ZTC Ryland that this was a problem for women managers. It was perhaps connected to a growing awareness within the company that women were under-represented at managerial levels, something which was perhaps connected to the willingness of men to talk of 'chauvinism'. The original managing director and later chairman of ZTC had publicly commented on the shortage of women managers and I was told by senior personnel people that deliberate attempts had been made to increase the number of women managers at Ryland. One personnel executive told me that he had 'no doubt that we let some through that would not have got through if we'd applied our normal criteria'.

An awareness that some kind of positive action of this kind might have occurred in itself added to the pressures on recently promoted women. Jane Trowell reported:

> 'There is a problem when you begin to get women into management and it is commented on in such a way that people can interpret it that "we needed to have more women and now we have more women", rather than "you deserve the position". The increase in women managers was open to the interpretation that it was just lip-service. That left a bit of a bitter taste. Nobody said it to me, but the thought that people might think it was rather irritating.'

This created a further pressure 'to show that you deserved to be where you are'. It was part of what another woman called 'a vicious circle' whereby you 'do well' and then have to counter the 'hint of resentment' among some of the men by 'doing even better'. She observed with a touch of bitterness that:

> 'You end up trying to make yourself fire-proof. But of course you are just making yourself more vulnerable to the big slip-up when it comes. The more fire-proof you think you are making yourself by completing everything on time and checking every move, the less fireproof you are becoming.'

The extra care which women managers feel they have to take with their work may influence their style of working; encouraging them to be more attentive to other people, for example. Some of the men suggested that women were, as women, more 'people-oriented' than male managers. This has been suggested by some researchers, like Carol Gilligan (1982). It is refuted by others, however. Sue Freeman (1990), on the basis of a study of forty American women managers, argues that women show greater diversity in their own styles than they differ from men. And in a review of the range of available research evidence, Powell concludes that 'the only meaningful difference between men and women may be in the environments in which they operate, with imbalanced sex ratio . . . contributing to stereotype-driven perceptions and unrealistic expectations for managerial women' (1988: 166). My observations of the behaviour and styles of the few women managers at ZTC Ryland suggested that they were far more influenced by having to handle a male-dominated organisational context than by any essential feminine qualities. They varied from each other considerably (and indeed were seen to by the men) and each found their own way of handling their identities and their careers as they shaped their performances to manage their managerial work.

Jane Trowell explained how, earlier in her career, she had gone out of her way to act 'professionally' and play down her femininity. It was an experience on a course that encouraged her to modify this:

'I went on a presentation course and I did mine on marketing. I was very very serious and very schoolmarmish, which I had a tendency to be. I was so composed and frosty it wasn't true. This guy suddenly said, "What do you do away from work?" I was absolutely pole-axed and only then did I relax. I had previously not talked about my outside life because I was so "professional". It took confidence to develop credibility before I felt able to lower the guards and say, "This is me; I love cooking and having dinner parties and I like doing some of the obviously female things".'

One of the obviously female things that a woman manager can do is to have children. And it is when a woman has children that the pressures really come to bear on her in ZTC, according to Jane Trowell, who was pregnant at the time:

'You know that it's part of the way of life here to stay late if you are in a senior job. I've coped with that in the past. But now I have to get away by six. I am probably managing better by being more efficient with my time and delegating better. But it is open to misinterpretation; "she's offloading". I'll be no less committed to the job when I have the baby. But the child-care arrangements won't stretch into the evenings. I'll have to get away to collect the baby. And I know exactly what sort of sarcy comments I'll get.'

The convention of managers staying late into the evening at Ryland had clear implications for women managers and was a deterrent to women remaining in management careers in ZTC. Each of the (admittedly small number of) women managers with children I met in ZTC Ryland was either contemplating an alternative career or actually left for a career in an organisation – a large hospital, for example – where women managers were less of a rarity. The 'staying late' pattern among Ryland managers had implications for male managers as well as for women, however.

HOME AND WORK, HUSBANDS AND WIVES

Many of the managers in ZTC Ryland, especially the senior ones, stayed at the plant as a matter of normal routine until between seven and eight o'clock at night. If there was extra pressure it would be expected that people would continue into the late evening to deal with it. Many of the managers were critical of this practice and felt that it could be reduced if people worked more effectively during the day and, for example, 'kept the length of bloody meetings under control'. I criticised one male manager for hurting the feelings of a woman colleague to whom he had joked, 'Having an early night?', as she left her office at 7.15 pm one evening:

'You know how committed and hard-working she is. Don't you realise that such pathetic jokes can hurt?'
'Yes. I plead guilty.'
'Don't you think that this staying late business needs to be re-thought, especially in the light of the equal opportunities issues we've been talking about?'

'Absolutely. I'm as guilty as any for perpetuating it. But I don't think it is a good thing at all, as a regular practice I mean. It does no good to anybody's family life. But I don't think it is good for the business either. It just breeds inefficiencies. To be honest, I think you get a lot of behaviour just like the shopfloor thing of stretching work in the day to make overtime for later. At least the ex-hourly-paid types get paid for overtime.'

'So why does it continue?'

'Uhu. It's daft isn't it. I suppose it's a status thing: "I'm too important to go home at the same time as the plebs." But, to be honest, I think – no, I know – there's another dimension to it. It suits a lot of blokes to get home after the kids are sorted out by the wife: "I'll just sort this paperwork and then when I get back the kids will be clean and pyjama'd and all the hassle over."'

'So it disadvantages women as wives as well as women as managers, then?'

'Absolutely. It really is a male thing. There's even the macho manager bit: "Look at me. What a big tough guy I am. Look at the long hours I can put in."'

'But you do it?'

'Pathetic isn't it?'

The practice of staying late, and working at weekends, came up repeatedly when I asked managers about the relationship between home and work in my interviews:

'The main issue is the messing up of the home life by working late. It is back to the culture thing again. I've tried to introduce some discipline to things here but the culture here is that overtime is a must and not a sin. I miss going to my allotment like I used to. It really helped, having a chat away from work and bashing the hell out of the soil.'

Many of the male managers spoke of the way their wives and families 'tolerated' this pattern of life, or were 'understanding'. Harry Basford said that 'work wins out' and that this was partly possible because he had 'a very good, very stable, family life'. I asked what he meant by work 'winning out':

'Oh it's time. And then, when I am there, not always giving 100 per cent attention. They understand, though. They are very good and understanding. I know all this seems contradictory. I know I am lucky in this and I think it might be different if my wife were at home all the time. She has a strong network of friends and contacts through her own work. She gets a lot of satisfaction and interest from work so she does not look to me for too much when my mind is on work. It could work out very differently if things were not like they are in my family life.'

Geoff Clifton told me:

'I have a very understanding family. If I went home and said "I am flying out to Munich tomorrow", I would not get too much aggravation. And I do that sort of thing.'

And Alan Bridgford observed:

'The wife knows that if I don't turn up at seven o'clock, I will turn up when I turn up. It doesn't become a major family issue.'

Whilst Dick Mansfield assured me:

> 'My wife understands that I have got a job to do and that I am intent on doing it properly and correctly and so be it. But the two things are distinct and separate. When I am not here, I am not here. My family understand that if I need to be here, I need to be here. That is a judgement I have to make and I am left to make it. My wife would not dream of trying to make that kind of judgement about, say, Saturday mornings or a Sunday.'

Another man said that his wife 'simply understands that I love my job and that it is part of the me she married', whilst another spoke of his wife accepting that he was a 'workaholic'. Don Smalley also used the term 'workaholic', but in a more self-critical way;

> 'I obviously (hmmn, why obviously?) work long hours and hence there has got to be a knock-on there. It makes problems. Is it because I am a workaholic or whatever? It affects social events and it affects holidays. Out of my twenty-five days allowance I only take ten or fifteen. Quite honestly, I do ask myself whether this is self-imposed and how much it is real work. If I took twenty-five days off, would it make the slightest bit of difference to me or the company? This is the same with a lot of people; they think they are more needed than they really are.'

It would appear that this practice of managers working considerably over their contracted hours could be put alongside many of the other elements of life at ZTC Ryland reviewed in Chapter 6 in which we see means becoming ends in themselves. Much late attendance appears to be purely ritualistic and a symbol of status, rather than a matter of doing necessary overtime. Robert Jackall argues that the long hours engaged in by the American managers he studied enabled them to engage in rituals like 'popping in and out of other managers' offices' with jokes and cartoons. This helped them maintain the kinds of social bond with each other which enabled them to operate as a managerial team (1988: 51). However, there is the suggestion on the part of some managers at Ryland that effectiveness is actually undermined by the time-wasting which is encouraged to fill the extended attendance time. There may thus be a cost to 'the business' as well as a cost to the quality of family life and, especially, to the interests of women, whether they be managers themselves or the wives of managers.

The relationship between people's home and family life involves more than issues of working hours. As Scase and Goffee say, there can be ambiguities in distinguishing the work and non-work roles of managers since 'although they may be apparently "relaxing" at home they may still be psychologically "at work"' (1989: 131). Over a third of the managers studied by Scase and Goffee reported that they 'often' found themselves becoming 'preoccupied with work-related issues during their free time' (1989: 139). This was especially so among senior managers and it is part of the *spill-over* type of relationship between work and non-work which Evans and Bartolomé (1980) found to be common among the managers they studied.

Clive Oxton had tried to stop the spill-over of work issues into his home life, but there was ambiguity even greater than that referred to by Scase and Goffee:

'I used to take work home in my head, if not in my brief-case. Now I try to put things at the back of mind. I may be fooling myself here, though, because I have been having these awful headaches and the doctor tells me it is tension. The only thing that could be causing tension is work. I feel I have got work in a separate compartment from home. But I wonder.'

Terry Carlton, in contrast to this, saw the two spheres of his life as 'complementary' because they both presented challenges:

'Work has a strain and discipline of its own, and so does home. They are complementary because they both provide stable bases from which to work. It's like logging in Canada, I once explained to somebody; I am happy jumping from log to log. It is falling down in between them that I am frightened of.'

In Evans and Bartolomé's terms this follows the *independent* pattern of work and non-work relationship. But Carlton also reports a positive *spill-over* effect from home to work:

'I think I learned most about negotiating skills from my boy. Kids are brilliant negotiators.'

Derek Draycott spoke of *spill-over* in the other direction. At work he had recognised the value of encouraging people to work out solutions to problems for themselves through a process of asking them questions, because 'It's better than you solving problems for them.' He found himself increasingly applying this to non-work relationships. He had been doing this with a friend who ran a small business, with his local vicar and 'I've even started to do it with the kids.' He was, however, 'less blunt in the questioning process than I am here'.

Spill-over between work and home can occur in either direction and it can be positive or negative in its effects. As Scase and Goffee (1989) also found, the direction was more typically from home to work in the case of women managers. Carol Rowsley explained:

You can't divorce one from the other, even though you try to separate the two. I suppose the main way that home affects work is that if school phones up and says my child is sick, I drop everything and run. Then, if I have to get something done desperately and have to work late, I do – if I can get a baby-sitter.'

Mary Southwell, however, with a chuckle, said she carried her managerial role over into the home:

'I just tell my husband to do the washing up and get the house cleaned!'

Some of the negative effects of work on home life are suggested by Phil Wollaton,

'It affects my wife and to some extent my children, because some of the frustration which I have I inevitably take home. They don't always understand the pressures. When I'm here I am paranoid about the need to answer telephones. When I get home, if the telephone rings and nobody answers I start to get cross. It's stupid, I know. It's got be answered but it doesn't really matter if nobody answers it at home.'

And Henry Dunkirk:

'I have a bit of a problem: I go home and switch off completely and I try to explain to Linda. But she'll say, "You're not talking". I'll put the tele on and I will switch off, because when you have been here all day – answering the phone and talking to people on the shopfloor – you don't feel like it. I don't think she really appreciates it because she has never worked in a factory. I say, "No, I am just resting."'

Eddie Elton felt better able to discuss work with his wife because she worked at ZTC, although not as a manager. This gave them 'something in common':

'We talk, perhaps whilst we're having dinner. I'll say, "How have you gone on today, love?", and she'll say, "A good day", or whatever. I am a good listener to her and she is a good listener to me. We help each other but sometimes you find yourself talking about information she shouldn't be privy to. But she is 100 per cent loyal. She never ever has let me down.'

Elton had been married before and painted a contrasting picture of his previous relationship (as well, perhaps, as a particular attitude towards conjugal roles generally):

'My first wife was a housewife and I had to listen to baby talk when I went home, or where she had been for coffee or what the neighbours had said, or whatever. I sometimes used to think "Oh, not again". You know; it doesn't change, does it? The things she did in any one day, because we had four kiddies, didn't really change. It was this neighbour or that neighbour or this shop or that shop. It does help when you have some topics in common.'

A younger manager spoke of the close partnership he had with his wife. She understood the interdepartmental tensions of life in ZTC Ryland:

'It would be different if I didn't have a wife who was working with me. We work as a team. We are in this together, so she supports me. She feels my frustrations at work. Last night I said to my wife, "I am furious". She said, "Don't tell me – Personnel." We share those problems. When I go home I can get anything off my chest.'

Inevitably, when we start considering the role that managers' marriages play in their lives we are getting into complex matters which touch on aspects of their lives and identities which will be unique to each of them. This takes us back to the issue of managers having to 'manage' their lives and identities, as well as their work responsibilities. Paul Ruddington spoke of how his wife and he had both been used to discussing their respective jobs. But her work, in another industrial organisation, became increasingly similar to his own:

> 'In some ways that may be a threat to me – as a person. When she was doing something different there was no problem. Tell me if I'm going too deep. It related to the sort of person I am. There was not too much problem at the surface. My wife has not been more successful than me or earned more than me. But when it began to creep towards that situation I suppose I saw threats coming. I admit that I do not have a particularly good self-image. I lack a lot in self-confidence. In my career I've not done badly. I could have done better. But there's a bolster; the professional life has helped with the personal. I can take comfort from my professional life when I have problems with my personal life. This in a sense is why my work is so important to me. I may not be able to do this and that, but I am still a valid person.'

Here again is the expression 'the sort of person I am'. Paul Ruddington gives us an insight into just one way in which being a manager can help an individual to manage their identity and maintain their sense of self-worth. Although there are patterns to the way people talk, live and manage to be managers, each is a unique individual who shapes their life in their own idiosyncratic way as they create their biographies and steer a course through their managerial career. When we come to considering what makes someone an effective or competent manager, in the next chapter, we will have to bear this in mind: each manager manages in her or his own way and is going to be successful or unsuccessful very much according to their notion of the 'sort of person they are'.

Chapter 9

Culture, Competence and Keeping Faith

'The culture in successful businesses is different from in failing businesses. It would be the same with a country or a city. You can see this when you go to Liverpool. I don't go there very often, but when I do I come back feeling really depressed. I could really weep when I look at it now; the way it has been destroyed. It has been destroyed by its own stupidity. I remember as a kid the docks, eighteen miles long. It is now dead. It is all a political problem; these areas have been starved over the years. It has been happening since the eighteenth century, so that these people have been downtrodden to the point where they expect to be downtrodden. They are totally suspicious of any change. They are totally suspicious of anybody trying to help them. They immediately look for the rip-off. They have also been educated to believe it is clever to actually get "one over on them". So they are all at it. And the demarcation lines that the unions have been allowed to impose in those areas, because of this, makes it totally inflexible to the point where it is destructive. I know it. I can see it.'

'And how does that relate to what is happening here?'

'Well, I was going to say, how do you change this sort of negative culture? We've done a lot here. But my greatest fear here is that they are going to destroy all the good work that we put onto this site if they keep pushing and pushing and pushing the bottom end like they are doing. I believe people will react in such a way shortly that they will destroy everything.'

'Bottom end?'

'Of the workforce; pushing them by getting rid, I mean. How the hell can you preach this flexibility, this personal and business development at the same time as you are getting rid? As someone said to me yesterday, an operator, "Why am I in here now doing the best I can getting this product out when tomorrow morning you can give me a brown envelope?" I had no answer.'

'But the good work you refer to?'

'Take IR. There has been a coordinated plan to withdraw the power from the unions and give it back to the managers and give it back to the workforce as well. That was going fairly well. But these continuing rounds of redundancies will give the opportunity to say "We told you so; we knew that was the ground plan all along." The union people can say, "You should have listened to us all the time."'

'And the other changes?'

'Developing Organisational Capability, winning culture, Business Improvement Plan, empowering and all that: I am totally committed to all of this in principle. These changes are the way forward. But what the company is doing

is going contrary to what all this is about. This is dangerous – raising
expectations and then smashing them. I believe the senior management has
a moral responsibility to its workforce and to employ. This firm is an integral
part of the society we live in.'
  'Which means?'
  'Any business has got to keep faith with all of those it deals with if it is going
to deserve to survive.'

MANAGERS, OWNERS AND CONTROLLERS

To contemplate managing organisations through culture rather than
through external controls, arm's-length relationships and tightly specified
calculative exchanges is, as I emphasised in Chapter 1, to navigate deep
and dangerous waters. Jack Hockley, after drawing parallels between his
perception of the problems of his home city of Liverpool and the negative
aspects of employment relations in a business, recognises this. He not only
points to the dangers of raising expectations which are subsequently not
met, he also sees organisational cultures as intimately related to the history
and politics of the social, economic and class context of the organisation.
Part of this context is the pattern of ownership of enterprises like ZTC.
And Hockley is clearly pointing to a powerful tension between what
managers like himself had been trying to achieve and the priorities, and
indeed values, of those in charge of the business.

I found it more common at Ryland to find managers expressing feelings
of antagonism towards the company's owning interests or 'top management' than towards those groups traditionally seen to be at odds with
managers, 'the workers' or 'the unions'. Management in ZTC is not a
united team sharing common aims and values. Jack Hockley spoke in
terms similar to those of many other managers, when he said:

  'The very senior management of this company take very short-term decisions,
  and very destructive decisions, in my view. But this is not just the senior
  management of this company. It appears to me that the whole of the country
  has this idea that if you are dirtying your hands, it is not a good thing. I
  personally think we are taking the short road to total destruction. The economy
  of this country is in danger of foundering. I believe we are losing at a rate that
  we will never be able to replace (a) the skill of manufacturing and (b) the
  development people are going to disappear with it. They must be prats to do
  this. It is a tragedy that our senior managers run down this track. We should
  get other products onto this site. It is a tragedy that we are losing all these
  people. They never look at the long-term. Look at the Japanese: they don't go
  round sacking their people.'

Jack Hockley's was an impassioned speech, made at an early stage in an
interview. He did not think there was any point in talking about detailed
aspects of managerial work without putting it in its 'broad context' which,
'whether you like or not, is political and moral'. I can only agree with this.
It is not my purpose here, however, to make personal judgements about

the allegedly 'short-termist' values of British companies and governments and about an anti-manufacturing bias in British culture at large. But my research in one British company – a part of a very large British enterprise owning a significant slice of British manufacturing capacity – suggests that a lot of its managers hold such critical views. Such views were held by men and women at the same time as they were working with a high level of commitment to achieve the continuation and success of ZTC Ryland. As various managers told me, this involved a considerable effort to resist becoming cynical.

Managers cannot avoid the fact that their appointment establishes them as the agents of the interests who own or ultimately control the organisation in which they work. As Peter Armstrong says, management is not a 'predefined set of tasks and functions', but involves acting, or appearing to act, 'so as to further the aims of more senior managers (and, ultimately, ownership) as these appear to the manager' (1989: 320). Armstrong's own research looks at the ways in which different managerial groups come into competition with each other – engineers with accountants, say, or personnel managers with production managers. He sees these as rivalries over how the interests of owners can best be represented (so enabling any given group to increase its share of the rewards available for serving dominant interests). However, an even more pluralistic view of managerial life (but which does not deny the ultimate dominance of owning interests) can recognise the potential for managers at least to attempt to influence the directing of the organisation's affairs so that it meets a wider range of interests than the owners might allow if left to their own devices.

I gave an account in Chapter 5 of attempts by managers in ZTC Ryland to influence the direction being taken by the company so as to enable themselves and other Ryland employees to escape the 'giant brown envelope' of redundancy. Similar attempts were made by managers in the American bank studied by Vicki Smith (1990). She shows how managers in some parts of the bank resisted various 'facets of the new managerial agenda' being imposed from above. These managers set about 'shaping their own workplaces' according to their own judgements about what would be best both for the company and for the people involved in those workplaces. These managers were not refusing to 'deploy their discretion to achieve certain corporate goals'. Their actions, rather, were 'shaped by an alternative sense of the corporate interest' (1990: 151). Although the Ryland managers achieved nothing on the scale of the managers studied by Smith, the logic of their attempts was the same. They saw their role as one of maintaining the long-term viability of the corporation. But they did not see that they should necessarily accept the definition of how this should be done that was held by the top management. There was no question of their challenging the ownership rights of the shareholders. But they chose to interpret their role as one of managing their work so as to serve simultaneously the interests of various other constituencies, or stakeholders; not least themselves.

MORALITY AND KEEPING FAITH

This analysis might be interpreted as suggesting simply that managers try to influence the strategies of top managements and owners to further their own sectional and personal interests and that, if this involves defending such interests as those of employees, then they are only doing this in order to retain a workforce which they can be employed to manage. My own strategic exchange view of human and group behaviour would not play down the role of such interests in shaping action (see pp. 25–7). But it would suggest that we avoid crude 'either-or' judgements about whether any given action is self-interested or altruistic. Ryland managers were anxious to resist what many of them viewed as the short-termist, cost-focused and hierarchically imposed decisions of the corporate management of ZTC and its masters in ZEC. There was clear self-interest in this, as such policies were seen as threatening their own careers. But they often had a value-based and moral objection to such policies as well. This can be related to the personal values of managers and to their concepts of 'self' and what we have met throughout this study as their notion of 'the sort of person I am'. Their involvement in managerial work was both an expression and a shaper of their notion of self and what is good and bad, right and wrong. Robert Jackall argues that managerial work forces managers to 'bracket' the values they hold privately and to follow the kind of morality, suggested to him by a former senior manager, who claimed that, 'what is right in the corporation is what the guy above you wants from you. That's what morality is in the corporation' (1988: 6). In spite of the existence of pressures towards such a state of affairs identified by Jackall, I believe that the majority of the managers I worked with at Ryland would be incapable of acting as amoral and unfeeling agents of remote financial interests.

The moral concerns of the Ryland managers were more than matters of personal integrity and private values, however, as Jack Hockley implies in choosing the words 'any business has got to keep faith with all of those it deals with if it is going to deserve to survive'. These managers recognised the moral basis of the very work in which they were engaged. I showed in Chapter 7 how managers can be seen as appreciating that a high level of trust and reciprocity is vital to achieving what I call 'productive coopera-tion': people who do not trust each other and have a strictly calculative concept of exchange are unlikely to achieve together work tasks of any complexity, or to solve organisational problems of any difficulty. The achieving of a high level of trust between the members of any group or organisation requires commitment to a shared set of values relating to their shared activities. This means a need for the organisation to function, as Peter Anthony argues, as a moral community (1986: 187–8). Such a view is supported by evidence other than my own. As Anthony, writing with Michael Reed, puts it:

> Accumulating evidence shows that managers (real managers, below the level of corporate manipulation . . .) depend for their effectiveness upon norms of reciprocity, upon trust, obligation and the maintenance of defensible social relationships . . . Reality, both social and economic, resides in the production and exchange of goods and services and that depends on the dialectics of control and cooperation, on leadership and community and, finally, upon authority, which is essentially moral.
>
> (1992: 608)

John Roberts (1984) draws on his own research among managers to argue that managers and management writers are mistaken if they believe that their work is a morally neutral activity which involves applying control techniques to achieve effective performance. Drawing, like Peter Anthony, on the writing of the philosopher Alisdair MacIntyre (1981), Roberts argues that manipulative techniques cannot work because of the endemic unpredictability of social life and, hence, the inadequacy of the social science knowledge upon which they are based. Technical managerial competence can achieve little real control. The only effective control that can be achieved is moral control:

> Such moral forms of control will not be realized merely by insisting that staff recognize that their interests are bound up with the survival of the 'company as a whole', whilst in their immediate practice, through coercion or manipulation, managers seek to deny or avoid this inter-dependence. Instead what is required is a form of *practice* in which there is a mutual recognition of one another as interdependent subjects; each recognizing his or her dependence on others' actions, whilst at the same time acknowledging the freedom of action of others.
>
> (1984: 301)

Roberts says that it is the 'interdependence of self-conscious subjects' that is, for him, the moral basis or condition of all social life. This insight, developed from the work of another philosopher and social theorist, Jurgen Habermas (1971), is denied or ignored by 'purely technical versions of management practice', says Roberts. I concur entirely with this and suggest that it helps us understand why the accounts given to me in Chapter 7 of managers' experiences of learning their craft said so little about managerial techniques or textbook theories that they had acquired. Their own 'theories', mixing the principled and the pragmatic, as we saw, were recognitions of the necessity of negotiating trusting and consistent relations with others.

We saw in ZTC Ryland that managers did not necessarily or consistently apply these principles in practice. I explained this as in part a result of the anxieties, frustrations and frailties of managers as individuals struggling to shape their own lives at the same time as shaping the activities of people around them (see pp. 178–81). But such problems appear to have been massively exacerbated by the insecurities and frustrations resulting from the apparent lack of recognition of the importance of reciprocity between top managers and others on the part of those at the corporate level in ZTC and ZEC. If we look back to the above summary by Anthony and Reed of the research backing for the importance of trust and reciprocity in managerial work, we will notice that they apply this only to 'real managers', people whom they differentiate from those who operate at 'the level of corporate manipulation'. This suggests that, at least in these commentators' reading of research evidence, it is not unusual for there to be a lack of the kind of two-way communication and negotiation between top managers and middle managers that these middle managers find necessary to develop within their own spheres of operation.

MANAGERIAL EMPOWERMENT AND EXCLUSION

Frances Westley also suggests, on the basis of her own review of research, that there is 'evidence of extensive dissatisfaction among middle managers, who often perceive that they are excluded from strategic processes' (1990: 337). The dissatisfactions found among the British managers surveyed by Scase and Goffee, and discussed in Chapter 3, were related by these researchers to what they feel is a 'growing divide between, on the one hand, senior executives and, on the other hand, middle and junior managers'.

Throughout this study I have deliberately avoided the concept of 'middle management'. It could be said that my study is a study of middle managers because, as well as giving little attention to 'supervisory' level managers, I pay only limited direct attention to corporate ZTC managers (there is plenty of 'indirect' attention to such people). But I did not want to impose such categories on the managers I was studying. I talked to people across the whole range of those who were officially called 'managers' on the Ryland site. Thus, when I refer to people as, for example, senior managers or directors, I am doing so because that is how they were referred to in the organisation. I wanted to avoid pre-judging and to allow whatever key distinctions between levels which might influence thinking and behaviour to be a matter of what would emerge as I got to know the organisation. And what turned out to be the key boundary was that between, on the one hand, managers located at Ryland (including directors of businesses within ZTC) and, on the other hand, corporate directors of ZTC and ZEC who were located in a city some forty miles away, or in London.

I have a further, and perhaps deeper, reason for not wishing to identify any group as a 'middle management' one. This goes back to my arguments about the nature of management which I set out in Chapter 2. There I identified management, whether we focus on it as a function, a set of activities or as a team of people, as a single logical entity. In principle the managerial part of an organisation is that part of it which is concerned with the running of the organisation 'as a whole'. The management could, at one extreme, consist of a single person and, at the other, could consist of every individual in the organisation (an organisation of partners, say, or a fully fledged cooperative). The pressures of size and complexity, let alone ownership preference, tend to take organisations away from either of these forms in practice. But what are likely to threaten significantly the performance of an organisation are situations like that argued by Scase and Goffee to be making British managers into 'reluctant managers'; a situation in which senior executives 'monopolize strategic decision-making' and the other managers 'are delegated routine administrative duties' (1989: 28).

The managers in ZTC Ryland were shown in Chapter 3 not to be 'reluctant' managers, yet neither were they like the managers identified by Dopson and Stewart (1990) who were finding themselves coming 'closer to top management and the strategic and policy area' (p. 63). We saw in Chapter 4 that the process of establishing the 'winning culture' for the organisation was explicitly based on principles of the company *not* having a 'top down' approach to strategy formation. Strategy was to emerge within an agreed 'strategic intent' and, as we saw, a good proportion of the Ryland managers had taken part in presenting training events where they used a script stating that there had to be a questioning in the company of the conventional wisdom that 'the bosses do the thinking and the rest of the organisation the executing'. Yet less than two years after all this had been pursued with such energy, even directors of ZTC businesses were complaining that they were remote from significant corporate decision-making. Having learned to encourage their staff to believe in 'empowerment', they were now asking where their own empowerment was.

The Ryland managers were not just frustrated at lacking a full opportunity to influence the destiny of their company. They had been trained in the company itself to expect such influence and had been educated in the intellectual grounds for such a highly participative style of strategy development. Within the Developing Organisational Capability programme they had been taught – and had taught others – that systematic research on what makes businesses successful showed that a 'fundamental condition' for ZTC's success would be the ability of the organisation 'to move information from the bottom to the top and back again in continuous dialogue' (see p. 97).

STRATEGIC CONVERSATIONS AND CULTURAL INTEGRATION

We noted in Chapter 4 that research by such people as James Quinn (1980) suggests that organisations which follow this 'logical incrementalist' style of strategy-making tend to be more successful than those which do not. And Frances Westley (1990) argues that 'middle managers' want to be included in what she calls strategic conversations not just because it strengthens their political power through giving them access to powerful coalitions, but because it gives them access to 'organisational sensemaking' (1990: 350). This takes us back to matters of culture – something which is often discussed using Clifford Geertz's claim that the human is 'an animal hanging in webs of significance he himself has spun' (1973: 5). As Westley says, if this is true then:

> the difference in experience between receiving a directive without access to the framing rules which underlie that directive, and entering into a strategic conversation where frames are open to negotiation would be akin to the difference between being the fly caught in the web and the spider who spins the web.

Middle managers, she says, need to be involved in the making of meanings in organisations, 'if organisations want a middle management group that is responsive as opposed to paralysed' (1990: 350).

To achieve the requisite level of productive cooperation for the organisation to survive into the long term, especially if the organisation is one involving the level of technological complexity and the degree of change in markets and competitive pressures occurring in the telecommunications field, it cannot afford to have a body of managers, outside the group of corporate top executives, who are paralysed. Going back to my brief and simple conception of management, this would make it impossible to *pull the organisation together and along to ensure its long-term survival*. The complexity of the web of human relationships which make up an organisation and its external stakeholders too readily gets out of hand if there is not a shared value base and sense of legitimacy. A clear culture (within which a variety of sub-cultures can still thrive) can counteract many of the tendencies which we saw in ZTC Ryland, especially that examined in Chapter 6 whereby means become ends in themselves and people go 'round and round in circles', throwing one initiative into the ring on top of another or sucking a new flavour of the month with every new page of the calendar. Such a culture can also help conflicts and political differences be played out in a way which, as one manager put it in talking of the need for a strong culture in ZTC, 'goes with the grain of the business, rather than against it'. Above all, a clear culture in an organisation enables people to see the essential simplicity which lies beneath the complex surface of organisational activities.

MANAGEMENT MADE SIMPLE: SEEING THE WOOD AS WELL AS THE TREES

We are moving back to one of the earliest arguments of Chapter 1 – that management is essentially the simple process of *running an organisation so that the variety of people who want something out of it will go on supporting it in such a way that it is able to continue its existence into the future* – but that this is made to seem more difficult because there is such an enormous variety of people, inside and outside the organisation, who want something from it. And many of these parties often have their own distinctive variety and mix of wants.

To reinforce the claimed value of cutting through the complexity of day-to-day managerial experience, I shall take further this 'management made simple' ploy. To manage an organisation you need a strategy, a structure and a culture, most analysts would agree. These too are simple matters:

- *Organisational strategy* is simply a broad idea of where the organisation is going and the basic way it is to get there.
- *Organisational structure* is simply a sharing-out of tasks and some rules and procedures to ensure that these tasks stay related to each other.
- *Organisational culture* is simply a set of shared understandings about what the organisation is there to do and what is important (right and wrong) about how it is done.

All of this is a little tongue-in-cheek. In reducing management to such simplicities, I am joking, am I not? Well, I have argued more than once along the route of this search for management, that jokes are always concerned with serious matters. In playing about with simple definitions I am like the comedian mocking pretension (if that is not utterly pretentious in itself). Management needs to be demystified and seen for the rather basic human social process that it is, with its dependence on language, dialogue and negotiation.

Management is a very practical, down-to-earth activity. There are no profound truths about it to be discovered and there are no hidden secrets to be uncovered about how to do it. Management is a very simple activity which involves bringing together people and resources to produce goods or services. It seems complex because it involves *people*, as I have said. But it also seems complex because whenever we get really involved in any activity we very soon find ourselves unable to see the wood we have entered because of the tangle of trees and undergrowth that surround and crowd us. If we concentrate too hard, work with too much seriousness at finding truths, we are going to learn little. It is a problem of focusing on the trees at the expense of seeing the overall shape of the terrain we are in, or of losing direction because we are looking down at our feet to see where each plodding step is taking us. The message is to lighten up a bit – be playful, agile and alert. That way we might learn more. That way we might get to wherever it is we want to go. The sort of truths which will then emerge will not be great profound statements that change our managerial lives, however; neither will they be a set of formulas for achieving career or business success.

THE VALUE OF GURUS AND THE DANGERS OF HYPE

It is perhaps ironic that Peters and Waterman in *In Search of Excellence* (1982) argued along similar lines. They cite James March's (1980) advice that we should 'supplement the technology of reason with a technology of foolishness' by allowing playful experimentation and risk-taking. Yet, for all their stress on 'looseness', the importance of common sense and there being nothing new under the sun, they have been pushed into the role of management 'gurus' whose books and seminars have taken on a near mystical role within the managerial tribe. As Graham Cleverley (1971) so effectively showed in his anthropological account of managers' use of 'magic' to help them tame 'the elements', managers often turn to management writers in the same way that the ancient Greeks turned to their myths and legends to comfort them in the face of the potential chaos of their existence.

Andre Huczynski, in his analysis of 'management gurus', takes a line similar to this and to my own one about the basic need of humans to create a sense of order to help them manage their existence. Management gurus like Peters and Waterman, says Huczynski, are meeting two principal managerial needs:

> First, the nature of organisational life places responsibility on managers to *perform* and *achieve* in a context where often they neither understand how their actions produce results, nor are able to influence the most volatile element in the organisation – other people. Second, partly as a result of this uncertainty, their assessment of themselves is also under downward pressure . . . For this reason, the two predominant managerial needs are, on the one hand, for increased predictability and control and, on the other, for increased social and personal esteem.
>
> (1993: 171)

I have observed an unfortunately rather snobbish attitude among some academic colleagues to what they often dismiss as 'pop management books'. Discussions with managers about these books suggest to me that very little of their content is remembered by those who have read them. Even less, however, is retained of what they have allegedly learned from more 'serious' works of academic management writers. The popular management books help managers engage in a brief standing-back from their everyday pressures and encourage them to reflect on what they are doing. A manager who had copies of books by Tom Peters, Rosabeth Kanter and Michael Porter in his bookshelf told me:

> 'Yes, I found them good for insights. I can't say that I have applied anything I've read in them. But they have often confirmed some of the things that I have worked out for myself or perhaps, sometimes, helped me go further down a line of thought than I might have felt confident to do.'

Where managers tended to be critical of what one man called 'gurus and big-name consultants' was when they indulged in 'hype', dressing up established and common-sense ideas in new guises. Tommy Bulwell observed:

> 'It's a sign of getting older, I think some days, but I more and more believe that there is such a tremendous amount of hype and bullshit about management and about technology and how to do things. When you get past half of the hype and the different words and descriptions you come back to a lot of very basic things that were either written in the basic sort of books twenty years ago. It's just names have been changed to call it added value or non-added value or a JIT programme instead of "Don't waste anything lads – get it made in the shortest time."'

Bulwell took an old work study book from his shelf and pointed to some basic principles which he said were still being 'recycled':

> 'It is all there. It has just been renamed a few dozen times by all sorts of people either writing books or trying to justify their consultancy tasks or whatever.'

But he connected this tendency to engage in 'hyped' ideas with a readiness to 'jump on technological bandwagons', again losing sight of basic simplicities:

> 'I think in organisations we don't look closely enough at the basic system: we could be using a quill pen to do something. We ought to consider how short and simple and effective we can make that before we decide to computerise it, automate it or whatever and have the balls sometimes to say it's good enough to use that simple system – we don't need to computerise it.'

However, Tommy Bulwell immediately went on to speak in terms which illustrates perfectly the way in which he has picked up some of the 'new management speak' (a term used by another manager) to articulate principles which he believed 'work':

> 'We don't close the loop anyway – getting people to own the problems – be sufficiently disciplined and positive. If you do, you probably don't need the robot to give you consistency and quality. If people identify with the job, they can do it themselves and they are more flexible. But we have to get them switched on and going with us.'

This piece of rhetoric stops short of using the word 'empowerment', but it is clearly consistent with the *empowerment, skills and growth discourse* which we saw in Chapter 5 as a set of discursive resources made available in ZTC for managers as a way of making sense of and adapting their managerial practice. It was taken up by Bulwell because it fitted with his view of the world, his values and his experience of practising management.

What Bulwell and others seemed to dislike was the tendency for fads, fancies and flavours of the month to be adopted (Chapter 6). This dislike of panaceas and prescriptions is taken up in a book *Beyond the Hype*, written by Eccles and Nohria (1992) and 'addressed to the thought-ful manager'. These critics are especially scornful of the tendency of management writers to be 'desperately seeking newness':

> Perhaps the most persistent rhetorical theme – one that has reached the most giddy heights today – is that the business environment is changing now like never before, that a new management paradigm and a new organisation must be created.
>
> (1992: 23)

And a key target for Eccles and Nohria are Hamel and Prahalad, who were, as we saw in Chapter 4, so central to ZTC's attempt to pursue a massively ambitious 'strategic intent' through what amounted to an entirely new approach to management for both of the companies which came together as ZTC. They note Prahalad and Hamel's (1990) claim that 'old prescriptions have potentially toxic side effects' and suggest:

> We would amend this quote slightly and observe that *all* prescriptions, old and new alike, have potentially toxic side effects if implemented poorly, too simplistically, or simply because circumstances have changed.
>
> (1992: 94)

We have seen that ZTC got itself into difficulties partly as a result of the kind of 'toxic side effects' referred to here. Eccles and Nohria nevertheless applaud Hamel and Prahalad for introducing 'language that managers have found helpful in taking action'. They are happy to see managers adopting new language which may help them frame their action differently but offer words of advice which would apply so well to the creators of ZTC: 'At the same time we would advise them to be careful about how any language for strategy, especially a new one, is adopted and used' (1992: 94).

Eccles and Nohria, had they been asked, would presumably have advised ZTC that they might use concepts like that of 'strategic intent' to 'challenge the prevailing organisational mindset, to open up new strategic possibilities, and to take action that can be more easily legitimized' under such a 'rubric' (1992: 94). In the phrase of Frances Westley (1990) which we met earlier, this terminology could have been used by managers within ongoing 'strategic conversations'. Instead, it was part of the 'DOC programme' and it was a potentially useful language which lost currency as DOC 'fell' along with the strategic intent growth targets which had been so optimistically adopted.

WHAT ABOUT HUMAN RESOURCE MANAGEMENT?

One three-letter abbreviation which ZTC's management did not make use of was 'HRM' – human resource management. This might seem strange, given the increasing currency of the term in the USA and in Britain. It is a term sometimes used as a mere synonym for personnel management, but it increasingly refers to an alternative style of managing the employment side of an organisation. HRM is seen as differing from personnel management, according, to such commentators as Beer and Spector (1985), Guest (1991) and Walton (1985), because it is 'proactive rather than reactive, system-wide rather than piecemeal, treats labour as social capital rather than as a variable cost, is goal-oriented rather than relationship-oriented, and ultimately is based on commitment rather than compliance' (Blyton and Turnbull 1992:5). This would fit much of what ZTC aspired to, and what I called the empowerment, skills and growth discourse used in the company could easily be labelled an 'HRM discourse'. To this extent one could treat our study of managerial processes in ZTC Ryland as an account of one organisation's search for HRM, in spite of the exclusion from its rhetoric of the 'HRM' expression.

The study of changing patterns of human resource management carried out by John Storey in a series of organisations characterised as 'mainstream employing organisations' in Britain shows companies pursuing a range of innovations like those we have seen in ZTC, ones which, as Storey puts it, have increasingly been related to the 'HRM theme' in 'attempts to 'make sense' of what was happening' (1992: 2,3). Across these organisations we see 'key levers' being pulled similar to those in ZTC: team-working, harmonisation, reduced job categories, performance related pay, marginalisation of shop stewards, and attempts to 'manage climate and culture'. Storey's observing of a general trend towards this type of relationship between managements and other employees puts the case of ZTC in context. ZTC was engaged in changes which were not wildly out of line with those being attempted in other 'mainstream' enterprises.

The present study complements investigations such as those of Storey (1992), Marchington and Parker (1990) or Starkey and McKinlay (1993) which look at 'HRM' and 'employee relations' innovations in British organisations. In the course of the present 'search for management' we have seen in some detail the difficulties which can arise with HRM-type programmes, especially when they are introduced alongside policies or styles which are are not in harmony with their claimed principles. Although the clash between two basic management styles, or between two key discourses, is especially striking in ZTC, we should not dismiss the ZTC case as simply a spectacular case of an organisation's management failing to be consistent in pursuing a new employment strategy. However well HRM policies are implemented, they will still have to cope with the deeper conflicts and contradictions underlying the type of society and economy of which they are a part. Karen Legge notes that the tensions and contradictions characterising employment relations in industrial capitalist societies, and analysed in my own earlier work (Watson 1977, 1986), are likely to challenge human resource managers no less than they have challenged personnel managers (Legge 1989: 37–8). They will continue to test the competence of all managers.

IN SEARCH OF COMPETENCE

A number of British companies introduced into their management selection and development processes statements of 'management competencies' in the late 1980s. These were lists of traits, qualities and personal characteristics which were felt to be desirable in managers working in those organisations. It had been decided at ZTC Ryland that they should have their own scheme and they had budgeted to employ consultants to help them with this. I argued that I could do this at considerably lower cost. I would bring together my own understanding of existing theory and research with the findings of my investigations at the Ryland plant to devise a scheme which would be incorporated into emerging management appraisal and development procedures. In this way I had a formal management task as part of the ZTC 'management team' which fitted perfectly with my need to interview managers and otherwise collect information for my personal research project.

The notion of management competencies goes back to efforts instigated by the American Management Association in the early 1970s to identify the characteristics of 'superior managers'. The outcome of those efforts was the scheme presented by Robert Boyatzis (1982) identifying twelve 'underlying characteristics' which a manager would need to be effective – as long as there was a fit between the individual's set of competencies, their job demands and the organisational environment. This approach was taken up in Britain not just by individual companies, but by a network of management development interests calling itself the Management Charter Initiative (hoping to correct the allegedly backward state of British management education and training identified in investigations and reports by Handy (1987) and by Constable and McCormick (1987) and by the British state). The British government announced its intention in a white paper (HMSO 1988) to develop 'a system of nationally recognised qualifications which embody the standards of competence required by employers and which allow for maximum mobility'. National management qualifications were to be developed which would be based on the competencies to be identified by such bodies as the Management Charter Initiative. The underlying principle was that managers would gain qualifications on the basis of what they could demonstrate that they could *do*, as opposed to what they *knew*.

I was personally involved in these national developments and had serious reservations about the whole trend, as had some fellow management academics. The development could be welcomed in so far as it switched the focus of management development from the acquisition of abstract knowledge to a demonstrated capability to act, but to translate this principle into a practice whereby management development might become a matter of gaining a series of 'ticks' on a list of bureaucratically presented characteristics was frightening and a potential case of means subverting ends to end all such cases. John Burgoyne raises the question of how any scheme could recognise such matters as the 'holistic nature of management', its 'moral and ethical dimensions' and its 'variability across situations' (1989: 60). Mangham and Pye argue that competence and effectiveness are 'judged through their expression in performance' and that this performance involves a continuity of action which means that 'the idea that any such performance can be broken down into component parts, being illustrative of this or that competence, exposes the central nonsense of the conceptualization' (1991: 132).

In my own search for management I have not attempted to assess which managers were 'better' than others, in so far as I could avoid this. Instead, I have tried to bring out in Chapter 7 the feelings, experiences and judgements of practising managers about what to them makes 'good' and 'bad' managers. There was little here to support the validity of the mechanistic type of competency scheme which Mangham and Pye characterise as an 'assembly process to management development – so much financial ability added to a bit of marketing and some strategic leadership together with some interpersonal skills and a hint of . . .' (1991: 133). The experiences of the Ryland managers of what seemed to them 'to work' when they reflected on the best and worst managers they had seen identified certain key principles involving such ethically tinged notions as trust, reciprocity and consistency. They also struggled to explain characteristics which Annie Pye describes, borrowing words from a David Lodge novel, as 'elusive . . . [appearing] like the moon, to shimmer on the water, seen but not grasped' (1991: 115). As Pye also comments, 'effective performance is relational' and the words of the Ryland managers draw our attention to how the best managers they had known possessed indefinable personal qualities which made it possible to influence people because 'that was the way they were'.

These interpersonal and influencing skills have to be related to wider concepts of the nature of management, if we are going to judge how competent or effective a manager is. I have argued throughout that one is a manager by virtue of one's involvement in the directing of an organisation as a whole towards its long-term survival. Competent managers are thus people who can appropriately influence the performance of those upon whom they depend for the fulfilling of the specific tasks associated with their post in such a way that a contribution is made to the performance of the organisation as a whole. This in turn means that a manager's competence is as much a matter of the structural and cultural context in which they are operating as it is of their personal qualities. This is where managerial competence and organisational culture link together so tightly: the necessary level of commitment, trust and understanding making possible productive cooperation depends both on the general web of meanings shaping people's relationship to the organisation and on the specific set of understandings negotiated between people and the managers working with them.

The management competency scheme which I developed for ZTC Ryland is reproduced in the Appendix. It was presented to the company as a 'stimulus to thought', a 'language for analysing and the matching of individual and business needs'. In the formal presentation I gave to the board of directors, I concluded with a slide saying that management competency schemes 'must not be used mechanistically' and 'Every manager is a unique individual', 'Every manager is effective or ineffective *in their own way.*'

My reservations about the whole exercise were soon confirmed, however, by a 'joke' made after my presentation by one of the group managing directors;

> 'Aha, this should come in useful when I have to decide which of my first line I am going to sack.'

This man was relieved of his own post not long after this event, but the personnel director and myself resolved that the scheme would only be introduced incrementally as part of other developments in personnel practices. At all costs we would avoid issuing a new document with a 'launch' which would look like the introduction of yet another 'flavour of the month' innovation. I left the scheme 'on the table' when I left the company and, as all of the senior personnel colleagues I had worked with on the scheme had left the company or the function or were about to, it probably faded away. I have chosen not to ask. I would only have been happy to have seen it used if it had been incorporated into decision-making and career development discourses; as a means to other ends, rather than as an end in itself.

Throughout this search for management, central attention has been paid to discourse and language, and in Chapter 8 particular stress was put upon what I called the intuitively developed mundane rhetorical skills of managers. A capacity to have fun, amusing oneself along with others, was also seen as a valuable accomplishment, not just because it helped handle tensions but because it helped shape interpersonal meanings and facilitate negotiated cooperative efforts.

All this suggests that managerial competence or effectiveness is indeed a subtle, multi-faceted and context-bound thing. It does not just involve skills and attitudes, but encompasses knowledge – even if that knowledge is 'stored' in the form of intuitions and is manifested in what Donald Schon calls reflection-in-action, whereby managers 'draw on repertoires of cumulatively developed organisational knowledge, which they transform in the context of some unique situation' (1983: 265). Schon refers to the manager engaging in 'a reflective conversation with the situation', an expression which accords with what I have argued about the process of thinking itself taking the form of an argument with oneself (see pp. 23–5). But the actions which result from such reflection must relate not just to the moment but to the wider and longer-term scheme of things. Eccles and Nohria, in trying to get beyond the 'management hype' and rediscovering the 'essence of management', use the concept of *robust action* here (1992: 40). This is action which 'accomplishes the short-term objectives while preserving long-term flexibility' (ibid.: 11). And, for them, rhetorical skill is as important as it is for me:

> Managers must use words to get others to act and to paint a picture of the world that is in line with other actions both taken and foreseen. For robust action, the rhetoric managers employ must be 'local' – it must pay attention to the particulars of the situation and the identities of the participants. On the other hand, the rhetoric managers use must be ambiguous enough and general enough to allow for flexibility and adjustment. They must spin a story that can evolve and yet retain its general integrity.

AND SO . . .

With this final reference to the work of others I shall end my attempt to weave the ideas and findings of other writers along with my own research, experiences, thoughts and observations into the tapestry recording my journey in search of management.

The image which has taken shape is one of management as essentially and inherently a social and moral activity; one whose greatest successes in efficiently and effectively producing goods and services is likely to come through building organisational patterns, cultures and understandings based on relationships of mutual trust and shared obligation among people involved with the organisation. Management is essentially a human social craft. It requires the ability to interpret the thoughts and wants of others – be these employees, customers, competitors or whatever – and the facility to shape meanings, values and human commitments.

How well all of this is done makes a difference to the quality of life of all of those in society who use the goods and services of factories, hospitals, shops, government and universities. This excludes no one. There is a lot to keep faith with.

Appendix

A scheme of management competencies devised for ZTC Ryland

A: PERSONAL ORIENTATION (WHAT A PERSON CURRENTLY IS)

1. Achievement and results orientation

Good managers set high but realistic standards of achievement for themselves and others, seek continual improvement in processes and results, and monitor progress against targets.

Bad managers muddle through without clear objectives, are happy with 'adequate' performance and judge success as the avoidance of trouble.

2. Initiative

Good managers seek and create opportunities, initiate actions and want to be 'ahead of the game'. They are 'proactive'.

Bad managers react to situations and passively follow the initiatives of others.

3. Decisiveness and self-confidence

Good managers believe sufficiently in their own judgement to make decisions and take risks; they accept the possibility of making mistakes from time to time.

Bad managers are unsure of themselves, they hesitate and procrastinate over decisions; they are risk averse and afraid of making mistakes.

4. Commercial orientation

Good managers have a strong sense of enterprise and a shrewd grasp of market opportunities; they are cost conscious but strongly aware of the importance of productive investment. They are interested in 'adding value' in what they do.

Bad managers have little awareness of or interest in the financial and market context of business; they either (i) pay little attention to costs – and consequently spend carelessly or (ii) keep down costs regardless of the possibility of later return on present expenditure.

5. Adaptability and capacity to learn

Good managers are flexible in coping with changing circumstances; do not panic in the face of crises or adversity; are constantly learning from their own experiences, from observations and from external sources (contacts, books, papers, media, etc.).

Bad managers continue to do things the way they always have, regardless of circumstances; they may panic or retreat when faced with threats or changes; they believe that they know all they need to know.

B: COGNITIVE STYLE (HOW A PERSON THINKS)

1. Vision and strategic thinking

Good managers can relate current activities to a clear and coherent image of a future state of affairs for the whole organisation and their part of it; they understand the links between everyday activities and the long-term effectiveness of the business – especially with regard to customers; they manage their segment (department, function, etc.) of the business as a contribution to the business as a whole. They appreciate the global context of the business and the need to work within an international cultural perspective.

Bad managers have a short-term perspective and an inward-looking approach to managing their responsibilities – their departmental or functional objectives are seen as ends in themselves rather than as means to more effective performance of the business as a whole. Minimal attention is paid to customers – whether these be internal or external ones and there is little awareness of or interest in the international setting of the business.

2. Information search

Good managers are constantly collecting and sifting information from a variety of sources and work hard to maintain an information network which will continually feed them with knowledge and intelligence of both a formal and informal nature.

Bad managers either (i) limit themselves to a few, usually formal, sources of information so that they have little knowledge of or 'feel for' what is going on around them, or (ii) allow themselves to be swamped with indiscriminatingly received information so that they quickly become dazed and out of touch.

3. Use of concepts

Good managers are able to sort and make use of information received and gathered by the use of conceptual schemes and models which enables them to see trends and patterns, to detect cause/effect relationships and to establish hypotheses which might be 'tested'.

Bad managers lack conceptual frameworks for bringing order to what they see to be going on; they cannot see the 'wood for the trees'; there is little idea of what causes any given phenomenon and there is little basis for trying out new ideas.

4. Creativity

Good managers are imaginative and innovative, devising both new things to do and new ways of doing what was done before.

Bad managers, at best, follow established practices and take the lead given by others; at worst, they are negatively conservative and resist new ideas.

5. Judgement and decision-making

Good managers critically and objectively evaluate information and decide upon actions in a logical and rational manner, making use of available evidence but balancing this, where appropriate, with intuition and informed risk-taking.

Bad managers' judgements are subject to bias and prejudice, their actions lack a clear logic and their reasoning may be either (i) coldly based on raw data without the addition of any degree of flair or imaginative interpretation or (ii) based on wild guesses, uninformed hunches, blind self-interest or malice.

C: INTERPERSONAL STYLE (HOW A PERSON RELATES)

1. Sensitivity and listening

Good managers are sensitive to the attitudes and feelings of all those they work with (at all levels, inside and outside the organisation); they treat others and their ideas with respect; they listen carefully to the ideas and viewpoints of others, working actively to elicit positive contributions from them.

Bad managers have little regard for the people they work with; they are insensitive to the feelings of others, concentrating on their own ideas, feelings and objectives regardless of the views or interests of others.

2. Impact and persuasiveness

Good managers have the personal presence and credibility to win support for proposed actions, values and strategies; they use persuasive arguments, symbols and rewards to gain support and they win compliance through setting examples to others.

Bad managers tend to be taken little notice of and, even when they appear to be given attention, they have little influence either on people's thinking or their behaviour.

3. Planning and organisation

Good managers set agendas for their teams and work with them to formulate plans, objectives and time targets which are supported with necessary resources.

Bad managers leave their teams unclear as to what is expected of them, with vague time horizons and haphazard access to resources.

4. Presentation and communication

Good managers ensure that information and ideas are communicated clearly and unambiguously, with the appropriate choice of communication medium to achieve maximum understanding on the part of the audience.

Bad managers have little appreciation of when to use which means of communication; their writing and their oral communication attempts are muddled, incoherent and ambiguous and they fail to check on how well their audience understands them in the course of their attempts to communicate.

5. Leadership, team building and maintenance

Good managers work with teams they lead to build up a positive climate, an efficient allocation of tasks and they ensure that information is shared and that skills are kept up to date and directed towards effective task achievement and continuous improvement. When they are a member of a team which they are not leading they contribute positively and constructively.

Bad managers work on their own and tend to maintain power by keeping information from others. The team they are responsible for is left to find its own way of working – this often leading to lack of focus, negativity, conflict and under-resourcing. If they are a member of a team and not a leader they only play a part when they perceive an opportunity to defend or further a sectional interest.

Bibliography

Alvesson, M. and Willmott, H. (1992) 'On the idea of emancipation in management and organisation studies', *Academy of Management Review* 17(3): 43–64.

Anthony, P.D. (1986) *The Foundation of Management*, London: Tavistock.

Archer, S. (1988) ''Qualitative' research and the epistemological problems of the management disciplines', in Pettigrew (1988).

Armstrong, P. (1989), 'Management, labour process and agency', *Work, Employment and Society* 3(3), 307–22.

Atkinson, P. (1990) *The Ethnographic Imagination*, London: Routledge.

Bahktin, M.M. (1981) *The Dialogic Imagination*, Austin, Tex.: University of Texas Press.

Baldamus, W. (1961) *Efficiency and Effort*, London: Tavistock.

Barnard, C.I. (1938) *The Functions of the Executive*, Cambridge, Mass.: Harvard University Press.

Baumeister, R.F. (1986) *Identity: Cultural Change and the Struggle for Self*, New York: Oxford University Press.

Becker, H.S. (1960) 'Notes on the concept of commitment', *American Journal of Sociology* 66.

Beer, M. and Spector, B. (1985) 'Corporatewide transformations in human resource management', in Walton and Lawrence (1985).

Bell, D. (1977) 'The return of the sacred? The argument on the future of religion', *British Journal of Sociology* 28:4.

Berger, P.L. (1973) *The Social Reality of Religion*, Harmondsworth: Penguin Books.

Berger, P.L. and Luckmann, T. (1971) *The Social Construction of Reality*, Harmondsworth: Penguin.

Bettelheim, B. (1976) *On the Uses of Enchantment: the meaning and importance of fairy tales*, New York: Knopf.

Billig, M. (1987) *Arguing and Thinking: a rhetorical approach to social psychology*, Cambridge: Cambridge University Press .

Blau, P. (1964) *Exchange and Power in Social Life*, New York: Wiley.

Blyton, P. and Turnbull, P. (1992) *Reassessing Human Resource Management*, London: Sage.

Boland, R.J. and Hoffman, R. (1983) 'Humour in a machine shop: an interpretation of symbolic action', in Pondy *et al.* (1983).

Boyatzis, R.E. (1982) *The Competent Manager*, New York: Wiley.

Braverman, H. (1974) *Labor and Monopoly Capital*, New York: Monthly Review Press .

Burgess, A. (1992) reported in *The Guardian*, 24 September.

Burgoyne, J. (1989) 'Creating the managerial portfolio: building on competency approaches to management development', *Management Education and Development* 20: 56–61.

Burnham, J. (1945) *The Managerial Revolution* Harmondsworth: Penguin.

Burns, T. (1955) 'The reference of conduct in small groups', Administrative Science Quarterly 6.

Carlson, S. (1951) *Executive Behaviour: a study of the workload and the working methods of managing directors*, Stockholm: Strombergs.

Carroll, D.T. (1983) 'A disappointing search for excellence', *Harvard Business Review* Nov–Dec: 78–88.

Carroll, S.J. and Gillen, D.J. (1987) 'Are the classical management functions useful in describing work?', *Academy of Management Review* 12(1): 38–51.

Cattell, R.B. (1966) *The Scientific Analysis of Personality*, Chicago, Ill.: Aldine.

Cawson, A., Morgan, K., Webber, D. Holmes, P. and Stevens, A. (1990) *Hostile Brothers: competition and closure in the European electronic industry*, Oxford: Oxford University Press.

Chapman, A.J. and Jones, D.M. (eds) (1980) *Models of Man*, Leicester: British Psychological Society.

Child, J. (1969) *British Management Thought*, London: Allen & Unwin.

Cleverley, G. (1971) *Managers and Magic*, London: Longman.

Clewlow, C. (1989) *A Woman's Guide to Adultery*, London: Michael Joseph.

Clutterbuck, D. and Crainer, S. (1988) *Makers of Management*, London: Macmillan.

Collin, A. (1986) 'Career development: the significance of subjective career', *Personnel Review* 15(2): 22–8.

Constable, J. and McCormick, R. (1987) *The Making of British Managers*, London: British Institute of Management.

Cooley, C.H. (1922) *Human Nature and the Social Order*, New York: Scribners.

Dalton, M. (1959) *Men Who Manage*, New York: Wiley.

Deal, T.E. and Kennedy, A.A. (1982) *Corporate Cultures: the rites and rituals of corporate life*, Reading, Mass.: Addison-Wesley.

Dixon, M. (1986) 'Ancient Wisdom with a novel twist', *Financial Times* 7 July: 14.

Dopson, S. and Stewart, R. (1990) 'What is happening to middle management?', *British Journal of Management* 1(1): 3–16.

Douglas, M. (1975) *Implicit Meanings*, London: Routledge and Kegan Paul.

Earl, M.J (ed.) (1983) *Perspectives on Management*, Oxford: Oxford University Press.

Eccles, R.G. and Nohria, N. (1992) *Beyond the Hype: rediscovering the essence of management*, Cambridge, Mass.: Harvard Business School.

Evans, P. and Bartolemé, F. (1980) *Must Success Cost So Much?*, London: Grant McIntyre.

Eysenck, H.J. (1953) *The Structure of Human Personality*, New York: Wiley.

Fayol, H. (1949) (originally published 1916) *General and Industrial Management*, London: Pitman.

Fineman, S. (1994) 'Organizing and emotion', in Hassard and Parker (1994).

Follet, M.P. (1941) *Dynamic Administration*, London: Pitman.

Fook, N.Y.M. and Watson, T.J. (1992) 'Culture, Environment and Survival in Further Education Colleges', Paper given to the British Academy of Management Annual Conference, September 1992.

Foucault, M. (1980) *Power/Knowledge: selected interviews and other writings*, Brighton: Harvester.

Fox, A. (1974) *Beyond Contract: work, power and trust relations*, London: Faber.

Fox, A. (1985) *Man Mismanagement*, London: Hutchinson.

Freeman, S.J. (1990) *Managing Lives: corporate women and social change*, Boston, Mass.: University of Massachusetts Press.

Freud, S. (1900) *The Interpretation of Dreams: Volume IV of the Complete Works of Sigmund Freud*, London: Hogarth Press.

Gabriel, Y. (1991) 'Turning facts into stories and stories into facts', *Human Relations* 44(8): 857–75.

Geertz, C. (1973) *Interpretations of Culture*, New York: Basic Books.

Giddens, A. (1984) *The Constitution of Society: outline of the theory of structuration*, Cambridge: Polity.

Gilligan, C. (1982) *In a Different Voice*, Cambridge, Mass.: Harvard University Press.

Goffman, E. (1958) *The Presentation of Self in Everyday Life*, Harmondsworth: Penguin.

Goldthorpe, J.H., Lockwood, D., Bechhofer, F. and Platt, J. (1968) *The Affluent Worker: attitudes and behaviour*, Cambridge: Cambridge University Press.

Gouldner, A. (1954) *Patterns of Industrial Bureaucracy*, New York: Free Press.

Gouldner, A. (1971) *The Coming Crisis of Western Sociology*, London: Heinemann.

Gowler, D. and Legge, K. (1983) 'The meaning of management and the management of meaning: a view from social anthropology' in Earl (1983).

Gubrian, J. and Silverman, D. (eds) (1989) *The Politics of Field Research* London: Sage.

Guest, D. (1991) 'Personnel management: the end of an orthodoxy', *British Journal of Industrial Relations* 29(2): 149–76.

Gulick, L.H. (1937) 'Notes on the theory of organisation' in Gulick and Urwick (1937).

Gulick, L.H. and Urwick, L.F. (eds) (1937) *Papers on the Science of Administration*, New York: Columbia University Press.

Habermas, J. (1971) *Towards a Rational Society*, London: Heinemann.

Hales, C.P. (1986) 'What do managers do? a critical review of the evidence', *Journal of Management Studies* 23: 88–115.

Hamel, G. and Prahalad, C.K. (1989) 'Strategic Intent', *Harvard Business Review* May-June.

Handy, C. (1987) *The Making of Managers*, London: NEDO.

Hannan, M.T. (1989) *Organisational Ecology* Cambridge, Mass.: Harvard University Press.

Hannan, M.T. and Freeman, J.H. (1977) 'The population ecology of organisations', *American Journal of Sociology* 82: 929–64.

Harré, R. (1980) 'Man as Rhetorician', in Chapman and Jones (1980).

Harvey, J.H., Weber, A.L. and Orbuch, T.L. (1990) *Interpersonal Accounts: a social psychological perspective*, Cambridge, Mass.: Blackwell.

Hassard, J. and Parker, M. (eds) (1994) *Towards a New Organisation Theory*, London: Routledge.

Huczynski, A.A. (1993) *Management Gurus: what makes them and how to become one*, London: Routledge.

Hughes, E.C. (1937) 'Institutional office and the person', *American Journal of Sociology* 43.

HMSO (1988) *Employment in the 1990s*, London.

Isabella, L.A. (1990) 'Evolving interpretations as a change unfolds: how managers construe key organisational events', *Academy of Management Journal* 33 (1): 7–41.

Jackall, R. (1988) *Moral Mazes: the world of corporate managers*, New York: Oxford University Press.

Kanter, R.M. (1977) *Men and Women of the Corporation*, New York: Basic Books.

Kanter, R.M. (1983) *The Change Masters*, London: Allen & Unwin.

Knights, D. and Morgan, G. (1990) 'The concept of strategy in sociology: a note of dissent', *Sociology* 24: 475–83.

Kotter, J.P. (1982) *The General Managers*, New York: Free Press.

Kotter, J.P. and Lawrence, P.C. (1974) *Mayors in Action*, New York: Free Press.

Lawrence, P.R. and Lorsch, J.W. (1967) *Organisations and Environment*, Cambridge, Mass.: Harvard University Press.

Leach, E. (1982) *Social Anthropology*, Glasgow: Fontana.

Leavitt, H.J., Pondy, L.R. and Boje, D.M. eds (1980) *Readings in Managerial Psychology*, Chicago, Ill.: University of Chicago Press.

Legge, K. (1978) *Power, Innovation and Problem Solving in Personnel Management*, London: McGraw Hill.

Legge, K. (1989) 'Human resource management: a critical analysis' in Storey, (1989).

Leith, D. and Myerson, M. (1989) *The Power of Address: explorations in rhetoric*, London: Routledge.

Linstead, S. (1985) 'Jokers wild: the importance of humour in the maintenance of organisational culture', *Sociological Review* 33(4): 741–67.

McCall, M.W. and Lombardo, M.M. (eds) (1978) *Leadership: where else can we go?*, Durham, NC: Duke University Press.

McGregor, D.C. (1960) *The Human Side of Enterprise*, New York: McGraw-Hill.

MacIntyre, A. (1981) *After Virtue: a study in moral theory*, London: Duckworth.

Mangham, I.L. (1986) *Power and Performance in Organisations*, Oxford: Blackwell.

Mangham, I.L. (ed.) (1987) *Organisation Analysis and Development*, London: Wiley.

Mangham, I.L. (1988) 'Managing the executive process', in Pettigrew (1988).

Mangham, I.L. and Pye, A. (1991) *The Doing of Management*, Oxford: Blackwell.

Mant, A. (1979) *The Rise and Fall of the British Manager*, London: Pan.

March, J.G. (1980) 'The technology of foolishness', in Leavitt, Pondy and Boje (1980).

March, J.G. and Olsen, J.P. (1976) *Ambiguity and Choice in Organisations*, Oslo: Universitetsforlagtt.

Marchington, M. and Parker, P. (1990) *Changing Patterns of Employee Relations*, Hemel Hempstead: Harvester Wheatsheaf.

Maslow, A.H. (1968) *Towards a Psychology of Being*, Princeton: Van Nostrand.

Mayo, E. (1933) *The Human Problems of an Industrial Civilisation*, New York: Macmillan.

Mills, W.C. (1970) *The Sociological Imagination*, Harmondsworth: Penguin.

Mintzberg, H. (1973) *The Nature of Managerial Work*, New York: Harper & Row.

Mintzberg, H. (1975) 'The manager's job', *Harvard Business Review* July–August.

Mintzberg, H. (1987) 'Crafting Strategy', *Harvard Business Review* July–August.

Mintzberg, H. (1988) 'Opening up the definition of strategy', in Quinn, Mintzberg and James (1988).

Montgomery, D. (1991) 'What's so Funny?', *Sunday Times Magazine*, 28 April.

Nash, W. (1989) *Rhetoric: the Wit of Persuasion*, Oxford: Blackwell.

Pascale, R.T. and Athos, A.G. (1982) *The Art of Japanese Management*, Harmondsworth: Penguin.

Peters, T.J. (1989) *Thriving on Chaos*, London: Macmillan.

Peters, T.J. and Austin, N. (1985) *A Passion for Excellence*, New York: Random House.

Peters, T.J. and Waterman, R.H. Jnr. (1982) *In Search of Excellence*, New York: Harper and Row.

Pettigrew, A. (1973) *The Politics of Organisational Decision Making*, London: Tavistock.

Pettigrew, A.M. (ed.) (1988) *Competitiveness and the Management Process*, Oxford: Blackwell.

Pfeffer, J. and Salancik, G.R. (1976) *The External Control of Organisations: a resource dependence approach*, New York: Harper and Row.

Poole, M., Mansfield R., Blyton, P. and Frost, P. (1981) *Managers in Focus*, Farnborough: Gower.

Pondy, L. (1978) 'Leadership as a language game', in McCall and Lombardo (1978).

Pondy, L.R., Frost, P.J., Morgan, G. and Dandridge, T.C. (eds) (1983) *Organisational Symbolism*, Greenwich, Conn.: JAI.

Potter, J. and Wetherall, M. (1987) *Discourse and Social Psychology: beyond attitudes and behaviour*, London: Sage.

Powell, G.N. (1988) *Women and Men in Management*, Beverley Hills, Calif.: Sage.

Prahalad, C.K. and Hamel, G. (1990) 'The core competence of the corporation', *Harvard Business Review* May–June.

Propp, V. (1968) *Morphology of the Folktale*, Austin, Tex.: University of Texas Press.

Pye, A, (1991) 'Management competence: "the flower in the mirror and the moon on the water"' in Silver (1991).

Quinn, J.B. (1980) *Strategies for Change: logical incrementalism*, Homewood Ill.: Irwin.

Quinn, J.B., Mintzberg, H. and James, R.M. (eds) (1988) *The Strategy Process*, Englewood Cliffs, NJ: Prentice-Hall.

Radcliffe-Brown, A.R. (1940) 'On joking realtionships', *Africa*, 13: 195–210.

Ray, C.A. (1986) 'Corporate culture: the last frontier of control', *Journal of Management Studies* 23(3): 287–97.

Reed, M.I. (1984) 'Management as a social practice', *Journal of Management Studies* 21:3.

Reed, M.I. (1989) *The Sociology of Management*, Brighton: Harvester Wheatsheaf.

Reed, M. and Anthony, P.D. (1992) 'Professionalizing management and managing professionalization: British management in the 1980s', *Journal of Management Studies* 29(5): 591–613.

Ritzer, G. (1993) *The McDonaldization of Society*, Newbury Park, Cal.: Pine Forge.

Roberts, J. (1984) 'The moral character of management practice', *Journal of Management Studies* 21(3): 287–302.

Roethlisberger, F.J. and Dickson, W.J. (1939) *Management and the Worker*, Cambridge, Mass.: Harvard University Press.

Rogers, C. (1961) *On Becoming a Person*, Boston, Mass.: Houghton Mifflin.

Rosen, M. (1991) 'Coming to terms with the field: understanding and doing organisational ethnography', *Journal of Management Studies* 28(1): 1–24.

Saunders, J. and Wong, V. (1985) 'In Search of excellence in the UK', *Journal of Marketing Management* 1(2): 119–37.

Scase, R. and Goffee, R. (1989) *Reluctant managers: their work and lifestyles*, London: Unwin Hyman.

Schein, E.H. (1978) *Career Dynamics*, Reading, Mass.: Addison-Wesley.

Schein, E.H. (1985) *Organisational Culture and Leadership*, San Francisco, Calif.: Jossey-Bass.

Schon, D.A. (1983) *The Reflective Practitioner*, New York: Basic Books.

Selznick, P. (1957) *Leadership in Administration*, New York: Harper & Row.

Shaw, M. (1990) 'Strategy and social process: military context and sociological analysis', *Sociology* 24: 465–74.

Silver, J. (1987) 'The ideology of excellence: management and neo- Conservatism', *Studies in Political Economy* 24: 105–29.

Silver, M. (ed.) (1991) *Competent to Manage*, London: Routledge.

Silverstone, R. (1981) *The Message of Television*, London: Heinemann.

Simon, H.A. (1957) 'A behavioural model of rational choice', in *Models of Man*, New York: Wiley.

Smith, V. (1990) *Managing in the Corporate Interest: control and resistance in an American bank*, Berkeley, Calif.: University of California Press.

Srivasta, S. (ed.) (1983) *The Executive Mind*, San Francisco, Calif.: Jossey-Bass.

Starkey, K. and McKinlay, A. (1993) *Strategy and the Human Resource*, Oxford: Blackwell.

Stewart, R. (1976) *Contrasts in Management*, Maidenhead: McGraw-Hill.

Stewart, R. (1983) 'Managerial Behaviour: how research has changed the traditional picture', in Earl (1983).

Stewart, R. (1989) 'Studies of managerial jobs and behaviour: the way forward', *Journal of Management Studies* 26(1).

Stewart, R. (1991) *Managing Today and Tomorrow*, London: Macmillan.

Storey, J. (ed.) (1989) *New Perspectives on Human Resource Management*, London: Routledge.

Storey, J. (1992) *Developments in the Management of Human Resources*, Oxford: Blackwell.

Strong, P. and Dingwall, R. (1989) 'Romantics and stoics', in Gubrian and Silverman (1989).

Taylor, F.W. (1911) *The Principles of Scientific Management*, New York: Harper.

Thompson, P. and McHugh, D. (1990) *Work Organisations: a critical introduction*, London: Macmillan.

Torrington, D. and Weightman, J. (1985) *The Business of Management*, London: Prentice-Hall.

Van Maanen, J. (1988) *Tales of the Field: on writing ethnography*, Chicago, Ill.: University of Chicago Press.

Walton, R.E. (1985) 'From control to commitment in the workplace', *Harvard Business Review* March–April: 76–84.

Walton, R.E. and Lawrence, P.R. (eds) (1985) *Human Resource Management: trends and challenges*, Boston, Mass.: Harvard Business School.

Watson, T.J. (1977) *The Personnel Managers*, London: Routledge.

Watson, T.J. (1982) 'Group Ideologies and Organisational Change', *Journal of Management Studies* 19(3): 259–75.

Watson, T.J (1986) *Management, Organisation and Employment Strategy*, London: Routledge .

Watson, T.J. (1987) *Sociology, Work and Industry*, London: Routledge.

Watson, T.J. (1994a) 'Towards a managerially relevant but non-managerialist organisation theory', in Hassard and Parker (1994).

Watson, T.J. (1994b) 'Managing, crafting and researching: words, skill and imagination in shaping management research', *British Journal of Management* 5(2).

Watson, T.J., Riggs, S. and Fook N. (1991) 'Participant observation and managerial work', *Proceedings of British Academy of Management Annual Conference*.

Weber, M. (1968) *Economy and Society*, New York: Bedminster Press.

Weick, K.E. (1979) *The Social Psychology of Organising*, Reading, Mass.: Addison-Wesley.

Weick, K.E. (1983) 'Managerial thought in the context of action', in Srivasta, S. *et al.* (1983).

Weir, D. (1993) 'Not doing the business', *Times Higher Education Supplement* 30 April: 22.

Westley, F.R. (1990) 'Middle managers and strategy: microdynamics of inclusion', *Strategic Management Journal* 11: 337–51.

Westwood, R. (1987) 'Social criticism: a social critical practice applied to a discourse on participation', in Mangham (1987).

Whitley, R. (1989) 'On the nature of managerial tasks and skills', *Journal of Management Studies* 26(3): 209–24.

Willmott, H. (1987) 'Studying managerial work: a critique and a proposal', *Journal of Management Studies* 24: 249–70.

Wilson, N.A.B. (1973) *On the Quality of Working Life*, London: HMSO.

Wittgenstein, L. (1953) *Philosophical Investigations*, Oxford: Blackwell.

Work in America (1973) *Report of the Special Task Force to the Secretary of Health, Education and Welfare*, Cambridge, Mass.: MIT.

Yin, R.K. (1984) *Case Study Research*, Beverly Hills, Calif.: Sage.

Author index

Subject index